FORT ST. JAMES AND
NEW CALEDONIA

FORT ST. JAMES AND NEW CALEDONIA

Where British Columbia Began

Marie Elliott

HARBOUR PUBLISHING

Harbour Publishing Co. Ltd.
P.O. Box 219, Madeira Park, BC, V0N 2H0
www.harbourpublishing.com

Edited by Betty Keller
Maps by Roger Handling
Cover design by Anna Comfort
Cover photograph by Marie Elliott
Printed and bound in Canada

THE CANADA COUNCIL | LE CONSEIL DES ARTS
FOR THE ARTS | DU CANADA
SINCE 1957 | DEPUIS 1957

BRITISH COLUMBIA
ARTS COUNCIL
Supported by the Province of British Columbia

Harbour Publishing acknowledges financial support from the Government of Canada through the Book Publishing Industry Development Program and the Canada Council for the Arts, and from the Province of British Columbia through the BC Arts Council and the Book Publishing Tax Credit.

Library and Archives Canada Cataloguing in Publication

Elliott, Marie, 1938–
    Fort St. James and New Caledonia : where British Columbia began / Marie Elliott.

Includes bibliographical references and index.
ISBN 978-1-55017-478-6

    1. Fort St. James (B.C.)—History. 2. Northwest, Canadian—History—To 1870. I. Title.
FC3849.F68E55 2009   971.1'82
C2009-900884-X

In memory of R.C. Harris, R.E.,
who researched, mapped and generously shared
his knowledge of British Columbia's historic trails

Contents

Acknowledgments

THE EXPLOITS OF JOHN STUART AND JOHN NOBILI provided the incentive for this book. In the early nineteenth century both young men came to North America ready for adventure: Stuart from Scotland, to earn a living with the North West Company, and Nobili from Italy, to establish missions for the Society of Jesus. Even though one company was commercial and the other religious, they bore striking similarities. Both were hierarchies that for efficient operation required regular, detailed communication, absolute dedication and the ability to endure great physical hardships. Stuart, latterly known as "old Aesop," and Nobili enjoyed writing about their adventures and were proud of their involvement in the history of New Caledonia. I feel honoured to bring their histories together after more than 150 years.

More recently a number of historians have influenced my research. Dominion Archivist and Librarian W. Kaye Lamb recognized the importance of editing and publishing the fur trade journals of Simon Fraser and Daniel Williams Harmon. His efforts on these and numerous other volumes about early explorers is valued by many students of British Columbia history. The ongoing scholarship of Sylvia Van Kirk and Jennifer Brown, regarding women and families in the fur trade, has infused social history research with new enthusiasm and purpose. Born at Stuart Lake, Lizette Hall has given us valuable information about the Carrier, and before her death, Yvonne Meares Klan conducted extensive research on New Caledonia.

Through his explorations, historical research and writing, the late R.C. Harris inspired us to recognize and enjoy the importance of British Columbia's heritage trails, most of them established by First Nations peoples centuries ago. Bob was always generous with his knowledge and his hand drawn maps, which I cherish.

The Hudson's Bay Company Archives, housed at the Provincial Archives of Manitoba, was the main source of material used for my research. Their services for distance researchers, especially the microfilm loan program, is superb and continues to improve over time. I am grateful for their prompt responses to my requests and for permission to quote from various records. I also deeply appreciate the trust and generosity of the Archivum Romanum Societatis Iesu in Rome who provided me with copies of John Nobili's correspondence and permission to publish it. Interpreter Cinzia Forasiepi has my admiration and thanks for patiently taking on the role of translator part-time, over two years. Permission to quote from published material has also been generously granted by Elizabeth Hawkins, Lorraine Huren, Bradley Lochner, the University of Oklahoma Press, University of Alberta Press, and the Champlain Society.

The collections of the University of Victoria McPherson Library and the library staff facilitated my local research, making it most enjoyable. I am also grateful for the collections and assistance of the British Columbia Archives, the Oregon Historical Society, the Jesuit Oregon Province Archives, Gonzaga University, Santa Clara University, the Glenbow Museum and Archives, the Fort St. James Library, and the Fraser-Fort George Regional Museum.

The support of my daughter, Carol, and advice from Tim and Merle Bayliff, Bill Quackenbush, Ronald Greene, Deidre Simmons,

Dr. Patricia Roy, Frances Gundry, Wayne Jacobs, Father John Brioux, OMI, and Father Gerald McKevitt, SJ, is acknowledged with special thanks.

A final extra special thanks is due to editor Betty Keller, Teresa Karbashewski, Erin Schopfer, Anna Comfort and all the staff at Harbour Publishing, and Roger Handling for the maps.

For the most part I have used Native names as given in the post journals, but added current names when appropriate.

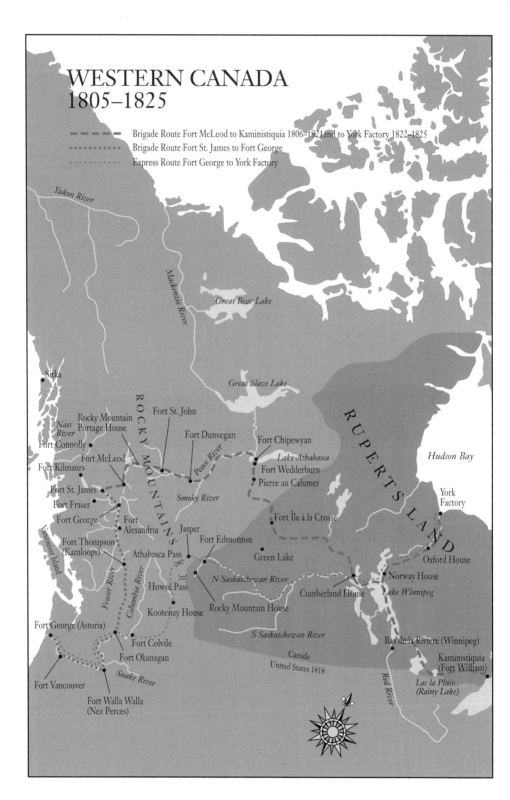

WESTERN CANADA
1805–1825

Brigade Route Fort McLeod to Kaministiquia 1806–1821and to York Factory 1822–1825
Brigade Route Fort St. James to Fort George
Express Route Fort George to York Factory

Yukon River

Mackenzie River

Great Bear Lake

Sitka

Great Slave Lake

R O C K Y   Fort St. John

Rocky Mountain
Portage House
Nass River   Fort Dunvegan
Fort Connolly   Fort Chipewyan
Fort Kilmaurs   Fort McLeod   *Peace River*   *Lake Athabasca*
                                   Fort Wedderburn
Fort St. James   Pierre au Calumet
Fort Fraser   M   *Smoky River*
Fort George   O   Fort
               U   Alexandria *Jasper*   Fort Île à la Crosse
Fort Thompson N   Fort Edmonton
(Kamloops)   T   Athabasca Pass
               A   Green Lake
               I   *N Saskatchewan River*
               N   Howse Pass
               S   Rocky Mountain House
                   Kootenay House

Hudson Bay

York
Factory

R U P E R T S   L A N D

Oxford House

Norway House

Cumberland House   *Lake Winnipeg*

Fort George (Astoria)   *Fraser River*   *Columbia River*

Fort Colvile   *S Saskatchewan River*
Fort Okanagan
                                        Bas de la Riviere (Winnipeg)
Fort Vancouver   *Snake River*   Canada
                                   United States 1818   Kaministiquia
Fort Walla Walla   (Fort William)
(Nez Perces)   *Red River*
                                               Lac la Pluie
                                               (Rainy Lake)

Vancouver Island

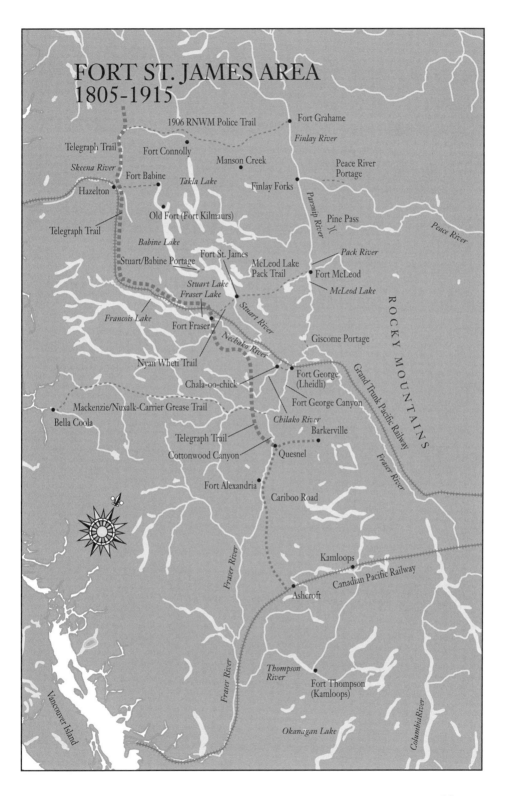

FORT ST. JAMES AREA
1805-1915

1906 RNWM Police Trail

Fort Grahame

Finlay River

Telegraph Trail

Fort Connolly

Manson Creek

Peace River
Portage

Skeena River

Fort Babine

Takla Lake

Finlay Forks

Hazelton

Telegraph Trail

Old Fort (Fort Kilmaurs)

Parsnip River

Pine Pass

Peace River

Babine Lake

Stuart/Babine Portage

Fort St. James

McLeod Lake
Pack Trail

Pack River

Fort McLeod

Stuart Lake
Fraser Lake

Stuart River

McLeod Lake

Francois Lake

Fort Fraser

Nechako River

Giscome Portage

ROCKY MOUNTAINS

Nyan Wheti Trail

Chala-oo-chick

Fort George
(Lheidli)

Fort George Canyon

Grand Trunk Pacific Railway

Mackenzie/Nuxalk-Carrier Grease Trail

Chilako River

Bella Coola

Telegraph Trail

Barkerville

Cottonwood Canyon

Quesnel

Fraser River

Fort Alexandria

Cariboo Road

Fraser River

Kamloops

Canadian Pacific Railway

Ashcroft

Thompson
River

Fort Thompson
(Kamloops)

Vancouver Island

Okanagan Lake

Columbia River

$\mathcal{I}$ ntroduction

THE 2006 BICENTENNIAL of Fort St. James celebrated one of the first permanent European settlements in British Columbia and 200 years of cooperation with First Nations people. It also celebrated the incredible courage and determination of the men and women of all races who took part in the exploration and fur-trading history of New Caledonia.

Today there are few reminders left of that mighty fur-trading empire that once stretched the length and breadth of New Caledonia (now British Columbia), south to California, east to Hudson Bay and the St. Lawrence River and then to Great Britain. Fortunately for those who wish to experience fur-trading activities first-hand, two of the New Caledonia forts have been restored and a number of the pack trails made accessible to hikers. One of these, Nyan Wheti, "the trail across," in the Central Interior was used for centuries by First Nations people to travel from Fraser Lake to Stuart Lake, and from 1806 into the early twentieth century it was used by fur traders and packers transporting dried salmon, furs and provisions and driving herds of livestock. Northeast of Prince George, the nine-kilometre Giscome Portage Trail, which connects the Fraser River to Summit Lake, offers hiking from Pacific to

Arctic watersheds. This ancient trail was utilized by fur traders transporting goods between the Fraser River and Fort McLeod and its outposts. In the Okanagan Valley it is possible to find evidence of the 1826–1847 brigade trail worn into the western slopes, and near Alexandria in the Fraser Canyon there are traces of the first brigade trail through the Cascades to Fort Langley.[1]

Although the buildings have long disappeared, the sites of most of the New Caledonia forts in the Central Interior can still be located. An unusual patch of grass in a rancher's field marks Fort Chilcotin, a park and a museum commemorate Fort George, and a cairn on Highway 97 north of Marguerite stands near the site of Fort Alexandria. Eighty miles north of Prince George, a small village marks Fort McLeod, Simon Fraser's first post west of the Rockies. To the west, Fort Fraser, Old Fort and Fort Babine can be found on contemporary maps. With the assistance of the Province of British Columbia, Parks Canada has restored both Fort Langley and Fort St. James in order that the public may experience the

Near the junction of the Nechako and Fraser rivers (upper right), Simon Fraser departed by canoe on his great voyage of discovery in 1808. One hundred years later the *BX*, the most powerful sternwheeler on the Fraser River, delivered supplies to a rapidly growing community eagerly awaiting the arrival of the Grand Trunk Pacific Railway. Fort George is a short distance upriver from the steamer. JASPER YELLOWHEAD MUSEUM AND ARCHIVES PA48-61

sights and sounds and investigate the structures required by the large fur-trading centres.

There have been numerous histories published about Fort Langley, but Fort St. James and its satellite posts have only received extensive attention in Adrian Morice's 1902 book, *The History of the Northern Interior of British Columbia*. However, this settlement deserves further examination because it was the major trading post in the Central Interior for over one hundred years. Between 1806 and 1826 it served as a collecting centre for furs packed at Fort McLeod and sent thousands of miles eastward by canoe brigades to Fort William on Lake Superior and later to York Factory on Hudson Bay. Between 1826 and 1847 the brigades departed from Fort St. James and travelled by canoe and horse trains south to Fort Vancouver on the Columbia River and from 1847 until 1863 to Fort Langley on the Fraser River. During the 1830s and 1840s Fort St. James was the centre of a region that supplied a good portion of the furs shipped by the Hudson's Bay Company to England, and following the Fraser and Cariboo gold rushes of 1858 to 1865 and on into the settlement era of the late nineteenth and early twentieth centuries, it continued to be an important fur-trading centre in what became the province of British Columbia.

This book is a history of the fur trade as it developed in central British Columbia. As the main themes of survival and cooperation unfold, it seeks to answer a number of questions: During the evolution of the fur trade in New Caledonia, how did the North West Company gain a secure foothold west of the Rockies in a land well populated by First Nations? After the merger with the HBC in 1821, how did the HBC maintain good relations with them until the rule of law was introduced in 1858? What were the special challenges in conducting the fur brigade to the Columbia River and to Fort Langley? And how were the forts of New Caledonia affected by the gold rushes, settlement and modern transportation systems after it became a British colony in 1858 and a Canadian province in 1871?

Adrian Morice did his best to answer some of these questions in 1902 but with limited access to original documents, he concentrated on writing a general, anecdotal history of New Caledonia. Unfortunately, the vast records in the HBC Archives in London were not opened to the public until the 1920s. North American historians rejoiced in 1974 when these records were "brought home" to Winnipeg to be housed at the Archives of Manitoba, and in June 2007 the United Nations Educational, Scientific and Cultural Organization (UNESCO) added the HBC Archives to its prestigious *Memory of the World* registry.[2]

All the major posts in New Caledonia kept daily journals, letterbooks and account books, and where extant these may be consulted. The entries in the journals help us to understand the interplay between First Nations and fur traders as they went about their daily routines, but we must accept the fact that not every important incident was recorded. The letterbooks corroborate the daily journal entries, and we gain an even broader understanding of events and administration by combining information from the posts' records with correspondence from the HBC's governor and committee in London, the governor and council in Rupert's Land, and from Governors George Simpson and Eden Colvile.

In addition to material in the HBC Archives, the letters of one of the few people not involved in the fur trade to visit New Caledonia prior to 1850, Jesuit priest John Nobili, provide a unique viewpoint, although Nobili could not have proselytized throughout New Caledonia from 1845 to 1848 without the assistance of HBC personnel.

To make the economic history of New Caledonia clearer, information from some of the most accessible financial reports has also been included. However, it is difficult to prove whether the district made a profit every year because not all expenses were identified. The fact that the HBC kept Forts St. James, McLeod, Fraser, Grahame, George and Babine open beyond 1900 suggests that the New Caledonia fur trade was a viable operation into the twentieth century.[3]

Despite its intensive trapping history in British Columbia, the beaver that was at the heart of the fur trade persists to this day, multiplying and building dams, much to the chagrin of officials in heavily populated municipalities who must cope with blocked culverts and flooded roads. In 2005 (the most recent statistic) trappers killed 3,878 beaver.[4]

Chapter One

"WHAT CANNOT BE CURED MUST BE ENDURED."

BY 1804 THE NORTH WEST COMPANY (NWC), based in Montreal, had overextended itself westward to the Athabasca District, its largest department with fifteen trading posts in the Peace, Athabasca and Mackenzie watersheds. Each year it took more than a month for the "wintering partners" at the company's distant posts to bring their collection of furs the many thousands of miles eastward by northern canoes to Lac La Pluie (Rainy Lake). There the Nor'wester brigades halted to unpack the furs while the wintering partners travelled another one hundred river miles to reach Fort William, the North West Company's post at the mouth of the Kaministiquia River on Lake Superior. At Fort William the partners met with the NWC directors who had travelled west from Montreal in their thirty-six-foot-long freight canoes or *canots des maîtres* to plan the distribution of personnel for the coming year. At the same time, the directors' Montreal boatmen or *engagés* continued on to Lac La Pluie with the annual provisions to exchange them for furs. Once business was settled and they had all enjoyed a grand *regale* and dance, the Montreal directors returned east in their fur-laden vessels, while at Lac La Pluie the wintering partners and their *engagés* loaded their canoes to the gunwales with provisions and trading goods and headed west.

Fresh possibilities for the fur trade began opening up in 1793 after Alexander Mackenzie, one of the company's partners, set out overland from Athabasca for the Pacific Coast on a journey that included about one hundred miles on a river that the Natives called Tacouche Tess. He thought it might be a branch of the Columbia River, but the need to return to Athabasca by winter forced him to leave the river and make an overland trek to the coast at Bella Coola. Seven years later only James Finlay had attempted to retrace Mackenzie's route through the Rocky Mountains, and he had only explored portions of the Parsnip River and another river that now bears his name.[5] By this time the directors of the North West Company were becoming convinced that they needed a port on the Pacific as a base for trading furs with China and that the mouth of the Columbia would be a good place to establish it. A port there would also allow the company to obtain provisions more efficiently for its western posts. Moreover, beaver were being trapped-out east of the Rockies, and based on Mackenzie's reports, there were rich possibilities for the fur trade beyond the mountains.

Alexander Mackenzie published an account of his journey in 1801 as *Voyages from Montreal Through the Continent of North America*, and it caught the attention of Thomas Jefferson, president of the United States (1801–1809), who began organizing an expedition to the west under Merriweather Lewis and William Clark. Their famous *Voyage of Discovery to the Pacific Ocean* began in May 1804 and by the following summer they had reached the confluence of the Snake and Columbia rivers, just as Simon Fraser, another of the NWC's wintering partners, was pushing westward up the Peace River to the Rocky Mountains. Fraser had not attended the NWC Council in Fort William in 1804 and no written decision has come to light, but it appears in that year the council ordered him to journey down the Tacouche Tess to

Brave, determined, loyal and reliable, Simon Fraser and his skilled crew, including two Lheidli T'enneh interpreter/ guides, completed the voyage of discovery of the Fraser River (Tacouche Tess) for the North West Company in the summer of 1808. GLENBOW ARCHIVES NA-1194-8

determine if it was the Columbia. Another NWC partner, David Thompson, was already exploring near the headwaters of the Columbia in the Rocky Mountains.[6]

WHY WAS FRASER CHOSEN to extend Mackenzie's exploration and not one of the other five wintering partners in Athabasca? Historian J.N. Wallace believes that it was not because of Fraser's superior qualities of courage and leadership, since all of the Nor'wester partners were exceptional men. Instead, he simply was the only senior trading partner available in 1805 to carry out this difficult and extensive expedition. Born in Vermont in 1776, Fraser had been brought to Canada by his widowed mother eight years later and entered the North West Company's service as an apprentice at sixteen. By 1799 he seems to have been in charge of Rocky Mountain Fort in the company's Athabasca Department, and he became a partner in 1801.

Fraser's second-in-command for the expedition, John Stuart, was an excellent choice for the job. He had been stationed at Rocky Mountain Fort in 1804 when the great explorer and mapmaker David Thompson arrived during his survey of the Peace River. Stuart seems to have received some previous training in navigation, but Thompson likely gave him more instructions and outlined his own plans for tracing rivers in the southern Rocky Mountains.[7] In addition to his navigating skills, Stuart was an expert canoe-maker. Whether a large northern canoe was needed for long distance hauling or a smaller craft for local transportation, he knew the right proportions. He also ensured that the necessary materials were in readiness—"raised" birchbark (removed from trees), wooden crosspieces prepared, tree sap and spruce roots (*watape*) collected to secure the bark onto the struts. In the northern regions where winter weather dominated six months of the year, precious time could be lost on a voyage repairing old craft or building replacements, so Stuart set a high standard of workmanship, often complaining that the canoes provided by other forts were "crazy," that is, in very poor condition. Even when flat-bottomed freight boats called *batteaux* were introduced from the Columbia River, Stuart still preferred canoes because they were faster and easier to handle in rapids. A few months before his final departure from New Caledonia in 1824 he specified that his new canoes must be "fully 31 inches middle post, 29 inches for the fore and just less than 28½ for the after post, echantillions [*échelons*] at least 25 inches. This size will not much increase their weight and it will enable them to travel in windy weather and be the means of preserving the property in good order."[8]

John Stuart, the "Father of New Caledonia," took charge from Simon Fraser in 1808 and worked hard for the North West Company, doubling the number of forts to six before transferring east of the Rocky Mountains in 1824.
BRITISH COLUMBIA ARCHIVES A-01876

James McDougall, whom the Sekani people called Mutsikanutlo, meaning "curly hair,"[9] was the third member of Fraser's expeditionary team. Somewhat older than Stuart and Fraser, he had served in the Peace River area since 1799. He proved to be a steady, reliable clerk, whether managing forts or taking the furs to Fort William. Both Fraser and Stuart were adept at setting up new forts and trading with unfamiliar Natives. More importantly, they shared an unwavering commitment to the North West Company.[10] Their spirit of cooperation provided a solid base on which the NWC could build its influence, and along with McDougall, they spear-headed the NWC expedition into the vast land beyond the Rockies that the company had dubbed New Caledonia by maintaining good relations among themselves and with the Natives.

Cooperation with First Nations was absolutely crucial if the fur trade was to survive in this new territory. In fact, without Native guides and interpreters neither Alexander Mackenzie nor Simon Fraser could have reached the Pacific Ocean, although countless illustrations fail to show that the canoes braving the rapids and whirlpools contained First Nations men and women as well as Metis boatmen, the European fur traders and their families. The fur brigades that followed in their wake also required Native men and women as packers, guides and dog train handlers to deliver tons of provisions to satellite posts, and all communication between forts as far away as the Columbia and Peace rivers relied on Native couriers who ensured that the mail reached even the remotest forts, often under severe winter conditions.

The daily journals of New Caledonia trading posts also verify the fur traders' dependency on Native labour for a broad spectrum of activities from building canoes and forts to fabricating snowshoes, moccasins and other wearing apparel. More importantly, Native people provided food for the many trading posts, especially game and fish, because post employees were either too few in number and didn't have the time or too unskilled to be successful as hunters and fishers. Preserving meat and fish by drying and smoking were time-consuming techniques that the fur traders also left to the Natives, and berry cakes made by the Native women from fruit gathered in late summer added variety to the fort personnel's winter diet. While James McDougall served in New Caledonia, he led the Carrier people and fort employees on an annual berry harvesting foray to Tache. Entire families were also involved in trapping and preparing furs for market. As a result of this interdependence, both the North West Company and, after 1821, the Hudson's Bay Company tried to avoid clashes by following a policy of respecting Native hunting and fishing territories.

Interpreters were vital to the success of a voyage of discovery, but Fraser's choice of the Metis Paul Bouché, also known as La Malice, caused him many problems. Perhaps La Malice was the only experienced man available, but he was cantankerous and often unreliable. He worked for the NWC for more than a decade before shifting his allegiance to the rival Hudson's Bay Company. He spent the winter of 1820–21 at Fort Wedderburn with his wife and children and advised Governor George Simpson on the best routes to infiltrate New Caledonia. Simpson, however, did not fully trust him although he considered La Malice's wife the most important interpreter at the fort because she was the only one who could speak Chipewyan. La Malice was still serving in New Caledonia in 1826 when he accompanied William Connolly's brigade to York Factory.[11]

Another Metis interpreter—and possibly a brother of La Malice—Jean Baptiste Boucher, known as Waccan, was also part of the New Caledonia expedition. He eventually gained immense status not only as an interpreter but also as a peacemaker and skillful labourer.

Young, strong, fearless boatmen or *boutes* were the other personnel needed to succeed. They were usually French Canadian Metis or Iroquois, although NWC trader Daniel Harmon later complained that he could not carry on a conversation with them because they were illiterate and ignorant: "All of their chat is about Horses, Dogs, Canoes and Women, and strong Men who can fight a good battle."[12] But they could paddle from sun-up to sundown day after day on meager rations, line canoes in turbulent, frigid water and fearlessly run the most dangerous rapids. When Jesuit priest John Nobili accompanied the brigade to Fort St. James in

1845, he was amazed at the boatmen's courage and endurance in the face of so many obstacles. He noted that the banks of the rivers were constantly caving in; at one site on the Stuart River an enormous slide had changed the channel and the outgoing brigade had to instantly chart a new course: "There were new islands, new rapids, with no time to turn back."[13]

Duplicating Mackenzie's strategy of a decade earlier, Fraser planned to establish two base camps to support his exploration, and in the fall of 1804 he sent James McDougall to construct the first one, Rocky Mountain Portage, on the eastern side of the Peace River canyon, just across the river from present-day Hudson's Hope. It became an important staging site for the ten-mile portage around the dangerous canyon that contracted to 150 feet and dropped 275 feet. Here canoes were readied for service and provisions stored, setting the scene for Fraser to breach the mountains the following year and establish his second base.[14]

At Trout (McLeod) Lake in 1805 Simon Fraser and James McDougall established the first fort west of the Rocky Mountains, to the left of the outlet of the Pack River. For the next twenty years all New Caledonia furs—up to 8,000 pounds annually—were shipped east by canoes from this collection centre after ice breakup in early May.
BRITISH COLUMBIA ARCHIVES I-51967

Immediately after returning from Fort William to the upper Peace River in the fall of 1805, Fraser set out to establish his second base camp on the west side of the Rocky Mountains before winter set in. His advance party included McDougall, La Malice and a small number of boatmen. They portaged around the Peace River Canyon, canoed upriver to Finlay Forks, then up the Parsnip and Pack rivers to Trout (McLeod) Lake. As Native trails going from north to south and east to west intersected here, Fraser built a small trading post and in late November returned to Rocky Mountain Portage with McDougall, leaving La Malice and two other men to trade with the Sekani during the winter. Eventually the two men deserted and returned to Rocky Mountain Portage; La Malice soon followed.[15]

During the winter of 1805–6 at Rocky Mountain Portage, Fraser gained further impetus for establishing posts on the west side of the mountains when he learned from the Carrier people that they were exchanging furs for ironworks and ornaments with the Babine Nation, who acted as intermediaries with Natives on the Pacific Coast. (They were given the name Babine or "large lip" by the NWC because the adult women of this tribe wore labrets in their lower lips.) While Stuart and Fraser made final preparations for the spring expedition, McDougall returned to the post at Trout (McLeod) Lake to explore the area and trade for furs with the Sekani people. However, he also ventured as far as "Carrier Lake," which is presumed to be present-day Stuart Lake, and discovered that there were hundreds of beaver ponds in the swampy, sub-boreal spruce forests there. In early May 1806 he sent fourteen ninety-pound packs of furs back to Fraser. These packs represented 50 percent of Fraser's winter trade at Rocky Mountain Portage, and their quality impressed him: "The furs are really fine. They were chiefly killed in the proper season and many of them are superior to any I have seen in Athabasca, being quite black and being well dried . . . "[16]

The Carrier people that McDougall met at the foot of Stuart Lake belonged to the Na-Dene or Northern Athapaskan linguistic group, languages that have recently been linked to the 5,000-year-old Ket language of Siberia.[17] While extending trading posts across the Prairies to the Rockies, the NWC had already encountered another member of this group, the Chipewyans, in Athabasca, but the three members located just east of the Rockies and in New Caledonia—the Beaver, Sekani and Carrier—were slightly taller than the Chipewyans, with straight black hair and longer faces. The Chilcotin, another Athapaskan group, lived to the southwest of the Stuart Lake Carrier, and the Atnah or Shuswap of the Interior Salish Nation to the south and southeast. The Carrier, Sekani and Chilcotin traded directly or through intermediaries with First Nations living on the Pacific Coast: the Tsimshian, Kwakiutl and Nuxalk.

McDougall discovered that, because of the salmon fishery, the cluster of Carrier villages at the foot of Stuart Lake formed an important stopping place in the vast network of trails and waterways that connected numerous First Nations sites. In late summer the Carriers installed weirs across the lake's outlet as well as on other major lakes in preparation for the annual salmon run. Although they caught some salmon in this way most years, roughly every fourth year there was a much higher yield and in these years they were able to dry and store thousands of fish for the winter. Stuart Lake also contained sturgeon of massive size, some weighing 300 pounds or more. Game supplemented the Carrier diet in both good and lean years. As a result of interdependency, large animals such as black and grizzly bears were more numerous during the years of the heavy salmon runs, and lynx and wolves increased during years with large rabbit populations. Local game birds such as grouse were available and in the spring and fall large flocks of migrating birds appeared on Stuart and Fraser lakes, which are located on the Pacific flyway for swans, snow geese, Canada geese (bustards), cranes and ducks. McDougall also learned from the Carrier that the Pacific Ocean could be reached from this point with only three portages, and recognizing

The conical *varveau* and woven weir fence stored to the left of the Nak'azdli house at Stuart Lake were used for catching salmon. BRITISH COLUMBIA ARCHIVES D-00454

the lake's central importance, he urged Fraser to include it in his exploration of the new country.

A late winter followed by spring freshets delayed Fraser's departure from Rocky Mountain Portage until May 1806, and when his party finally reached Trout (McLeod) Lake, inclement weather and the need to construct new canoes caused further delays. When they finally set out again on June 23, Fraser left James McDougall in charge at the lake. The next part of the journey southward proved extremely difficult as the usual hazards of driftwood and rocks were compounded by swiftly flowing waters, but eventually Fraser's party reached the main river—the Tacouche Tess. After travelling down it for a few hours, he easily found the island-studded mouth of the Nechako River that Mackenzie had missed a decade earlier, and his party camped overnight at this junction, which the Carrier people called Lheidli.[18]

Fraser and his men then took another fifteen days to work their way up through the rapids of the Nechako and Nak'azdli (Stuart) rivers because they were now in flood, and the canoes, hastily made at McLeod Lake only a month earlier, leaked constantly. By the time they reached Nak'azdli (Carrier or Stuart) Lake, the men were exhausted and food was running low.[19]

Based on McDougall's report, Fraser expected to find a thriving community here with plenty of fresh fish and game and many beaver pelts on hand, but only a few starving Natives met them— with neither furs nor food. He learned that the annual salmon run was not due for several weeks, berries would not ripen until the end of August, and the Natives lacked fishhooks to catch sturgeon.[20] However, Fraser's initial contact with the Carrier here was an omen for the future as they offered little resistance to the newcomers and they were not well armed.

His greatest challenge now was the threat of starvation. Although they had a bountiful harvest every fourth year, three years out of four the salmon run at the lake was small or non-existent. There were no moose in this region and other large animals such as caribou and bear were seasonal or only attracted by large salmon runs. The Natives could follow their food supplies, but a fixed trading post required defending and careful management of its larder.[21] To make matters worse, at this important first contact with the people of this settlement, Fraser lacked the large supply of trading goods that NWC traders traditionally relied on to barter for food and to ensure a good reception. He tackled this difficult situation with a strong practical sense and the simple philosophy of "what cannot be cured must be endured."[22] He immediately set his men to work to build a shelter and then wrote to Archibald Norman McLeod, his superior at Fort Dunvegan on the Peace River, urging him to fulfill his obligations:

> To form establishments this summer certainly depends upon us—but to render them productive will depend upon the attention you Gentlemen will pay them. We had but few trading goods on leaving the [Rocky Mountain] Portage, and tho few of you can imagine what it costs to feed the people in this quarter, there are none of you but know that exploring new countries and seeing strange Indians is expensive, was it only

to procure a welcome reception. As we are at present we have scarcely a sufficient apportionment of goods to feed all hands during the winter.[23]

McLeod, however, had only arrived at the site of Dunvegan in the fall of 1805 and had spent the winter building palisades, bastions and block houses. He had to feed the forty-five men employed there constructing the fort as well as the company's officers, Native hunters and their families. As a result, it would be late 1807, after the brigade returned to the Peace River, before he sent Fraser any provisions or trading goods, and this lack of supplies not only prevented Fraser's exploration of the Tacouche Tess in 1806–7 but also required additional personal sacrifices from both Fraser and Stuart. Fraser had been slated to go out on rotation to Montreal in 1808 and Stuart had signed on only until 1807. They were now forced to delay their voyage of discovery until the spring of 1808.

Meanwhile, Fraser and his men were forced to survive on short rations while they built their new trading post, Stuart Lake Post (known as Fort St. James after 1821), at the foot of Nak'azdli Lake (now known as Stuart Lake), but in August 1806 he learned from the Natives that, even when there were no salmon in the Nak'azdli, there was often a salmon run on another branch of the Nechako River to the southwest. Not wanting to face six months of starvation, at the end of August he sent John Stuart southwest to find the half-mile-long Natleh (Nautley) River that drains a large lake (which Fraser named for himself) into the Nechako River. Fraser followed him there a few days later to establish a post. This was a wise decision because for many decades to come the dried fish secured from the Natives at Natleh and at Stella, a village at the western end of the lake, would help to support Forts St. James, McLeod, George and sometimes Alexandria.

John Stuart passed the winter of 1806–7 at Stuart Lake while Fraser remained at Fraser Lake until December in order to secure a good supply of fish. The two men, with Stuart's wife and child, celebrated Christmas and New Year's at Stuart Lake, and Fraser

Established in 1806 at the foot of Stuart Lake, Fort St. James received the full force of winter winds and snow. This picture was taken November 12, 1912, by surveyor Frank Swannell. BRITISH COLUMBIA ARCHIVES H-04827

returned to Fraser Lake in the early part of 1807. Through the lonely winter days he kept in touch with Stuart, James McDougall at McLeod Lake and his superiors at Dunvegan by frequent letters delivered by La Malice and other couriers.[24]

However, Fraser was not entirely alone during his stay at Fraser Lake. Although he had left a Native woman behind in the Athabasca district when he set out to establish the New Caledonia forts, he acquired another country wife during this first winter at Fort Fraser. It would appear that the children from Fraser's previous union(s) resided at Fort McLeod under the care of James McDougall because Fraser gave him instructions to charge his account for "anything that the children are in want of and that can be had . . ."[25] While many of the Nor'westers remained with their partners for life, Fraser was an exception, and there is no record of how his Native wives and children were cared for when he returned east of the Rockies in 1809 or when he retired to Upper Canada in 1816. This aspect of his life sits in sharp contrast to his assistants, Stuart and McDougall and later Daniel Harmon, who maintained stable relationships with Native and Metis women.

In *Strangers in Blood*, Jennifer Brown states that Nor'westers treated Native women as commodities, buying and selling them among themselves and not generally marrying. Simon Fraser was very rough with his French Canadian boatmen when they wanted to take Native women as partners. He didn't hesitate to remove a woman as punishment for bad behaviour by one of his men, and he accepted payment—as much as 300 livres—from the woman's new partner. Archibald McLeod at Fort Dunvegan and Hugh Faries also followed this policy. The NWC Resolve of July 1806 prohibited company men from taking Native wives because the cost of feeding and caring for the increasing number of women and children was taxing the company's resources. Although men were fined £100 each at St. Mary's and lower Red River for breaking this rule, it was impossible to strictly maintain it west of the Rockies. Senior personnel such as Fraser, McDougall and Stuart were exempted.[26]

Cooperation with the Native peoples was crucial for the white traders because the Natives far outnumbered them. At a much later date John Stuart recorded in his letterbook how the NWC had kept the Native people under control:

> The dread of the Beaver Indians has long, perhaps more than anything else, kept the Carriers in awe . . . From the first establishment of Western Caledonia in 1806 the Natives were invariably told that any murder committed would be severely punished & that the Beaver Indians was one of the means that would be resorted to.[27]

Although they shared the Athapaskan language with the Carrier, the Beaver from the eastern side of the mountains were known for their ferocity. They had made earlier contact with the NWC, and having been armed with guns by the 1780s, they had been able to drive the Sekani out of the Peace River region into New Caledonia and had stolen their women during raids.[28]

NWC personnel in New Caledonia also used a display of arms and fisticuffs to keep the Natives in line. When clerk Daniel Harmon managed Fort Fraser, he recorded an encounter with the senior Carrier chief Qua or "Kwah." Harmon took offence when Qua insulted him during an argument and he knocked the chief to the ground. Harmon quickly regretted his actions, but when Qua invited him to a feast shortly afterwards, he and his men attended, but they went fully armed with pistols and a sword. Thereafter Harmon was known to the Carrier as "Big Knife." He also used a show of arms in January 1817 to subdue a group of angry Natives after one of them had been "given a drubbing" for stealing.[29]

Respect for First Nations customs was another way in which both the NWC and HBC maintained peaceful relations with the Native people throughout their time in New Caledonia. The NWC respected the Native celebrations for the arrival of the first salmon and the cremation of their dead—although the white men described the ceremony in dramatic, Victorian Gothic fashion. Both the NWC and HBC made a practice of recognizing headmen or chiefs at an annual ceremony where the post manager presented them with outfits of clothing and enough tobacco to share with the other Natives in attendance. And the feasting and dancing at New Year's Day celebrations brought together the fun-loving French Canadian *engagés*, sombre Scots and First Nations in a happy encounter.

Chapter Two

THE TACOUCHE TESS

SIMON FRASER'S LONG-AWAITED PROVISIONS arrived in the fall of 1807 from Dunvegan, delivered by two reliable Nor'westers, Jules Quesnel and Hugh Faries. Both men were Canadians, born in Montreal, but only Quesnel had served in Athabasca, as an assistant to David Thompson. Faries had transferred from Rainy Lake and would spend two terms in New Caledonia. Fraser placed Faries in charge of a temporary trading post at Lheidli (later to be called Fort George) at the junction of the Nechako and Tacouche Tess, where the canoes would be built for exploration in 1808. Most likely because of his service with Thompson exploring and mapping the rivers on the southeastern side of the Rocky Mountains, Quesnel was chosen to accompany Fraser and Stuart on the voyage of discovery.[30]

The historic expedition to the sea began at 5 a.m. on May 28, 1808, when Fraser set off from Lheidli in four canoes with Stuart, Quesnel, Jean Baptiste Boucher (Waccan), eighteen voyageurs and two local Carrier, Little Chief Tyee-as and his brother Ka-ha from Chala-oo-chick on the Nechako River, who acted as guides and interpreters.[31] On his first journey up the Nechako in 1806 Fraser had no choice but to portage around the rapids below

Chala-oo-chick, and it is possible that he had met the chief and his brother at the settlement at that time, although since it was early summer most of the young men would have been away hunting. However, when Fraser returned in 1807 they would have become acquainted because the Nor'westers were building their small outpost at Lheidli and travelling back and forth to villages on the well-worn Native trail that connected the two, saving themselves fourteen miles of river travel.

The Letters and Journals of Simon Fraser, 1806–1808 contains Fraser's description of the journey, including the terrifying encounters with rapids and whirlpools in narrow, steep-walled canyons. Frequently John Stuart went ahead of the canoes with Quesnel to reconnoitre dangerous sections of the river. Fraser wrote, "I scarcely ever saw anything so dreary, and seldom so dangerous in any country; and at present while I am writing this, whatever way I turn, mountains upon mountains, whose summits are covered with eternal snows, close the gloomy scene."[32] To Fraser's great relief, the Natives along their route were helpful and a few even acted as guides. They willingly provided food and in one generous instance accepted only two calico nightgowns in exchange for two desperately needed canoes.

Fraser wisely heeded their advice about avoiding surprises and always sent a Native interpreter ahead to inform new tribes of his impending arrival. With the assistance of local chiefs he carefully planned meetings with the many Native bands along the way, employing a combination of polite courtesy and extreme caution, arming both himself and his men. Near the village of Kumshene at the junction of the Fraser and Thompson rivers he may have felt a bit overwhelmed when a principal chief introduced him to a gathering of 1,200 people, but Fraser claimed that he shook hands with every one of them.[33] The explorers' most difficult confrontation with the Natives duplicated Mackenzie's experience a decade earlier when he and his men had been forced to turn back at Bentinck Arm. Shortly after Fraser reached tidewater, hostile Musqueam forced his party to make a hasty retreat upriver.[34]

Despite many accidents and life-threatening experiences, Fraser's expedition returned safely to Lheidli, taking only one more day than on the journey south. Although bitterly disappointed that he had not found the Columbia or even a totally navigable river on which to transport furs, he could take solace in the fact that there were no serious injuries or any loss of life among his men. His success was due in great measure to the reliable Metis boatmen, Native guides and interpreters, and the calibre of the NWC men who accompanied him. John Stuart proved an excellent second-in-command, keeping a record of meridian measurements throughout the voyage. Fraser included six of them in his journal, and all except one—the one for June 24—were accurate.[35]

Immediately after returning to Lheidli, Fraser handed leadership over to Stuart and left to report to his superiors at Dunvegan and Fort Chipewyan. He spent the winter at Rocky Mountain Portage, and in the spring of 1809 after James McDougall and Hugh Faries brought out the New Caledonia furs, they journeyed together to Fort William. While Fraser continued on to Montreal to take his deferred rotation, McDougall and Faries returned west with the provisions for 1810.

Fraser never recrossed the Rocky Mountains, remaining in the Athabasca Department, where the country and Natives were familiar to him. During the War of 1812 he apparently went east again to Montreal and enlisted as an officer in the Corps of Canadian Voyageurs, which was led by William McGillivray, the principal director of the North West Company. Along with other Nor'westers Fraser became involved in transport on the St. Lawrence River. He wanted to retire in 1815, but William McGillivray talked him into serving another year in Athabasca, and a year later as Fraser was en route to Fort William for the annual council, Lord Selkirk arrested him and other Nor'westers for having taken part in the Seven Oaks Massacre at Red River. Although he may have been aware of the Red River plans, Fraser had not been physically involved, and following his acquittal, he retired to Lower Canada. In 1820, when he was forty-four, he married Catherine MacDonell, and they settled on farmland near the Raisin River in St. Andrews, and raised eight children. Fraser and his wife died within one day of each other in 1862.[36]

Although his achievements are outstanding, Fraser's presence in New Caledonia spanned little more than two years. His faithful second-in-command, John Stuart, his interpreter Jean Baptiste Boucher, and clerks James McDougall and later Daniel Harmon deserve the credit for cooperating with First Nations, ensuring the survival of the fur trade in New Caledonia and the transition to Hudson's Bay management in 1821. Twenty years later, George Simpson, governor of the Hudson's Bay Company, commented on the quality of life in New Caledonia and paid homage to Stuart's service:

> ... there is not a District in the country, where the Servants have such harassing duties or where they undergo so many privations; to compensate for which, they are allowed a small addition to the Wages of other Districts. But the present duties of the District, as regards the labour and suffering of the people, are no wise to be compared with what they were during the early part of the administration of Chief Factor John Stewart [sic], who may be considered the Father or founder of New Caledonia; where for 20 years of his Life he was doomed to all the misery and privation, which that inhospitable region could bring forth, and who with a degree of exertion, of which few men were capable, overcame difficulties to which the business of no other part of the country was exposed; bringing its returns to near about their present standing, and leaving the District as a Monument of his unwearied industry and extraordinary perseverance, which will long reflect the highest credit on his name and character, as an Indian Trader.[37]

However, Stuart was honest enough to admit that it was McDougall, with his long record of faithful service, who was really the father of New Caledonia, although McDougall never rose above the position of clerk and received little recognition from the HBC.[38]

DURING THE SUMMER OF 1809, while McDougall and Faries were absent with the brigade, provisions ran low at Fort St. James. Leaving Quesnel in charge, Stuart went to Fort Dunvegan to collect enough supplies to last until the brigade returned in the fall. Before heading back with supplies, he explored the rolling countryside with thirty-one-year-old Daniel Harmon, the son of a Vermont innkeeper, who had joined the NWC nine years earlier as a clerk. The two men discovered they had a mutual interest in theology, but it is also possible that Stuart, knowing Quesnel would leave the NWC when he completed his contract in 1811, may have been assessing Harmon as Quesnel's replacement. Fortunately, on October 7 when the incoming brigade under the leadership of Archibald McLeod arrived from the east at Dunvegan, it included three canoes loaded with over four tons of supplies for New Caledonia, enough to provision the forts adequately for another year.[39]

By now the routine at Fort St. James had been well established, and with a few exceptions it was probably similar to other NWC forts. Once freeze-up occurred, while the Natives hunted fur-bearing animals, the NWC men used small dogsleds called *traineaux* to distribute dried fish obtained locally and

Daniel Harmon's book about his experiences in the fur trade reveals close family ties among Nor'westers in New Caledonia. GLENBOW ARCHIVES NA-1194-13

provisions brought in by the brigade to the outlying forts. Horses would not be introduced to this area for another decade, but two dogs could pull a 250-pound load plus food for themselves and the men, making close to 300 pounds in all. In years of salmon scarcity after 1822 the dogs would be sent from Stuart Lake to either Babine or Fraser Lake where salmon was more plentiful. Post journals kept careful track of the dogs' whereabouts and how many pups were born because, although dog flesh was considered a delicacy by the French Canadian *engagés*, the animals were in limited supply, and post managers only served it on special occasions. However, an exception was made for *engagés* on long treks who found it necessary to slaughter one or two animals when their food rations were exhausted, but they could be punished by fines if they had slaughtered a dog without due cause.[40]

Every spring the furs were transported to McLeod Lake where they were made into ninety-pound packs and sent east with the outgoing brigade. The handful of men left in charge for the summer at the New Caledonia forts were assigned local chores such as building maintenance and gardening. Stuart insisted that his

Every year for twenty years, *engagés* packed four tons of New Caledonia furs over a ten-mile portage to avoid these dangerous rapids in the Peace River Canyon. When the brigade returned in the fall they brought a winter's supply of provisions back across the trail. The W.A.C. Bennett hydro dam was built at this site in the 1960s.
LIBRARY AND ARCHIVES CANADA 1960-125 NPC PA-020161

men should not go out to Native villages on trading expeditions when the brigade was away because it was too dangerous. During the cold, stormy days of winter, life at the outlying forts was dreary as the men were forced to stay inside, trying to keep warm beside smoking fireplaces.

In the spring of 1810 Quesnel was left to manage Fort St. James while Stuart and Faries took four canoe loads of furs to Rainy Lake. On October 6, en route back to New Caledonia, they stopped at Dunvegan where Faries left the brigade for a new appointment in the Peace River area. But the brigade's mail included an official letter for Daniel Harmon from three of the wintering partners, requesting that he transfer to New Caledonia. They gave him the choice of working under Stuart or taking complete control, but well aware of the region's difficulties with food and provisions, Harmon chose the first option.

Late fall was not the best time of the year to set out for a new posting west of the mountains. Snow and rain plagued the brigade as Harmon, his Metis wife, Lizette, and young son George journeyed with them up the Peace River. Quesnel met the canoes at McLeod Lake on November 1 and, accompanied by thirteen labourers, escorted the family overland to Fort St James.[41] Stuart assigned them to Fort Fraser for the winter, but first Quesnel and his labourers had to restore some of the buildings, so it was not until December 29 that the Harmons moved to Fraser Lake and celebrated New Year's Day in lively fashion with Stuart and Quesnel in attendance:[42]

This being the first Day of the year our People have past it as is customary for them—Drinking & fighting. Some of the principal Indians of the place desired us to allow them to remain at the Fort to see our People drink, but as soon as they began to be intoxicated and quarrel among themselves, the Natives were apprehensive that something unpleasant might befall them also, therefore they hid themselves under beds & elsewhere, and said they thought the White People had become mad. But those who were in the fore part of the Day the most Beastly, became in the afternoon to be the quietest, they therefore observed that their senses had returned to them again, at which change they appeared to be not a little surprised.[43]

In the spring of 1811 Harmon moved his family back to Fort St. James before going to assist with brigade preparations at McLeod Lake. This time Stuart took the furs to Rainy Lake accompanied by McDougall and Quesnel, the latter being eager to leave the fur trade and return to Montreal. In 1809 Quesnel had complained to a friend, "In New Caledonia there is nothing to be had but misery and boredom." He felt that joining the NWC was his misfortune and that the isolation and endless diet of dried salmon were ruining his health.[44] At Harmon's request, Quesnel agreed to take three-year-old George with him and deliver him into the care of Vermont relatives for education. When the brigade departed McLeod Lake, Harmon felt deeply the loss of his only son, but on returning to Stuart Lake his sadness was somewhat alleviated by the birth of a baby daughter, Polly.[45] When Stuart arrived at Fort William that June, he was made a partner in the NWC. He appears to have spent the following year on rotation because Mc-Dougall returned alone with the brigade to Fort St. James in the fall.

David Thompson did not attend the annual meeting at Fort William in 1811 because he was completing his epic journey down the Columbia River. Like Mackenzie and Fraser before him, his great achievement was also tinged with disappointment. He arrived at the mouth of the river on July 16 to find that the American merchant John Jacob Astor had recently established a trading post, Fort Astoria, there for his Pacific Fur Company (PFC). Thompson spent a week at the fort and on his return journey up the Columbia sent a letter by Native courier to Fort St. James, informing Stuart and Harmon of his accomplishment. The letter, dated August 28, 1811, at Ilk-koy-ope (Kettle) Falls, passed from tribe to tribe, reaching Harmon in April 1812—a remarkable example of Native cooperation. As a result of Thompson's explorations on the Columbia, the NWC now began competing with the PFC, building trading posts at Spokane, the mouth of the Okanagan River and at the junction of the Thompson and North Thompson rivers.

David Thompson, satisfied that his exploration for the NWC was completed, commenced the long journey to eastern Canada with his family. When he stopped at Fort William to attend the 1812 NWC Council, they granted him time off on rotation and then retirement; he was now 42 years old and had spent 28 years in the service of the company. He also received £100 per annum for the next seven years as a retired partner in order that he could finish drawing up his maps. A few years earlier Simon Fraser had named the Thompson River in his honour, and now Thompson repaid the favour. The river that had been named Tacouche Tess by Mackenzie and published as that on Arrowsmith Maps was changed for posterity to the Fraser River.

Chapter Three

THE PRICE OF ADVANCEMENT

AFTER A YEAR ON ROTATION John Stuart returned via Fort Chipewyan to McLeod Lake on October 28, 1812, with orders to take charge of all of New Caledonia and combine "Plans & operations with the Gentlemen on the Columbia." New Caledonia at this point meant the region west of the Rockies and east of the Coast Range between latitudes 56° and 51°, which encompassed Bear (Connolly) Lake in the north to the height of land north of the mouth of the North Thompson River. Stuart was to go to the mouth of the Columbia the following spring and await the supply ship there. In the meantime, he spent the winter at Fort St. James with Harmon and their respective families. Also present were twenty-one labourers, one interpreter and three other women.[46] Because the government of the United States had declared war on Great Britain in June 1812, all of the company's wintering partners had been warned to have two years' provisions on hand in case supply lines from eastern Canada were cut off, and perhaps it was for this reason that Stuart waited for Harmon to make a trip to Dunvegan and back in the spring of 1813 before he set off for the Columbia in May.

Until this time New Caledonia had only maintained connections with forts east of the Rockies by way of the Peace River, but the Thompson River area and the Okanagan Valley had recently been infiltrated from the east by both Astor's Pacific Fur Company and the NWC. On this trip Stuart went by canoe partway down the Fraser River, then overland to the Thompson River. At the junction of the North and South Thompson rivers he passed the fort built by Joseph Larocque for the NWC the previous year and an adjacent one built by the Pacific Fur Company, both now abandoned, and proceeded south through the Okanagan Valley to Fort Okanagan on the Columbia River. After building *batteaux* there, he continued his journey to the mouth of the Columbia, where he met with John George McTavish, who had been empowered by the North West Company to purchase the assets of the Pacific Fur Company, Astor having been forced to surrender his interests on the Pacific Coast as a result of the war. Stuart remained with the Columbia Department of the NWC throughout 1813, although he apparently went east to Fort William in the summer with Joseph McGillivray and Alexander Stuart. He returned in the fall, just in time to be a signatory to the sales agreement between the Pacific Fur Company and the NWC on October 13.

Stuart's journey marked the historic first step in establishing a brigade route south from New Caledonia and a second NWC commercial headquarters west of the Rocky Mountains. Harmon noted in his journal:

> Should Mr. Stuart be so fortunate as to discover a water communication between this and the Columbia we shall for the future get our yearly supply of Goods from that quarter, and send our Returns out that way which will be shipped [from] there directly for the China Market in Vessels which the Concern intends building on that Coast—but while those deep laid plans are putting in execution, I in a more humble sphere it is true, but full as sure of succeeding in my undertakings shall attend to the little affairs of New Caledonia and pass the Summer at this place.[47]

From this date on, because of Stuart's frequent absences, Harmon and McDougall—along with their clerks and interpreters—were in charge of the New Caledonia forts most of the time. Stuart usually ended his departing instructions to them with the admission that they knew more about fur trading that he did and it would be presumptuous of him to give them detailed orders.

DURING FEBRUARY 1814 John Stuart and Alexander Henry searched along the Columbia for a new site for a NWC headquarters. They surveyed as far as the Willamette River and considered the *jolie prairie* at Point Vancouver on the north side of the Columbia but decided that it was too far from the sea. At last they returned to Astoria, which had been renamed Fort George by officers of the British naval sloop *Racoon,* who took formal possession of it on December 13, 1813. It would be used as the NWC's headquarters on the Columbia River for another decade.[48] It was not until Governor George Simpson visited the Columbia in 1824 that the *jolie prairie* was utilized by the HBC to establish Fort Vancouver.[49]

The acquisition of the Pacific Fur Company and its merger with the NWC created a huge fur-trading empire west of the Rockies. However, its administration was still conducted from Montreal, and like the Romans in ancient Gaul and Britain, the company had extended itself too far. Administration costs were high and the beaver "felt furs" collected along the Columbia were not of the high quality that sold well in China. The NWC Columbia Department lost more than £45,000 in 1813–14 and there were considerable losses for three or four of the next five years.[50] It remained for the HBC a decade later to develop the region's potential. The NWC tried provisioning Fort St. James from the Columbia, but they were only successful for three years—1813, 1814 and 1820—and they continued to transport New Caledonia furs east to Fort William by brigade.

During these years it was important that the northern forts be kept informed of the proceedings at the mouth of the Columbia River, and it was found that communication with trading posts on the upper Peace was most efficient if routed through New Caledonia to include Fort Fraser, Fort St. James and Fort McLeod. For this task the NWC employed Native couriers when their *engagés* weren't available. Natives had delivered Thompson's letters to Harmon in the spring of 1813, and they brought one from Stuart in September. In early November Joseph Larocque arrived from Dunvegan with the incoming brigade; acting on Stuart's orders he had taken on the role of courier between the Columbia River and Fort Chipewyan and was returning south via New Caledonia. For Harmon, however, the growing excitement about NWC activities on the Columbia were set aside in December 1813 when he received a letter from his brothers, advising that his son George had died following a brief illness the previous March. Harmon was so overcome with grief that McDougall and his family accompanied him back to Fort St. James to help break the news to Lizette. The two families spent the Christmas holidays together.

In January 1814, Harmon, Larocque and fourteen men went to Fraser Lake to trade furs and barter for salmon. Then on January 9, despite the extreme winter conditions when travel could only be accomplished by snowshoe and dogsled, Larocque left for the Columbia River with a package of letters. A month later Donald McLennan arrived from the Columbia with letters for Harmon and for John McGillivray, the factor at Dunvegan, confirming the NWC purchase of the Pacific Fur Company. Harmon had planned to have McLennan spend the spring and summer with him at Fort St. James, but McGillivray wanted his mail to the Columbia delivered as soon as possible, so McLennan departed in April, leaving Harmon with only ten men for the summer while McDougall went east with the brigade. On October 13 Larocque returned from the Columbia with ten men and two canoes laden with provisions, and Harmon put him to work restoring Fort Fraser before winter set in. When Stuart returned with McDougall and the incoming brigade at the end of October, Harmon moved to Fort Fraser and Larocque departed for the Columbia.[51] At the end of the year Stuart, McDougall, Harmon and their families once again celebrated New Year's together at Stuart Lake. Stuart spent all of 1815 at Fort St. James while presumably McDougall took the brigade east.

In April 1815, Stuart wrote to Ross Cox at Spokane House, expressing his concern for the new establishment on the Columbia, and offering advice on how to deal with Native hostility. He was obviously relieved to be back in New Caledonia:

> Although I deeply regret my absence from my friends on the Columbia, I have no cause to complain of my lot; for here, if not perfectly quiet, we are at least *hors de danger*. Messrs. Mc-Dougal [sic] and Harman [sic] are with me in the department. They are not only excellent traders, but (what is a greater novelty in this country) real Christians, and I sincerely wish that their steady and pious example was followed by others. We are at separate posts; but as we feel great delight in each other's company, we visit as often as the situation of the country and our business will permit; and in their conversation, which is already rational and instructive, I enjoy some of the most agreeable moments of my life.[52]

When Stuart once more took charge of the outgoing brigade in April 1816, he was due for a rotation and did not expect to return to New Caledonia. His luggage contained a copy of Harmon's journal to be delivered to relatives in Vermont. Harmon had been making copies of his journals ever since he joined the NWC in 1800 and was likely planning to publish them when he returned home, but a number of his close relatives had died while he had been in New Caledonia, and fearing that he might never see the rest of them again, he wanted them to have a record of his career west of the Rockies.[53]

New blood was added to the ranks when James McDougall's brother, George, arrived at Fort St. James in 1816. George had been employed for a year in Athabasca by the Hudson's Bay Company when he was captured by the North West Company, a victim of the increasing conflict between the rival companies. Upon

First established by Simon Fraser in 1806, Fort Fraser became a major source of dried salmon and agricultural products. The climate and soil were more conducive to raising vegetables and grain than at Fort St. James and Fort McLeod. BRITISH COLUMBIA ARCHIVES A-04216

release, he fled to New Caledonia where Harmon promptly hired him for two years, placing him in charge of Fort Fraser. Although later Governor George Simpson would express a low opinion of McDougall, he quickly became another mainstay of the NWC's New Caledonia administration. He did not leave until he was assigned to Great Slave Lake in 1830; he retired from the company while at Lesser Slave Lake in 1849.[54]

After six years in semi-isolation, Harmon was now looking forward to leaving New Caledonia, but Lizette was pregnant again, and a second daughter, Sally, arrived in February 1817. He presumably signed on for another two years and with the assistance of James and George McDougall managed New Caledonia to the best of his ability, but he preferred to remain in New Caledonia each summer while James McDougall accompanied the brigade to Rainy Lake. His local activities included a short *derouine* visit to the Native settlements on the Fraser River each January and the occasional special trip to Dunvegan or Fort Chipewyan. He also planted the first vegetable gardens west of the Rockies, first at Fort Fraser and then Fort St. James.

In 1819 as the time neared for Harmon's final departure from New Caledonia, he had a major decision to make. Should he take his family with him or place them under the care of another NWC employee? In October 1805 when he had taken Lizette Duval as his wife *à la façon du pays* (in the fashion of the country), he had thought that he would leave her behind when he returned east as he was well aware that other NWC Native and Metis wives had found it difficult to adjust to white society. But after fourteen years together, sharing many joys and sorrows, including the deaths of newborn twins at Dunvegan and then little George, his attitude had changed and he wrote a moving passage in his journal that expressed his deep love for his family:

> We have children still living who are equally dear to us both. How could I spend my days in the civilized world and leave my beloved children in the wilderness? The thought has in it the bitterness of death. How could I tear them from a mother's love and leave her to mourn over their absence to the day of her death? Possessing only the common feelings of humanity, how could I think of her in such circumstances without anguish? On the whole, I consider the course which I design to pursue as the only one which religion and humanity would justify.[55]

And so on May 8, 1819, the canoe bearing Harmon, Lizette and their two daughters, Sally and Polly, was eased into the Pack River by six boatmen. Ice dams hindered their progress, but once they crossed Rocky Mountain Portage, they travelled safely with the outbound brigade to Fort William. Six days after their arrival Lizette gave birth to a son. She and Daniel were formally married at the fort before setting out on the final leg of their journey to Vermont.

Harmon established his family near relatives, then resumed service with the NWC for a few more years. He was posted to Rainy Lake and granted chief trader status at the time of the merger of the HBC and NWC. In 1820 he published his fur-trading experiences as *A Journal of Voyages and Travels in the Interior of*

North America; it illuminates the day-to-day life of a fur trader as well as the role of a husband and father in New Caledonia. Harmon claimed that four-fifths of his time was free for his own pursuits, but his journal entries suggest otherwise. Given the modern valuation of labour, where double time for overtime and weekends off are standard expectations, Harmon, who was always on duty, certainly earned his free days.

Chapter Four

THE INVASION

For more than a century after its founding in 1670 the Hudson's Bay Company had been content to maintain forts on Hudson Bay and let the Natives bring furs to them. Their first inland post was not built until 1774 when Samuel Hearne established Cumberland House near the Saskatchewan River, and gradually more trading posts were added. But ever since Alexander Mackenzie's explorations in the 1790s, the NWC had been making attempts to move into HBC territory. And as the NWC extended their trading posts up the North Saskatchewan River and into New Caledonia, they didn't hesitate to intercept furs bound for "the Bay." These inroads drastically affected HBC dividends, which fell from 8 percent to 4 percent between 1800 and 1808 and to zero between 1809 and 1814. In 1810 the Hudson's Bay Company reorganized in an effort to give personnel more incentive to maintain the trading posts. Fixed salaries were reduced and senior employees received a share of the dividends.[56]

HBC men in the field were now expected to be firm and unyielding to NWC aggression although their actions were to be tempered by prudence. An HBC circular to post managers made this very clear:

We have always been and still are desirous that you should avoid all occasion of violent conflict with any commercial rivals . . . We expect that you will defend like men the Property that is entrusted to you; and if any person shall presume to make a forcible attack upon you, you have arms in your hands and the Law sanctions you in using them for your own defence. The peril is on the head of the aggressor. We should very much regret if you were to go one step beyond what the Laws of your Country will fully justify.[57]

On the other hand, the HBC's establishment in 1812 of the Red River Colony right across the Nor'westers' main trade routes had made a confrontation between the two companies unavoidable. Their rivalry for control of Athabasca and New Caledonia escalated after March 1816 when the HBC's governor, Robert Semple, captured and destroyed Fort Gibraltar, the NWC's post at Red River. Then on June 19 of that same year, when Semple was leading a party of armed Scottish settlers, a group of Metis under Cuthbert Grant killed him and twenty of his men at a place known as Seven Oaks. The HBC claimed that this "massacre" had been instigated by the NWC, but while a number of Grant's followers were indicted for murder, no one was ever convicted.

Meanwhile, the men of the NWC continued to fight hard to maintain their advantage. As the HBC traders moved cautiously along unfamiliar waterways, the Nor'westers went boldly ahead of them, frightening away game and warning the Natives not to trade furs with the enemy. As the result of this policy, eight HBC men starved to death in 1816 at an Athabasca post, and HBC clerk George McDougall and another eighteen men surrendered to the NWC to avoid the same fate. Afterwards, McDougall was allowed to travel to the west side of the mountains to join his brother in New Caledonia.

John Stuart, who had survived an attack by the HBC on his canoes at Green Lake, took an active role in the rivalry. (Peter Skene Ogden and Samuel Black also harassed HBC traders in this region.)[58] In December 1819 at Pierre au Calumet, which is on the Athabasca River just below the mouth of the McKay River, Stuart struck a hard bargain with HBC employee Aulay McAulay and his starving men. When they appealed to him for provisions, he provided meat and grease valued at 2,780 *livres* but demanded a large security in return: McAulay had to hand over all his trading goods, valued at 13,777 *livres*, withdraw from the region and return to Fort Wedderburn. Furthermore, McAulay had to ensure that he and his men would remain idle until June 1 and that HBC servants would not trade with the Cree in the neighbourhood until September 1, 1820. The conditions were impossible to fulfill, but Stuart refused to repay the balance of the security when he learned that McAulay and his men had been employed during the winter.[59]

The HBC had begun investigating access to New Caledonia in 1818, shortly after an international treaty guaranteed free commerce to both Britain and the United States between latitudes 40° and 54°40'. During the winter of 1818–19 the HBC established an advance post, Fort St. Mary's, on the north side of the upper Peace River across from the mouth of the Smoky River. However, a shortage of men and provisions delayed further action until February 1819 when José Guabin took a band of free (not under contract) Iroquois across the mountains to trade for furs and promise the arrival of the HBC soon in New Caledonia. To avoid contact with personnel at Fort McLeod, they had followed the Smoky River southwest from the new fort, then crossed the Rockies by way of a pass near Mount Robson, but an interpreter named Donald Fleming verified their presence after George McDougall sent him out on reconnaissance from the NWC fort on Stuart Lake.[60]

In 1820 Ignace Giasson was ordered to cross the mountains with five men, but they were not to approach the New Caledonia forts except when "business or the nature of your mission absolutely required."[61] As interpreter and guide, he hired the Metis-Iroquois Pierre Bostonais (sometimes recorded as Hatsinaton), who was generally known as Tête Jaune because of his blond-streaked hair. Tête Jaune was obviously familiar with the location of the NWC forts because Giasson later sent George Simpson a map showing his proposed HBC posts marked in red—near Trout Lake (Fort McLeod) and twenty days further by canoe, which would be the vicinity of Stuart Lake.[62] He persuaded the New Caledonia Natives to save their furs for trading when the HBC brigade arrived from York Factory in the fall, but this carefully planned rendezvous did not take place because the HBC *engagés* took too long partying at Norway House. The Native trappers grew tired of waiting and traded their furs to the NWC—a loss of fifty or sixty packs to the HBC. Giasson had to cache six packs of his own furs to be retrieved the following spring.

When the intense rivalry continued unabated, the HBC in London sent George Simpson to Red River to strengthen company resistance. By this time William Williams, who had become the HBC's governor-in-chief of Rupert's Land in 1818, was under indictment in the Lower Canada courts for assault and the false arrest of a number of Nor'westers, although he had managed to evade arrest. Simpson, however, had been primed to take his place. Trained as an accountant in a London sugar brokerage, he had no experience in the rough tactics of fur-trading rivalry, but at age thirty-three he was mentally tough and analytical with excellent skills in diplomacy. His departure from London was hurried and unexpected, but he took it as a great adventure and optimistically assumed he would

Governor George Simpson fought to win New Caledonia for the Hudson's Bay Company during the winter of 1820–21. He valued its rich fur trade and made a personal visit in 1828. He was knighted by Queen Victoria in 1841. BRITISH COLUMBIA ARCHIVES PDP02186

return to England in the spring of 1821. In fact, he remained in Canada for the next five years.[63]

Arriving in the fall of 1820, he found Williams firmly in charge at Red River and agreed to travel on and spend the winter in Athabasca. When he reached Fort Wedderburn, HBC headquarters, he set about immediately to extend HBC trading into New Caledonia. He already knew the region produced one hundred packs of good quality furs annually and that trade with the Natives was inexpensive:

> The Natives are unacquainted with the use of Spiritous liquors; Blankets, Cloth and many other high priced European articles may also be dispensed with, unless like the other tribes throughout the Country they get spoiled by opposition; the present standard of Barter is very high, in the ratio of 20 Beaver skins for a short Gun, 10 to 15 for a copper kettle according to size, and 1 for 3 inches of Tobacco so that the Trade must yield enormous profits.[64]

But in spite of his determination, Simpson had a healthy regard for the ferocity of the NWC defences:

> The North West Co'y will know that if we once get firmly established in the New Caledonia the ruin of their Athabasca Trade is consummated; they mean therefore to stretch every Nerve to foil us in that quarter, and I have every reason to believe that the most desperate measures will be resorted to on their part.[65]

Simpson relied on the Iroquois to play an important role in the HBC's fight for control of New Caledonia. They had come west as highly skilled boatmen from Montreal, and when their contracts expired, they remained in the country as free trappers, married into local tribes and adjusted easily to the nomadic life and its challenges. Harmon had noted in his journal that in 1818 Iroquois had been trapping beaver indiscriminately in New Caledonia, which upset the Carrier people.[66] Since the Iroquois owed allegiance to no one, Simpson reasoned that, when the HBC arrived on the scene, they could be lured to their forts by better tariffs (prices).

In the spring of 1821 Simpson asked Giasson to lead a party into New Caledonia again, but he refused because his contract with the HBC had expired and he was determined to return east. The job then went to William Brown who had been in charge of Fort Wedderburn during the winter. Two canoes with twelve men were to depart about June 10 in order to build two posts, one at McLeod Lake and the other at Stuart Lake. They were to secure enough salmon for the winter and twenty men in four canoes would bring supplies to them from Norway House to Rocky Mountain Portage in early September. Simpson wrote, "La Malice the Guide has wintered at both places, knows the Country well, and thinks we have no danger to apprehend either from the Natives or on the score of living."[67]

Simpson expected the fight for New Caledonia to continue for a number of years and planned to use Fort de Pinnette, near present-day Fort St. John, as his staging post. He wanted a strong attempt:

> The complement of Officers and Men for this District appears large, but after mature reflection I considered it best to err on the safe side, as in my humble opinion it would be better not to establish the Country at all than run the risk of losing all our prospects by making a contemptible figure at our entrée. The Indians will now see that we are not the petty intruders that the North West Company have represented us, and they will join us with a confidence and security which nothing but a formidable appearance can infuse.[68]

Pulling a final ace from his sleeve, Simpson encouraged his senior officers to form alliances with Native women in New Caledonia:

Connubial alliances are the best security we can have of the goodwill of the Natives. I have therefore recommended the Gentlemen to form connections with the principal Families immediately on their arrival, which is no difficult matter as the offer of their Wives & Daughters is the first token of their Friendship & hospitality.[69]

However, the winter of 1820–21 was so severe that the Peace River forts used up most of the provisions set aside for the planned New Caledonia spring expedition, so Brown's departure was rescheduled for that fall after the incoming brigade arrived. By that time the Hudson's Bay Company and the North West Company had been merged, and Brown learned that he had been promoted to chief trader.[70]

Chapter Five

DEFENDING NEW CALEDONIA

UNTIL 1820 New Caledonia had been on the fringes of the NWC/ HBC rivalry, but in the final year before the union of the two companies it could not avoid being drawn into the melee as rumours spread amongst the Natives that HBC traders had once again breached the Rocky Mountains. The news surfaced at Fort St. James on June 11, ten days after Hugh Faries, who had returned to New Caledonia to replace Daniel Harmon as clerk in charge, had departed for the Columbia to collect the annual supply of provisions. Carrier Natives informed James McDougall that an HBC clerk named Ignace Giasson, together with three men and a number of Iroquois hunters, was distributing goods and tobacco at the forks of the Fraser and Nechako rivers, promising a fort there in the fall. McDougall wrote in his Fort St. James journal: "They will play the deuce with the Natives . . . I have neither the means nor the men to ascertain the truth."[71]

Already short of provisions because the previous year's provisions brigade had been cancelled and now on the verge of starvation because of a late salmon run, McDougall spent a miserable summer worrying about the impending invasion. Meanwhile, thousands of miles away, the HBC canoes had departed from York

Factory in July, loaded with trading goods for New Caledonia. Near the HBC's Fort de Pinette on the upper Peace River, Samuel Black, one of the most irascible NWC traders, waited to harass them as they passed by. He was a huge man with a "slow and imposing manner of speech," and he went about armed with a dirk, sabre and pistols. When one HBC man protested Black's Nor'westers dragging Natives out of the Bay's canoes, he drew his sabre and told the intruder in his broad Scots accent to "hold your noise or I will send your head flying into the lake."[72]

On this occasion, however, not only Giasson's strategy but Black's, too, was foiled by the HBC brigade's fun-loving boatmen who again partied too long at Norway House. The brigade had to halt until the crew sobered up, and as a result they could not reach the upper Peace River before freeze-up. Reassigned from his planned ambush to briefly help out in New Caledonia, Black brought a large supply of leather with him. He arrived at Fort St. James on September 5, and McDougall sent him and a young interpreter to Fort Fraser to assist Donald Fleming in trading for salmon. Black found Natleh village in disarray because many of the Natives had died from dysentery, and the others had deserted.[73]

Meanwhile, Hugh Faries, who had departed Fort St. James on June 1 with Waccan and seven men in three canoes, was en route to the Columbia River. Waccan was necessary because Faries was totally unfamiliar with the route to Fort George (the new name for Fort Astoria) on the Columbia. The brigade got off to a bad start when two of the boatmen drowned after their canoe sank in the whirlpools of Fort George Canyon, the most treacherous rapids on the river route between Fort St. James and the portage site. Two rocky outcrops in the canyon split the river into three deep channels filled with whirlpools; the middle channel was the most dangerous and never used. (In the years to come the canyon claimed many more lives, canoes, and even steamboats. The federal government did not remove the outcrops until the winter of 1908–09.[74])

The treacherous rocks and rapids of Fort George Canyon claimed the lives of many fur-trade people. In later years they also sank numerous steamboats, including the famous *BX*. THE EXPLORATION PLACE P989.1.2

Faries' two remaining canoes managed to reach the portage site where Fort Alexandria would be built in 1821 (about twenty-eight miles south of present-day Quesnel), but the guide and horses promised by Joseph Larocque at Fort Thompson were not waiting there for them. Faries and his men were starving as they made their way 150 miles overland to the North Thompson (near present-day Little Fort) and then to the fort, and en route they learned from Natives that their guide had been murdered. When the brigade finally reached Fort Walla Walla on the Columbia, they had to make two trips down the river to Fort George in order to bring up the generous outfit of eighty-nine pieces.

Upon Faries' safe return to Fort St. James at the end of October, Black departed for Fort Chipewyan in Athabasca where NWC/HBC rivalry had reached its zenith. On October 23 the HBC's George Simpson and his men had brazenly captured NWC leader Simon McGillivray Jr. and incarcerated him at Fort Wedderburn. Incensed at their audacity, the NWC were counting on Black's cunning to gain McGillivray's release.[75]

For several years the NWC had promised a trading post to the Natives at the forks of the Nechako and Fraser rivers where Faries had built a temporary outpost in 1807 to expedite Simon Fraser's great journey downriver. Now, in view of the continuing threat from HBC traders, he wasted no time in deploying George McDougall to re-establish this outpost. McDougall left Stuart Lake on October 26 with a large stock of trading goods. Once there, apparently fearing that HBC traders were still in the vicinity, instead of constructing a fort at the forks, he built a small outpost near the village of Chala-oo-chick on the Nechako.[76]

In early January 1821, five years after he thought he had left New Caledonia for good, John Stuart returned to Fort St. James via the Columbia River. He immediately read the post journals in order to bring himself up to date and learned that "unbounded extravagance" had taken place during his long absence. Personnel had not followed the rules for trading practices he had set down in 1815, and as a result most traders had been too generous, permitting Natives to obtain supplies by the debt system.[77] Despite his chagrin, Stuart took part in the traditional New Year's celebrations, which were held several weeks later than usual. The description of this event in the Stuart Lake post journal leaves little to the imagination:

Monday, January 22 [1821]. It being customary every New Year to give the men a treat, Mr. Faries has promised them that whenever they would be altogether he would give them a couple of days to rest & divert themselves; therefore they now being all here before our departure for the Babine it was intimated to the men last evening that this would be fete. They got some guns & paid the general compliment by firing in the morning, upon which they were called in & got each three drams & cakes, then got each a pint [of] rum, 1 lb. flour, grease, 3 large beaver among them with potatoes & fish. They drank and ate all day, some got as drunk as pipers but behaved well. In the evening they had a dance in the Hall but there being few they drank little having only employed 2 flacons of rum & 1 of shrub [a mixture of rum, sugar and lime juice]. After the ball was over Msrs. Stuart & Faries gave them a two gallon keg of rum to drink to the Company's health, so that they have had this day 6 gallons produced spirits which they have almost made with [——] them and few of the Canadians that drink, but the Iroquois have been in their glory and if they eat little made up for it by drinking.[78]

"Good New Year's feast," Stuart wrote in the margin.[79]

Stuart departed for the Columbia River again on February 24, leaving Fort St. James with 2,554 dried fish in the storehouse, enough to last until April. His parting instructions to personnel included tactics for dealing with the threat of the HBC invaders. In his letter to James McDougall at McLeod Lake he recommended that every possible obstacle be put in their way. A "strict watch ought to be kept night & Day in the Parsnip River to prevent a possibility of their arriving or passing unknown to you."[80]

Because Hugh Faries had only a few months left to serve in New Caledonia, Stuart designated him acting manager to reside at Fort St. James. When Faries and his family took their final departure with the spring brigade, James McDougall assumed leadership but remained at McLeod Lake until Stuart's return.[81] His brother George took over management of Fort St. James, assisted by a staff of two interpreters and five Canadians. By now the fort buildings needed to be replaced, and Stuart left orders to commence erecting a bastion and a 120-square-foot house at a nearby site during the summer. Other chores included planting the garden and collecting enough hay to winter the three or four horses that had been brought to the fort for manure purposes, not transportation.

Stuart did not use canoes when he departed in February, and he stressed to George McDougall at Fort St. James that of "more consequence than all the rest put together is to get canoes made to meet me on the Tacoutak [Fraser] River on our return from the Columbia with the outfit." McDougall was to accompany the canoes, leaving Fort St. James August 20 and arriving at Faries Portage (Alexandria) by September 1. Under no circumstances was he to run the rapids below Chala-oo-chick, "nor will it be permissible to attempt running down any other that may appear bad." He was to bring interpreter Jose Carrier and his woman and property and be prepared to take charge of a new fort. If Stuart's family arrived at Fort St. James wanting passage they could also be brought down. When trading furs, extravagance should be avoided and all gratuities to Natives, even down to a single salmon, should be noted in the journal.[82]

As McDougall made the daily journal entries, he scarcely concealed his annoyance with the latter part of Stuart's orders; "When ice is broken, it is not difficult for a person to avoid falling into it," he wrote. Extravagance was necessary, he wrote, because the fort was dependent on the Natives for food; by May there were only 231 dried salmon on hand. "Starvation was not the time to break Indians of extras. We must depend on [Chief] Qua for fish." Although McDougall would as "soon see the devil come to the fort as Qua" because he was always demanding something, there are many entries that record the Carrier chief, his wives, children, and brother Hoolson bringing fish to the fort for bartering, proving the extent of the fort's dependence upon him.[83]

Stuart had remained at Fort St. James for only a month before setting off for the Columbia again, but this mid-winter trip had been a departure from his usual itinerary, suggesting that he had been ordered to Fort St. James to help prepare for the merger. Since early 1820 the majority of the NWC partners had realized their company had serious financial problems and that the British government was also pressing the HBC for a resolution to the conflict between the two companies. In fact, negotiations were actually taking place in London, but at this point the outcome was still uncertain. (Even George Simpson, on his way out from Athabasca in June 1821, was surprised to learn of the final agreement.[84])

This painting of Fort Thompson is presumed to have been executed by John Tod.
BRITISH COLUMBIA ARCHIVES PDP00170

In August 1821 Stuart returned from the Columbia with the provisions for the northern posts, apparently still unaware that the merger of the companies had taken place. Acting on the assumption that the brigade route to the Columbia would continue, he ordered George McDougall to establish a new fort at Faries' Portage; it was to be called Alexandria in honour of Alexander Mackenzie. Soon after reaching Fort St. James, Stuart learned of the merger, and he quickly wrote letters to all of the New Caledonia forts, reassuring the clerks that the NWC had received fair treatment in the merger agreement and that there would be opportunities to rise in the ranks. It was probably at this time that he also received the news that he was now a chief factor.

THE UNION OF THE NWC AND HBC under the name and charter of the Hudson's Bay Company gave the company an exclusive twenty-one-year licence to conduct all of the fur trade west of the Rocky Mountains. Under an agreement of joint occupation with the United States, HBC trappers could roam as far south as California and as far east as the height of land in the Rocky Mountains, but New Caledonia was the real prize because for the next two decades it provided the finest and the greatest number of furs. The NWC's Columbia and New Caledonia departments were now included in a vast HBC Northern Department that stretched from Lac La Pluie north to Hudson Bay and west to the Pacific, and George Simpson became its governor. (He became governor-in-chief of both northern and southern departments in 1826.[85])

Simpson's immediate challenges were to close duplicate NWC and HBC forts, diplomatically blend the personnel of the two rival factions, and find positions for those displaced by the closures. The governor and committee in London wrote to Simpson in February 1822 approving his decision to single out a few HBC clerks and NWC wintering partners who had expected to become chief traders for special salaries of £175 annually because they would not be promoted immediately. Included in this group were Francis Heron and James McDougall.[86] However, Simpson and his Northern Council denied promotion to Samuel Black and Peter Skene Ogden because they had been so treacherous during the years of rivalry. But the two renegades were not about to accept this decision meekly and went to London during the winter of 1822–23 to lay an appeal before the governor and committee. When their pleas for chief tradership were granted, Simpson had no choice but to accept the outcome, but to ensure future peace, he separated the two men. He assigned Black to head a Rocky Mountain expedition to investigate the sources of the Finlay River and the unexplored country now known as the Cassiar and sent Ogden a thousand miles south to supervise the Snake River trapping expeditions in the Columbia District. Ogden gained chief factor status in 1834 and after 1846 served with distinction in the triumvirate that managed Fort Vancouver following McLoughlin's retirement. Black received his promotion to chief factor in 1837.

Simpson also had a surplus of clerks to disperse, so the incoming 1821 brigade from Athabasca brought a number of HBC men to John Stuart at Fort St. James; they included Thomas Hodgson, James Murray Yale, Duncan Livingston and William Brown. Stuart sent Hodgson, a boat builder from Hudson Bay—"very slow but honest"—to briefly man Chala-oo-chick outpost until Yale replaced him in November. Because Yale was short in stature and youthful looking, Stuart requested Hodgson to introduce him to the Natives as his son "& acquaint them that I expect they will consider & attend to him as such." Since there was no longer any fear of opposition, he ordered Yale to move all the buildings George McDougall had built at Chala-oo-chick to the forks of the Nechako and Fraser. This was the real beginning of Fort George, presumably named for George Simpson.[87]

In February 1822 the governor and committee in London wrote to Simpson concerning manpower, at the same time recommending that in future New Caledonia should be outfitted from Norway House or York Factory rather than the Columbia because they thought it was a more economical procedure. The Columbia, however, would still receive goods from England and ship furs to Canton, as had been previously arranged by the North West Company. The letter—which Simpson did not receive until he arrived at York Factory in early summer—also stated:

> We understand that hitherto the trade of the Columbia has not been profitable, and from all that we have learnt on the Subject we are not sanguine in our expectations of being able to make it so in future. But if by any improved arrangement the loss can be reduced to a small sum, it is worth a serious consideration, whether it may not be good policy to hold possession of that country, with a view of protecting the more valuable districts to the North of it; and we wish you to direct the attention of the council to this subject and collect all the information which you can obtain from individuals acquainted with the Country.
>
> . . . Should the result of all your enquiries be unfavourable to the plan of continuing the trade of Columbia it will be

proper to consider whether it will be better to continue the trading establishments there, until the goods are nearly all expended, or to transport those remaining after the business of the Winter 1823/24 is finished to New Caledonia.

The Russians are endeavoring to set up claims to the North West Coast of America as low as Latitude 51, and we think it desirable to extend our trading posts as far to the West and North from Frazer's river in Caledonia, as may be practicable, if there appears any reasonable prospect of doing so profitably. It is probable that the British government would support us in the possession of the Country, which may be occupied by trading posts, and it is desirable to keep the Russians at a distance.[88]

Meanwhile, having received no instructions from the new governor, in the spring of 1822 Stuart, taking Brown and Livingston with him, departed again for the Columbia for provisions but at the same time he sent one hundred packs of furs out with the brigade to York Factory. He also gave the brigade a letter for Nicholas Garry, a member of the HBC's London headquarters committee who had been sent out to Rupert's Land to help establish the terms of the merger. The letter was an attempt to guide the future conduct of the company:

This part of the Country was never much stocked with Beaver or other animals of the fur kind but they are to be found all over, and when well conducted the Department continued to yield a yearly increase of returns from its first establishment to the present moment, and unless too much is attempted it will continue to do so for years to come. In all new countries the trade must be extended gradually and one Post ought to be properly established before another is attempted in the same quarter. Was it nothing else, too great a surplus of People sent into the Department in one year, before provisions are made for them, would cause the natives to starve, and we should starve with them . . . one faux pas committed would destroy the fruit of years of well conducted labour, and in making the selection of Gentlemen required particular care ought to be taken that none but persons of principle are sent. The Natives throughout this Continent will adopt the vices but not the virtues exhibited by their traders, and as education commonly makes the man, I would recommend that none but such are sent to New Caledonia . . . . To the Gentlemen who shared with me in the toil of establishing the Country, I may be supposed to be partial, and I am so to the good qualities of all I know, but it arises from a knowledge of them. And had the good fortune of Messrs. James McDougall & John McDonnell been equal to their length of service and merit, instead of being Clerks they would be among the first on the list of Chief Factors. The former may be considered the father of New Caledonia and the latter as an Indian trader is second to any that ever crossed the Rocky Mountains, and it will be both an act of Justice and for the Interest of the Company to provide for them, and being the best situated to promote the general interest, make their remaining in the country worthwhile. A salary of from two to three hundred pounds, until otherwise provided for, would attach them to the service and I know no other way in which an equal sum would be disposed of equally advantageously to the concern.[89]

When Stuart returned in September, he found the new Fort Alexandria in the good hands of George McDougall, but Yale had become involved in an altercation with the Carrier and had not removed all the buildings from Chala-oo-chick. For a second time Stuart ordered him to complete the work before winter, but Yale's insubordination foreshadowed difficulties that ensued the following year.[90]

Acting on instructions from Simpson and the council, in October 1822 Stuart sent William Brown to Babine Lake to reconnoitre for the site of yet another fort. With the assistance of interpreter

Waccan and eleven men, Brown established Fort Kilmaurs, named after his home in Scotland, at the point between the two northern arms of the lake where Old Fort stands today. He selected this site because it lay near the village of Nah-tell-cus that contained twenty-four families; another thirty-nine families lived in two other nearby lakeside villages to make a combined total of 250 people. In addition, there were approximately 750 people living near the mouth of Simpson's River, and Brown made contact with the people in four more large villages to the west and northwest. All of these people traded with one another and with the Natives at Fraser Lake as well as with middlemen from the coast.[91]

Babine Lake quickly became another important source of salmon for the trading forts of New Caledonia because the salmon arrived there a month earlier than at Fort Fraser as the migration route via the Skeena River was shorter. Thus, in years of poor runs on the Fraser, Fort Babine would usually have a good supply of dried salmon already prepared for delivery.[92] However, Brown faced an unusual trading problem at Fort Kilmaurs because the Carrier there could obtain most of their provisions by trading salmon and then demand the highest prices for their furs. If they

In 1910 Fort George was well cared for by Shetland Islander James Cowie. THE EXPLORATION PLACE P985.2

were not satisfied with HBC prices, they traded with middlemen associated with coastal traders or used their furs to gamble. Moreover, in years of plenty the Carrier did not feel compelled to hunt for beaver at all.[93]

Because of Kilmaurs' remoteness, communication was difficult in the winter, and Stuart came to regret the day Simpson had ordered it built. In 1823 he complained to James McDougall at Fort St. James, "That cursed place has caused me more trouble and anxiety in the space of not fifteen months than the rest of Western Caledonia during the seventeen years it has been established."[94] Brown had a keen interest in recording daily events and his *Journal of Transactions and Occurrences in the Babine Country* from October 1822 to February 1823 is clearly written and informative. It is possible that he planned to follow Daniel Harmon's example and publish a book about his adventures even though his superiors had previously criticized his writing activities. When George Simpson had spent the winter of 1820–21 with Brown at Fort Wedderburn, he noticed that journal writing occupied a good part of Brown's day. Simpson then asked him to maintain "a concise Journal of the Post for the inspection of his superiors" and made it clear that company business should not be incorporated into a private document. Then, to make sure he was following orders, a month later Simpson had warned Brown that he would demand the journal in the spring and lay it before the governor and council.[95]

Brown's entries in his Fort Kilmaurs journal detail the challenges of establishing a new fort among the Carrier, improving the ancient Native portage between Stuart and Babine lakes, and documenting the bullying and cajoling that ensued between Natives and newcomers as both sides tried to establish supremacy. He also incorporated copies of his letters to other New Caledonia traders and occasionally inserted information he had requested from the accountant at Fort St. James. Stuart looked the journal over in March 1823 and made a critical notation on the flyleaf:

The foregoing Journal being, contrary to my expectations, committed to me for perusal, it was with reluctance I opened but in conformity to a long established rule in New Caledonia I read it through and find it to be what I had suspected: more calculated for the mandarins of Fenchurch Street [HBC London] and the [York] Factory than for that of New Caledonia men. I however have not the smallest objection to any part of it but consider it extremely unfair to have the letters and replies by the writer inserted without inserting those received in answer also and am happy to find that as far as can be judged from the Journal and conformable to the idea I myself had formed of the writer of it, ample justice has been done Kilmaurs.[96]

When Brown left New Caledonia for good in 1826 because of ill health, Hugh Faries was in charge of conducting the brigade from Athabasca to York Factory, and he left all Brown's papers, a cassette and a writing desk at Fort Chipewyan in order to accommodate his own family in the canoes. Upon reaching York Factory, Brown complained to Simpson, and the matter was laid before the governor and council. The council fined Faries £10, which Brown donated to the fund for the relief of the distressed families and settlers of Red River Colony.[97]

Chapter Six

"THE BLOOD OF MY CHILDREN"

THE ADDITION of Forts George, Alexandria and Kilmaurs doubled the number of forts in New Caledonia within two years of the merger between the North West Company and the Hudson's Bay. Yet John Stuart, who returned to New Caledonia in 1821, found that all the new clerks sent to assist him at these new forts were HBC men and all, with the exception of Thomas Hodgson, were single and reluctant to follow the strict orders of a former rival. This situation led to a tragic incident.

Prior to conducting the brigade to York Factory in the spring of 1823, Stuart's departing instructions stressed the importance of the clerks remaining at their posts during his absence. Furthermore, they were not to bring Native women into the forts because this behaviour inevitably led to trouble. The previous September he had cautioned Yale that in his dealings at the new Fort George:

No danger whatever is to be apprehended from the Natives & affability to all, added to a little kindness and attention to the most deserving, will go a great way towards gaining the good will of all, and by shewing them that it will be no less their own interest than ours, may in the end teach them to become industrious.

In the wake of Stuart's departure, the general feeling in New Caledonia was that he would not return. And so in early August, a time of little trading activity, Yale ignored Stuart's instructions and left Fort George with his Carrier interpreter, Joseph Porteur, for a visit to John McDonnell at Fort Fraser and James McDougall at Fort St. James. Fort George was left to the supervision of Baptiste Beignoit, who was considered "a good middleman and has some education," and Belonie Duplanté, "a perfect chatterbox but a good man."[98] It wasn't until the morning of August 27 that Yale departed from Stuart Lake to resume his charge of Fort George.

Two weeks later a letter arrived for James McDougall at Fort St. James from McDonnell, conveying the startling news that Beignoit and Duplanté had been murdered. Their bodies had lain unburied until Yale returned, and during that time dogs had mauled Duplanté's corpse. Yale soon identified the murderers as Zill-na-hou-lay and Un-ta-yhia, the latter being the son of Carrier elder Nandzul, but he could not venture out to apprehend them as he had to guard Fort George's buildings, there being no *engagés* to spare at the other posts, and the brigade led by Stuart or his replacement was not expected to arrive for another month.[99]

Meanwhile, at York Factory

James Murray Yale's New Caledonia career got off to a bad start at Fort George, but his courage and determination eventually won him the charge of Fort Langley. BRITISH COLUMBIA ARCHIVES A-00900

Stuart met with Governor Simpson for the first time and may have informed him that two new forts, Simpson on an island at the confluence of the Mackenzie and Liard rivers (on the site of the NWC's temporary Fort of the Forks, built in 1804) and George at the confluence of the Nechako and Fraser, had been built during the previous year and named in his honour. Stuart had prepared his annual report at Norway House, while en route to the depot, and delivered it to the council with an impressive amount of paperwork. This was in obedience to Resolve 110 of the Minutes of council held at York Factory in July 1822 that required chief factors, chief traders and clerks in charge of districts to deliver into the hands of the general accountant within forty-eight hours after arrival "the District Books, Servants accounts, Journal, report, List of Engaged & unengaged men, and general account Current completed under Penalty of £10 Sterling to be applied as a fund for charitable purposes." They were also to submit their orders or "indents" for their next outfits for examination by the council.[100]

In late October 1823 Stuart did return to New Caledonia—for one more year—accompanied by yet another surplus HBC trader, John Tod. At York Factory Stuart had been warned that Tod was a difficult employee—a "Wolf or rather fox in sheep's clothing," and en route west with the brigade he noted in his journal that on two occasions Tod had tried to create trouble.[101] He had, however, no recourse but to take him. At Rocky Mountain Portage he met with McLeod Lake Natives who told him that all Fort McLeod's buildings had been washed away in a flash flood. A week later when the brigade was still two days away from McLeod Lake, William Brown came to meet them with the news of the murders at Fort George.

Until this time, Stuart had been able to boast of a perfect record: not one white man or Metis had been murdered by Natives in New Caledonia since the NWC arrived in 1805. Like a grieving Moses, he declared, "the Blood of my Children" had now been shed. At McLeod Lake, he went without sleep for two nights, writing to Simpson and to all the New Caledonia post managers, setting out the tactics they must employ to secure the guilty parties. He even went so far as to write Samuel Black, who was at Dunvegan for the winter, urging him to send Beaver warriors by the end of the year to impress on the Carrier the need to locate and destroy the murderers.

Black, however, did not respond immediately because there was a crisis in the north as well. At Fort St. John on November 2 and 3 Beaver Natives, motivated by the fact that the HBC was closing the fort in favour of the post at Rocky Mountain Portage, had murdered trader Guy Hughes and four of his men. And there may have been a secondary reason: when at Fort St. John a few months earlier, Samuel Black had taken one of the wives of a Beaver Native known as "Sancho."[102] In response to the murders William McGillivray had set out from Fort Chipewyan with a punitive expedition of sixteen men, mostly Cree, but they were soon recalled because Governor George Simpson felt that the Beaver would resolve the injustice themselves.[103]

When Stuart learned of the Fort St. John tragedy he feared that the murderers might flee into New Caledonia, placing the outlying posts at risk. He wanted to close Fort Kilmaurs immediately, but Brown managed to change his mind. However, the general unrest did cause Stuart to cancel his plans to establish a fort in the Chilcotin.

The most effective, non-violent punishment of the local Natives for the death of Beignoit and Duplanté would be to close down Fort George, even though the number of furs collected that winter would be affected. But after considering this and various other strategies, Stuart finally settled on the policy of letting the Carrier people take responsibility for locating the Fort George murderers. The HBC would stay out of the retribution business because they could not risk their men in a series of vindictive strikes. Besides, Chief Qua had set a precedent for this policy several years earlier when he had arranged for the revenge killing of a Carrier who had murdered an Iroquois employee at Fort St. James.[104]

Samuel Black, finally responding to Stuart's request for Beaver Indians on December 15, 1823, from Rocky Mountain Portage, expressed his belief in the Native people's ability to bring the killers to justice:

> I think subjects in this Country (besides *Engagés*) could be got to assist us in so just a cause for to my knowledge I never knew injustice or Tirany practiced in the Country; to the contrary we are Slaves to them or are we ever prepared for such dreadfull occurrences. We are like Lambs in the midst of Wolves. We are here as Traders, not as Warriors, but let them not rouse the Concern to exertion for they have the power to inflict punishment on those atrocious Villains too Common in the Country and who hitherto have in my opinion only been deterred from Villiany by temporary and local circumstances.[105]

In a letter to John McDonnell, Stuart reflected on the policies he had laid down to guide the fort managers while he was absent:

> I ever disapproved of exposing the lives of any of the Company's Servants by going in Summer to the Indian villages in quest of either provisions or other things, nor do I think or ever did [that] too much precaution can be used in guarding against the machinations of the designing, and I regret the whole of the Establishments are not in a better state of defence; but I know much of the Indian in general, or Western Caledonia in particular, the safety of our Establishments do not so much depend on actual strength in the number of people in them as it does on the conduct of the person in charge.

And in the McLeod post journal he set down his thoughts about the traders' relationships with Native women:

> It is long since I apprehended that too free Intercourse with

the Carrier Women would be the ruin of the Company's affairs in this quarter. The North West Company provided in a great measure against it by prohibiting any of them from being taken into keeping, or suffered to reside in the Company Forts, and on my being transformed into a Chief Factor of the Honourable Hudson's Bay in the very first letter I ever wrote to the Governor & Council of the Northern Factory I apprized them of the evil tendency of sending people into this quarter who had no women of their own and without presuming to say that the prevalent custom lately introduced into Western Caledonia, not only in opposition to my order but altogether unknown to me, of taking Native Women into keeping is owing [to] the Murder of their Servants and the almost total ruin of their Trade in this quarter. I would fain hope that the Governor & Council of the Northern Factory will publish a law prohibiting the admission of Native Women into their Forts. Mr. Yale has already of himself discarded the one he had and so has Mr. McBean. But there are still two at Kilmaurs who in 1823 deserted their husbands Beds & left the Company's Fort, but was afterwards admitted in direct opposition to my wishes.[106]

Stuart's attempts to unravel the motive for the Fort George murders resulted in half-truths and a host of unsubstantiated rumours from Yale and Tod at Fort George. Then, acting on Stuart's orders, George McDougall questioned the inhabitants of the various lodges at Chala-oo-chick and learned that one of the murderers had stayed there for several days before being sent away. In the final analysis, however, it appeared that Yale, ignoring Stuart's orders, had "bought" the wife of a local Carrier and taken her to live with him at the fort. During Yale's absence in August, the woman's former husband had come to visit her and, when Beignoit or Duplanté threatened to inform Yale, they were murdered.[107]

When George McDougall arrived at Fort George to investigate the murders, he discovered the Iroquois trapper Tête Jaune and his brother Baptiste there, and he took the opportunity to hire them as guides for the winter, paying them the wages of middle-men. They requested some clothing before taking the Alexandria furs to McLeod Lake.[108] But apparently they were better guides than trappers because the following July the Fort Alexandria journal recorded that "two confounded vagabonds, Tête Jaune and brother Baptiste, have destroyed beaver," resulting in the loss of three or four packs of furs.[109]

As New Year's Day 1824 approached, Stuart realized that Mc-Dougall and McDonnell would be keeping New Year's at Fort St. James as he had once done, and he sent them an extra supply of flour, sugar, "shrub" and other liquor for their *regale*.[110] Meanwhile, Stuart celebrated in traditional NWC fashion with cakes and French brandy for the Fort McLeod men and a glass of wine for himself. Despite all his difficulties, there were a few accomplishments to be thankful for. By the end of November his men had erected a house, twenty by thirty-eight feet, and he had stored away the tent he had been living in for the previous 137 days. A month later all furs and provisions had been secured under lock and key in a new shop and store, and there were enough dried salmon on hand to last the winter.

He still had many problems to cope with, but the expectation that he was spending his last few months in New Caledonia must have ameliorated some of the stress. First on the problem list was Chief Qua's behaviour, as McDougall had sent Stuart a letter in late December complaining about the chief's attitude. A gun had been held in Qua's name for purchase, but when he brought in his furs, the chief complained that the price of sixty skins was too high. In the past Stuart had rewarded Qua for bringing in good hunts and given him an annual set of chief's clothing—coat, shirt and leggings—but he had always had a see-saw relationship with the chief, and now he replied to McDougall immediately:

Yours of the 27 ult. La Pierre delivered me this afternoon & however sorry I might be that in the existing circumstances

Qua should give you cause to be dissatisfied at his conduct, I am no wise surprised at it. He is a greedy beggar and downright fool that seldom knows what is best for himself, and as for the Gun neither him nor others with my consent will get it for less than the fixt price. And he ought to be thankful that I had not forgotten him when far removed from him. La Pierre tells me that Qua intends going down the River and he will do no good there. I wish he could be prevented, and after getting this warning should happen there to meet with what he deserves, it will be his own fault. I never thirsted for the Blood of any one but if I find that Qua, as I strongly suspect, will endeavour to dissuade the Indians below from punishing the perpetrators of the murder committed at Fort George, it will confirm the opinion I have long entertained of himself and his Brother that they are at heart ill disposed towards the Whites and that nothing but self interest has prevented them from committing themselves what they approve in others. Had Qua acted as he ought to himself, seeing the others have not done it, would we now have destroyed the Murderers, and by so doing prove his abhorrence of the deed.[111]

Qua's manipulative relationship with company personnel continued until his death in 1840.

Yale had remained for the winter at Fort George with John Tod, but rather than keep a low profile, the two men caused more grief in February 1824 when they savagely beat Joseph Porteur. As Stuart held a high regard for the long-time interpreter, he dealt swiftly with Tod, who had already earned his ire by spreading unsubstantiated rumours about Yale and the Fort George murders. He wrote to Tod:

You are suspended from all duty to the Company, and that your Wages will cease until cleared from the stigma under which, through you, the whole of the Company's Servants must appear in the Eyes of the Indians from your unwarranted assault on the Interpreter (while engaged with another that neither required nor thanked you for your untimely assistance), a man, who, though an Indian, has served the Company for an equal length of time, and equally faithful as you! Consequently equally entitled to protection; and one who, on this side of the Mountains, is of so much more consequence to the Company than yourself that was it not in Consideration of your former Services I would, as an example to others, dismiss you from the Company Service at once! An injury intended for myself alone I can both forgive & forget; but am in duty bound equally to protect the whole of the Company's Servants, and guard against the General Interest of the Concern being injured, either by the whims or Caprices of Individuals.[112]

Accompanied by Yale and George McDougall, Porteur arrived at McLeod Lake in February, still badly bruised and barely able to walk. Stuart was appalled by his condition and prescribed a strengthening plaster to ease his pain. He kept him at McLeod Lake until his health improved.[113] Within a short time Tod had exonerated himself by laying the whole of the blame for Porteur's beating on Yale. Although Stuart hoped Tod would resign, when he didn't, he eventually reinstated his wages and his position as clerk but exiled him to Fort McLeod where he remained until 1832. He assigned Yale,

John Tod was considered "A wolf in sheep's clothing," and his recollections of New Caledonia don't always match the written record. BRITISH COLUMBIA ARCHIVES C-08882

despite his protests, to Fort Alexandria where he would be supervised by George McDougall. In April 1824, when the Natives still had not given up the murderers of Beignoit and Duplanté, Stuart abandoned Fort George.

The emotional toll on Stuart is clearly evident in his letterbook for the spring of 1824, but he took the time to care for Porteur and to write to Donald McKenzie, a new *engagé* at Fort Alexandria, offering to bring his wife with the incoming brigade: "Should your *cher amie* be at Split Lake, and willing to visit Western Caledonia, she will have a passage on board the canoes, and will not want for anything that will be in my power to give." McKenzie, however, did not take advantage of this ploy to keep him in New Caledonia because he planned to return east with the brigade to seek medical attention.[114]

Reprisals by the HBC caused more difficulties for chief traders in the Peace River district than in New Caledonia, and in the early spring of 1824 after the Fort St. John massacre, trader Francis Heron, fearing there would be more attacks, closed Rocky Mountain Portage House. This closure was a great loss to the outgoing brigades as the men at the fort had always ensured that canoes and a large supply of pemmican were on hand there; in fact, the previous year Hugh Faries had sent seven canoes from Fort St. John to the Portage with 1,000 pounds of fresh meat and 224 pounds of pemmican. Now Heron warned Stuart he must bring enough provisions to get his brigade as far as Dunvegan.[115] A year later a murder at Dunvegan led to that fort's closure until 1828, but Simpson refused to reopen any other forts on the upper Peace during his entire twenty-six years as governor.[116]

Despite his concern that the number of furs collected in New Caledonia would be fewer than average, when Stuart and his family left for the last time in early May 1824, he brought out the fourth largest returns for all of the HBC districts, valued at £4,800. Only the Athabasca, Saskatchewan and Columbia Departments were higher that year.[117]

Stuart's baggage also contained the annual reports for all the trading posts of New Caledonia as well as the traders' responses to the questionnaire that Governor Simpson had instituted soon after the union of the companies in order to provide a good annual assessment of each district. The 1823–24 report for Fort St. James, which had been prepared by James McDougall and dated April 26, 1824, gives an excellent picture of the fort at that time. McDougall and three common labourers manned the fort. McDougall's Metis wife also lived there and they cared for the son of Baptiste Bouvier, an HBC employee at English River. Both McDougall and Stuart fostered the young sons of HBC personnel as it was an inexpensive way to gain extra help while training them for future service. Salmon was their dietary staple, augmented by white fish, sturgeon and carp. Their annual supply of provisions amounted to four kegs of fish roe, 3,000 dry carp, 2,000 fresh carp, 7 large sturgeon, 1,000 fresh salmon, 2,800 white fish and 6,500 dry salmon. An additional 8,600 dry salmon were used during winter travel.[118]

McDougall listed five Native villages attached to the fort: Nacausly, Pinche, Tache, Kinchi and Iya-quo. All were located around the shores of Stuart Lake or on tributary streams. They were home to a total of 260 men, women and children, and they traded an average of twenty packs of furs annually, although he estimated the trade had been thirty-five to forty packs in the years before Kilmaurs was established.[119] McDougall saw no way that the trade could be increased, but he did not believe that it would decrease because the Natives always received immediate payment for their furs. He wrote:

> I can see no alterations that could benefit the trades. It is even doubtful with me whether a reduction in the price of goods would have the desired effect, for a Carrier when he wishes for an article will work hard to get it, let the article be dear or not, and when he has no inclination to get it, let it be ever so cheap, it will not cause him to kill one marten more or less.[120]

STUART ARRIVED WITH HIS BRIGADE at York Factory in July 1824 and attended the Northern Council meeting there. He probably expected the council to make a formal statement about the Fort George murders and Yale's position with the company, but the governor and council waited until the following year to comment, even though London headquarters had called for an inquiry:

> This melancholy occurrence in New Caledonia is much to be regretted, more especially as it seems to have originated in the indiscretion of one of our own clerks in taking an Indian woman and quitting his post, contrary to the instructions which he had received. We think the conduct of the Clerk Mr. Yale ought to be investigated by Council and if it is found that he disobeyed the orders of his superior he ought to be fined or even dismissed . . . It is much better to prevent all risk of quarrels than to resort to an exertion of force to secure the safety of our servants and we must trust to your discretion to adopt such measures as may be found necessary to protect the lives of our servants there and elsewhere, but care must be taken not to involve the innocent in any attempt to punish the guilty, and if culprits are apprehended, the punishment ought to be inflicted by the Chiefs of their own tribe and not by our people, which may be accomplished by explaining your motives and suspending all intersect with the tribe until this is done and by making use of other means of influence with the Chiefs . . . Every exertion should be used to obtain the good will and confidence of the Natives in all the Countries to the West of the Rocky Mountains . . . Every assurance should be given them that our object is confined to carrying on a trade which must be beneficial to them and that we have no desire to possess or cultivate their lands beyond the little gardens at the Trading houses.[121]

In the end, the Northern Council decided there was not enough evidence to dismiss Yale, and he remained employed in New

Caledonia for several more years before being transferred to Fort Langley, which was administered from Fort Vancouver.[122] It was not until 1828 that his New Caledonia replacement, William Connolly, and clerk James Douglas gained retribution for the Fort George murders.

Stuart completed his own report on Western Caledonia after he reached Norway House. In this document, dated August 18, 1824, he encouraged the building of a fort on the lower reaches of the Fraser River and expressed himself in favour of using the Columbia route over the eastern trek to York Factory for delivering furs and obtaining provisions. He also pointed out that one of the main disadvantages of living west of the Rockies was the reliance on dried salmon as nourishment for hard labour. "Seldom any, even the most robust [*engagé*], without destroying his constitution, can remain in N. Cal. more than two or three years."[123] In fact, the constant chewing on the tough *barder* wore down their teeth, and young recruits were reminded to put a file in their luggage. When they asked why, they were jokingly told "to sharpen your teeth."[124]

Stuart took on a new posting at Fort Carlton in what is now Saskatchewan, followed by Bas de la Riviere and the Mackenzie River District. He took great pride in faithfully attending the annual council meetings from 1823 until 1831; he retired in 1839. Newlywed Letitia Hargrave met him in London a year later, prior to sailing with her husband to York Factory. To her Stuart was "a wearisome horror" because he had changed his mind about marrying his country wife, Mary Taylor, in Scotland and sent her back to York Factory in 1839 for Letitia's husband to cope with. Stuart died at Springfield House near Forres, Scotland, on January 14, 1847.[125]

Chapter Seven

WILLIAM CONNOLLY

IN AUGUST 1821 Governor George Simpson had sent a party of Hudson's Bay men west to conduct an inspection of the NWC posts on the far side of the Rockies, and they concluded that the Columbia posts could be made profitable if excess personnel were eliminated. They also felt that the Columbia district was strategically important because it kept the Americans out of the rich fur-bearing areas of New Caledonia. As a result, the HBC committee in London, determined to compete more aggressively with the Americans, ordered Simpson to visit the area to see if it could be made more efficient. He left York Factory on August 15, 1824, and arrived at the mouth of the Columbia on November 8, a journey of just eighty-four days—twenty days less than anyone who had previously made the trip. En route he caught up to former Nor'wester John McLoughlin, who had been assigned to take charge of Fort George (Astoria) at the mouth of the Columbia. From then on the two men travelled together. Having played a key role in bringing about the merger of the two companies, McLoughlin's strong leadership abilities would prove invaluable to Simpson in managing this area.

Simpson found the inland forts of Thompson, Spokane and

Walla Walla, all supervised from the Columbia, well-stocked with expensive imported luxuries—"all this time they may be said to have been eating Gold"—and he immediately made changes to improve profits for the district, changes that inevitably affected New Caledonia.[126] He began by recommending to London that coastal trade be extended and that New Caledonia be combined with the Columbia district to form the Columbia Department. He also decided that, starting in 1825, the fur brigade to York Factory would be cancelled in favour of using the Columbia route once again, just as Stuart had suggested. Only a leather party would be sent east of the Rockies in the fall of each year to obtain moose and buffalo hides—unavailable west of the Rockies—for moccasins, leather ties, *apachemons* (saddle blankets) and snowshoe lacing. These were generally supplied by Forts Carlton and Edmonton, which were in buffalo country, and sent on to Dunvegan or Jasper House for pickup by the New Caledonia party.

Fort Vancouver, which Simpson had built one hundred miles upriver from the Columbia's mouth during the winter of 1824–25, would be the new terminus for the Columbia brigade. He also began contemplating the construction of a new fort near the mouth

Fort Vancouver, the terminus of the New Caledonia fur brigade 1826–1847, provided a brief touch of luxury for the traders and a once-a-year opportunity to carouse for the *engagés.* GLENBOW ARCHIVES NA-1274-19

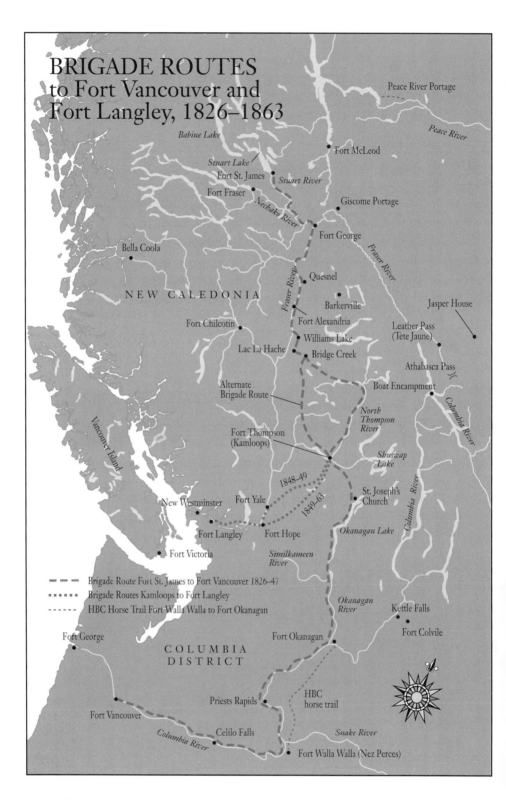

BRIGADE ROUTES
to Fort Vancouver and
Fort Langley, 1826–1863

Peace River Portage

Peace River

Babine Lake

Fort McLeod

Stuart Lake
Fort St. James
Fort Fraser

Stuart River

Giscome Portage

Nechako River

Fraser River

Fort George

Bella Coola

NEW CALEDONIA

Fraser River

Quesnel

Barkerville

Jasper House

Fort Chilcotin

Fort Alexandria

Leather Pass
(Tete Jaune)

Williams Lake

Lac La Hache

Bridge Creek

Athabasca Pass

Alternate
Brigade Route

Boat Encampment

Columbia River

*North
Thompson
River*

Fort Thompson
(Kamloops)

*Shuswap
Lake*

Vancouver Island

1848–49

St. Joseph's
Church

Columbia River

New Westminster

Fort Yale

1849–63

Fort Langley

Fort Hope

Okanagan Lake

Fort Victoria

*Similkameen
River*

--- Brigade Route Fort St. James to Fort Vancouver 1826–47
••••••• Brigade Routes Kamloops to Fort Langley
- - - - HBC Horse Trail Fort Walla Walla to Fort Okanagan

*Okanagan
River*

Kettle Falls

Fort George

Fort Okanagan

Fort Colvile

**COLUMBIA
DISTRICT**

HBC
horse trail

Priests Rapids

Fort Vancouver

Celilo Falls

Columbia River

Snake River

Fort Walla Walla (Nez Perces)

of the Fraser River that might in time replace Fort George on the Columbia, although while still at York Factory in July 1824 he must have ascertained from Stuart that the Fraser was not a viable route for transporting furs from the Interior to the sea. Consequently, in November 1824 he sent a party under chief trader James McMillan to explore the lower section of the river. McMillan reported that the valley contained rich soil and that the local Natives had assured him that the river was navigable as far as Fort Thompson. He also chose a site for a fort at the junction of the lazily meandering Salmon River and the Fraser, but Simpson was not yet ready to build there. Simpson had spent five months totally reorganizing the company's Columbia district. He wrote:

> I have the satisfaction to feel that the present visit has been productive of most important advantages to the Honble Coy's interests; the Work of reform is not yet however thoroughly effected and to put the whole Machine in full play I find that my presence is absolutely necessary on this side [of] the Mountain one more Winter at least. I can scarcely account for the extraordinary interest I have taken in its affairs . . . In fact the business of this side has become my hobby and however painful dangerous and harrassing the duty may be I do not know any circumstance that would give me more real satisfaction and pleasure than the Honble Committee's authority to take a complete survey of and personally superintend the extension and organization of their Trade on this Coast for 22 or 18 Months and if they do so I undertake to make its commerce more valuable to them than that of either of the Factories in Rupert's Land.[127]

Simpson's request to "personally superintend" reforms to the Columbia district was not granted, and his last action before leaving for the east in March 1825 was to place chief factor John McLoughlin in charge of it.

Carrying out Simpson's reforms in New Caledonia became

the task of William Connolly, who took John Stuart's place there in 1824. Born at Lachine, Quebec, around 1786, Connolly had joined the NWC as a clerk when he was just fifteen. It was while he was serving at Cumberland House from 1818 to 1821 that he became a chief trader. Connolly attended the council meeting at York Factory in early July 1824, and by July 16 four northern canoes had been readied to take him to Fort St. James where he would be joined by his Cree wife, Miyo Nipiy (also known as Susanne Pas-de-Nom), and several of his six children, including his grown daughter Amelia. However, his departure was delayed for ten days while he tried to recruit his full quota of thirty-six men. The company had just approved a wage increase for the New Caledonia boatmen, allowing *boutes* (steersmen and bowsmen) £27 sterling and *milieux* (middle boatmen) £22 with an additional £4 and £3 respectively when employed with the brigades to and from York Factory. But even with this offer of the highest wages possible in the service, Connolly could hire only six of the ten new *engagés* he required because New Caledonia's reputation for bad food was well known at York Factory. And not one of the boatmen who arrived with Stuart would sign on with Connolly although they readily re-engaged for other districts.

Connolly began his Fort St. James journal on July 27, the day his brigade finally left York Factory:

> The reluctance evinced by the men to engage for Western Caledonia arises not so much from the great distance that District is from the Depot as from the bad quality of the provisions that Country produces and which can hardly support men who have such laborious duties to perform throughout the winter . . . No probability appearing of the compliment being made up, and as all attempts to that effect would only have occasioned a further loss of time which the advanced state of the season could by no means admit upon, I in consequence resolved upon leaving Y Factory . . . [128]

Connolly arrived at Fort Chipewyan to find that two middlemen had deserted Black and Manson's expedition to the Finlay River and surrendered to Francis Heron at Ile-à-la-Crosse on July 25. Since Connolly was short of *engagés*, he took the two men on and kept them over the winter in New Caledonia. The following spring they were transported to York Factory where they were handcuffed and publicly exposed on the roof of the factory for one day before being imprisoned for a week and fed only bread and water. They were then sent to Fort Churchill and Fort Severn for the winter.

From Dunvegan, Connolly wrote to Simpson requesting that six good canoes, thirty pounds of gum and eighteen pounds of *watape* for repairs should be held there the following spring for the use of the outgoing fur brigade to York Factory. Although large animals were scarce in the Peace River area, he also wanted forty-two bags of pemmican to be procured for his boat crews, interpreter and "gentlemen."[129] In the past John Stuart had repeatedly made requests for adequate provisions for the New Caledonia brigades, and it may have been for this reason that he was assigned to Carlton, as that post and Edmonton were responsible for securing the Athabasca brigade's meat supply.[130]

Although Simpson had ordered that, starting in the spring of 1825, the fur brigade from New Caledonia should go south over the Columbia route, a short supply of *engagés* at Fort Vancouver and of horses at Fort Alexandria prevented Connolly from complying. Instead, he sent a small brigade to Fort Vancouver for provisions but took the furs to York Factory, where he attended the council meeting. On his return he sent the minutes of the meeting to his second-in-command, William Brown at Fort Kilmaurs, advising him to keep them "secret." He also passed on Simpson's orders that mild measures should be employed as discipline. The beating system used by Yale and Tod must be avoided in the future.[131]

In the spring of 1826 William Connolly, accompanied by clerk James Douglas, used the Columbia route for the first time to carry

New Caledonia's furs for shipment abroad. It was by this time considered such an important transportation route that, the following year when hostilities between the Shuswap and Chilcotin people threatened the safety of Fort Alexandria, Simpson would not allow that fort to be closed even temporarily.[132] However, maintaining a large enough herd of brigade horses at Alexandria during severe winters was difficult if the previous summer's hay crop had been poor because many of the weaker horses, especially pack animals worn down by transport, perished from starvation and the cold weather. Replacements had to be brought in from Fort Thompson in time for the brigade's departure in May.

Between 1825 and 1830 the combined production of Forts McLeod, Fraser, Alexandria and St. James accounted for 81 percent of the large and 85 percent of the small beaver pelts traded in New Caledonia. Fraser Lake collected 25,136 pelts, Stuart Lake 19,825, Alexandria 16,432, McLeod Lake 13,571, Babine Lake 12,331, Connolly Lake 4,339 and Fort George 2,222. Almost half of them were beaver pelts.[133]

As a young New Caledonia clerk, James Douglas earned the enmity of the Carrier Natives. But his sterling leadership abilities in the Columbia District and at Fort Victoria won him the position of governor of the colonies of Vancouver Island and British Columbia, and a knighthood from Queen Victoria. LIBRARY AND ARCHIVES CANADA 1958-157 NPC C-003316

Although Simpson was mainly interested in maximizing the efficiency of the Columbia District, he was also alert to any possibilities for greater efficiency in New Caledonia. Thus, when Iroquois trappers at Boat Encampment at the northernmost bend of the Columbia River (now under the waters of Kinbasket Lake) supplied information about new routes through the Rockies to Fort George on the Fraser River, he thought it might be possible for furs and provisions to be transported eastward from Fort George through a pass near Jasper, rather than using Rocky Mountain Portage.[134] However, while this pass, which would come to be known as Leather Pass and eventually Tête Jaune Pass, proved satisfactory for bringing in leather and new recruits for New Caledonia, it was too difficult for outgoing brigades loaded with furs.

The efficiency of the Babine fur trade continued to be threatened by the spectre of the Russians on the seacoast even though that danger would be resolved by the conventions of 1824 and 1825 in which the Russian government would agree to withdraw any claims to the northwest coast below 54° 40'. Simpson was, therefore, eager to have William Brown at Fort Kilmaurs undertake a voyage of discovery west of Babine Lake and all the way to the sea, but by this time Brown's health was failing, and he did not carry out the expedition planned for the summer of 1825 or that planned for the following winter. He was finally granted leave of absence in the spring of 1826. He died in Europe a year later, leaving behind a Native wife, Fanny, and their children at the Native village of Pinche on Stuart Lake.[135]

In 1825 Simpson received instructions from London that all the Interior posts should establish farms in order to become self-supporting:

> We do not consider it necessary to transport provisions from the Coast for the use of the people at the Wintering grounds. Indeed we consider that no provisions ought to be taken from the Depot except what may be required for the inward voyage and that the different departments ought to furnish sufficient for the voyage to this Depot, to which end we recommend that due attention be paid to raising grain and potatoes at every post, also to the rearing of hogs and cattle and that the progress made in those respects be particularly noted in the Annual Report.[136]

When Simpson passed on these orders from London, Connolly introduced stock raising, adding swine, chickens, oxen, horses and cows to the various forts' properties. Stuart had already introduced horses to Fort St. James a few years earlier, and now Connolly was able to use them to plough and seed the larger fields with barley, oats and peas.[137] In the fall the harvests were threshed and stored for the winter.

In 1827, more than two years after a site had been chosen for a fort on the lower Fraser, Simpson ordered its construction, and work began on August 1. To be called Fort Langley in honour of Thomas Langley, an HBC director, this fort would become invaluable for the 800-hectare farm that surrounded it, but in the end it did not become a replacement for Fort George on the Columbia as Simpson had anticipated.

Meanwhile, Simpson had become so overly zealous in cutting costs that in 1828 London took him to task:

> So far from thinking your Indents extravagant, we have for some time been of the opinion that they were not sufficiently large. We consider it bad policy to be short of goods either for the trade of the Districts or the supply of the people. We shall therefore send out every article indented for, and as there will be more goods than the *Prince Rupert* will be able to carry, we have chartered a vessel of 200 Tons to take what the *Prince* cannot store, and should there be any spare tonnage in the hired vessel it will be filled up with such useful articles of trade as can be obtained at a short notice. The Indents for the Southern Departments and the Columbia will also be complied with together with a further requisition to a small extent, which has been received from C. Factor McLoughlin.[138]

In the same letter the Committee members in London set out their reaction to the report written by Chief Factor John McLoughlin describing his retaliation for the murder in March 1828 of a trader named Alexander Mackenzie and his four *engagés* by the Clallum

Natives of Puget Sound. The victims had been travelling from Fort Vancouver to Fort Langley when they were slain and the Native wife of one of the men kidnapped. In the revenge attack ordered by McLoughlin and commanded by Alexander Roderick McLeod, a Clallum village was razed and ten or more Natives were killed. The kidnapped woman was rescued but the murderers escaped. The governor in London advised Simpson that:

> We observe that Mr. McLoughlin thought it necessary for the future safety of our people to send an expedition against the Indians who murdered Mr. McKenzie and his men. We have already explained to you what we consider the proper course to be pursued in such cases with the Indians on the East side of the Mountains; but we are aware that those upon the shores of the Pacific are not so dependent upon us for their necessary supplies and that their character and condition may probably require a different treatment from what is found to be sufficiently efficacious with the Indians in our own Territory. We have not received a copy of the instructions under which Mr. A.R. McLeod acted and we shall expect to receive a more detailed report of the proceedings of the party employed in the expedition than Mr. McLoughlin has given us. Until we do so we cannot form any opinion upon this unfortunate occurrence. The principle ought to be to inflict no more injury upon the Indians who may be guilty of such atrocities than may be considered sufficient to deter them from a repetition of them and if possible a compromise of the quarrel or some compact of peace for the future should be [made].[139]

Simpson may not have received these instructions before he visited McLeod Lake and Fort St. James in 1828, but his attitude towards revenge and punishment in the future was very much guided by the London Committee.

IN THE SUMMER OF 1828, when Simpson set out on his second tour of New Caledonia and the Columbia District, he was accompanied overland from York Factory by his country wife, Margaret Taylor, sister of his personal servant, Tom Taylor; a Highland piper, Colin Fraser; Dr. Richard Julian Hamlyn and Archibald McDonald, who had just been promoted to chief trader and was en route to Fort Langley to take over its management. While passing through Athabasca they also took on William McGillivray, his wife and young child. Simpson thought that McGillivray was drinking too much and hoped to smarten him up with a placement in New Caledonia. (He had demonstrated this same personal involvement in managing troublesome employees on his visit to the Columbia in 1824 when he transferred Alexander Ross and John McLeod east of the mountains. In future years Simpson arranged "sobering" transfers to New Caledonia for chief traders Alexander Fisher and Simon McGillivray, Jr., and clerks Donald McKenzie and William Lane.[140])

When Simpson arrived at Fort McLeod in September 1828, he found John Tod, who was in charge there, extremely low on provisions because Connolly's brigade had not yet returned from Fort Vancouver. Simpson noted in his diary:

> In regard to the means of living, McLeods Lake is the most wretched place in the Indian Country; it possesses few or no resources within itself, depending almost entirely on a few dried Salmon taken across from Stuart Lake, and when the Fishery there fails, or when any thing else occurs to prevent this supply being furnished, the situation of the Post is cheerless indeed. Its compliment of people is a Clerk and two Men whom we found starving, having had nothing to eat for several Weeks but Berries, and whose countenances were so pale and emaciated that it was with difficulty I recognized them.[141]

Even though he left some of his baggage with Tod, Simpson and his party took three days to cover the overland route from McLeod Lake to Fort St. James. Clerk James Douglas, who was in charge in the absence of William Connolly who had taken the brigade to

Fort Vancouver, knew that Simpson liked to enter each new fort with a flourish in order to impress the Natives, and he arranged a welcoming barrage from the fort's cannon. Archibald McDonald's description of the grand arrival has become a classic:

> The day, as yet being fine, the flag was put up; the piper in full Highland costume; and every arrangement was made to arrive at Fort St. James in the most imposing manner we could, for the sake of the Indians. Accordingly, when within about a thousand yards of the establishment, descending a gentle hill, a gun was fired, the bugle sounded and soon after, the piper commenced the celebrated march of the clans, "Si coma leum cogadh na shea" (Peace; or War, if you will it otherwise). The guide, with the British ensign, led the van, followed by the band; then the Governor on horseback, supported behind by Doctor Hamlyn and myself on our chargers, two deep; twenty men, with their burdens, next formed the line, then on loaded horse, and lastly, Mr. [William] McGillivray (with his wife and light infantry) closed the rear. During a brisk discharge of small arms and wall pieces from the Fort, Mr. Douglas met us a short distance in advance, and in this order we made our entrée into the Capital of Western Caledonia. No sooner had we arrived, than the rain which threatened us in the morning now fell in torrents.[142]

Simpson's "country wife," Margaret Taylor, and McGillivray's wife and baby daughter were welcomed by Connolly's wife, Miyo Nipiy, and her daughter Amelia. It had been only four years since they had entered New Caledonia via the same difficult Peace River route.

When Simpson addressed the assembled crowd of Carrier Natives and fort inhabitants, he made reference to the need to seek retribution when Natives killed HBC employees. A few weeks earlier, while ascending the Peace River, he had seen the crosses on the riverbank that marked the site of the murder of Guy Hughes and four men in 1823. He also alluded to the murder of trader Alexander Mackenzie and four *engagés*, the death of clerk Duncan Livingston at Fort Kilmaurs in April 1828 that had been quickly avenged by Waccan, and the recent death of Zill-na-hou-lay, one of the Fort George murderers.[143]

James Douglas had been involved in the capture and death of Zill-na-hou-lay, who had apparently been found hiding in Chief Qua's house. When Qua learned about Douglas's act of trespass and revenge, he came to the fort with a group of Natives to seek compensation. There are numerous versions of what happened at this point. John McLean, a clerk in New Caledonia from 1833 to 1836, claims that James McDougall's daughter Nancy, who was married to Waccan, helped to resolve the crisis. Other accounts state that William Connolly's daughter Amelia—recently married to Douglas—saved her husband's life by throwing down trading articles into the crowd. Carrier historian Lizette Hall learned a similar version from her father, a grandson of Qua, but in her version no goods were offered.[144]

Amelia Connolly was married to James Douglas by her father, William Connolly, in February 1828 at Fort St. James. This photograph was taken in Victoria about 1858, the year that James became governor of the colonies of Vancouver Island and British Columbia. BRITISH COLUMBIA ARCHIVES A-01679

Connolly did not hear about the events at Fort St. James until he reached Alexandria with the incoming brigade on August 31. His trek to Fort Vancouver and back had not gone well. On the outward trip three of his *engagés*—Andre Laforte (also known as Plassis), Felix Vinette (also known as Larent), and Pierre Kanatagonit—drowned when their boat broke up going down Priests Rapids on the Columbia River.[145] On the return trip Connolly had planned to go west from Fort Alexandria to visit the Chilcotin and establish a post there, but the letters waiting for him there from Douglas advised that Zill-na-hou-lay had been killed on August 1. Connolly noted in his journal:

> The circumstances here alluded to is the death of the last survivor of the murders of our Fort George men which was effected on the 1st of this month in the Indian village of Stuarts Lake by Mr. Douglas with his men. This villain, it appears, renewed a practice he had of skulking about the establishments in the summer when he supposed that no danger existed. But in this instance he did not escape with his usual impunity, having paid with his life both for his audacity and for the time by which he was forfeited. This was effected without any noise or creating any disturbance among the Stuart Lake Indians, but intelligence of it having been carried to Frasers Lake before Mr. Douglas could acquaint Mr. McDonnell of it, that latter gentleman was exposed to much risk and an attempt had actually been made upon his life by a wretch of the name of Attas, but fortunately without effect.
>
> I much fear that some further attempt of that nature will be made which the weakness of the Establishments and our very long absence are likely to invite, but in the event of this succeeding the whole district will inevitably be thrown into confusion. I am far from imputing any blame to Mr. Douglas for what he had done, circumstanced as he was, to redeem our credit, which had suffered not a little for having allowed the murder of our people to go so long unpunished. He could not do otherwise than he did. All I have to regret is that it happened at a season when the means for repelling any attack, should such be contemplated by the Natives, are so very limited. I further learn that one of the murderers of the unfortunate Duncan Livingston had been met by Waccan in the Babine Lake who immediately put an end to the scoundrell's existence, but having no circumstantial account of this affair

all I can say about it as well as of the preceding is that if neither of them lead to any unpleasant results before my arrival
with the brigade, that I will have every cause to rejoice.[146]

Because his canoes were in poor condition and one man had deserted, Connolly's brigade took another thirteen days to travel
upriver to the last campsite above the rapids at Chinlac. There
Connolly placed James Murray Yale in charge of a cache and two
canoes and left shortly after midnight on September 17 on a forced
march to Stuart Lake. He arrived at three in the afternoon to find
George Simpson waiting for him. When Chief Qua subsequently
approached the fort with some of his men, Connolly would not
allow him to enter the building because of his recent misconduct.
In his journal he wrote:

> This circumstance of which through Indians I had heard
> something previous to my arrival is as follows. Some days
> after that affair had taken place, this old rogue Qua, with as
> many others of his tribe as he could muster, entered the fort
> and made their way into the house all armed. Mr. Douglas,
> suspecting that they had come with some evil intention, im-
> mediately seized his arms as also his men but neither of them
> were able, from the crowd which surrounded them, to use
> them in turning their intruders out of the fort. It is true that
> the Indians on their part used no other violence than to en-
> deavour to preserve themselves from injury and declared that
> they had no other view in this than to enter into an explana-
> tion with Mr. Douglas. But as that could have been done with-
> out such a display, the most favourable construction which
> can be put upon their conduct is that their intentions were by
> intimidation to extort what they might think proper in com-
> pensation for the death of their relative. And nothing but the
> determination Mr. Douglas evinced of defending himself to
> the last saved him from being pillaged and perhaps from be-
> ing killed. On several occasions previous to this, I am told,

for I never witnessed it myself, that similar scenes had been exhibited and those insults having been tamely submitted to; they thought no doubt that in this instance they would escape with equal impunity. They now however have been taught to entertain more respectful opinions of the whites and that the days of trifling are at an end. Prior to that affair the conduct of the Indians attached to this post had been everything Mr. Douglas could have wished, and subsequently also they have not given the smallest cause of offense.[147]

Yale brought the brigade to Fort St. James a few days later. He had been on sick leave at Fort Vancouver but had taken part in the Puget Sound expedition to revenge the death of Alexander Mackenzie. Now with little time to rest, he was chosen to accompany Simpson down the Fraser, possibly because in November 1826 he had explored by canoe as far as Kumshene at the confluence of the Thompson and Fraser rivers, the site of present-day Lytton.[148]

While another canoe was built for Simpson's expedition and his excess baggage retrieved from Fort McLeod, he spent a miserable week at Fort St. James. It rained every day, and the fort's meagre supply of salmon had to be augmented by rabbit and game. Nevertheless, he was impressed with Connolly's administration. In his famous "Character Book," where many employees received a poor rating, Simpson described Connolly as "an active useful man whose Zeal and exertions have generally been crowned with success, whose Word may be depended on in most things, and whom I consider incapable of doing anything that is mean or dishonorable." On the negative side he noted that:

> His temper, however, is violent to madness when roused, he is at times Hypochondriacal, always tenacious of his rights, priviledges and dignity, disposed to magnify his own exploits and to over rate his Service which nonetheless are valuable, rather domineering and Tyrannical, but on the whole a respectable and useful Member of our Community."[149]

Simpson reported the total furs for 1828 from Fort McLeod constituted thirty packs and were worth £2,500; twenty-five packs worth £2,000 had been shipped from Fort St. James; thirty packs worth £3,000 from Fort Fraser (the most valuable post in New Caledonia) with the possibility of an increase of eight more packs; twenty-five packs worth £2,000 from Fort Alexandria; fifteen packs worth £1,300 from Fort Babine; and fourteen packs worth £1,200 from Connolly's Lake. Between them the six posts had produced 130 fur packs with a gross value of £12,000. Expenses amounted to £3,000, making £9,000 profit. If the Chilcotin post could be established, Simpson estimated it could provide another fifteen packs worth £1,200, and he wanted Fort George re-established because it would supply an estimated twelve packs valued at £1,000. Thus, in a year or two profits could be raised to £10,000 or £12,000 "beyond which it cannot materially rise, as its Trade does not appear to me capable of further extension."[150]

EVER SINCE SIMPSON'S VISIT to the Pacific Coast in 1824, he had nurtured the idea that the Fraser might be navigable to the ocean, though he was not prepared to run the entire river. Thus, at five on the morning of September 26, 1828, his canoes made their way through the fog at the mouth of the Nechako River into the rapidly flowing Fraser, with the ruins of the abandoned Fort George barely visible on the right. When he arrived at Fort Alexandria the following day, he changed to horses and, accompanied by Archibald McDonald and Dr. Hamlyn, took the brigade trail overland to visit Fort Thompson. Meanwhile, James Murray Yale and Simpson's best boatman had continued the trip to Kumshene where Simpson planned to rendezvous with him.[151]

Simpson's inspection of Fort Thompson went well. At a large gathering of the local Natives he read letters written by two of the Native boys from the Columbia district who were being educated at Red River. Chief Nicola was not present, but before departing, Simpson left him a gift—a red-lined HBC cloak. Nicola looked af-

One of the most dangerous rapids of the Fraser Canyon, Hell's Gate was also a First Nations fishing site. Photographed by F. Daly in the 1860s. GLENBOW ARCHIVES NA-674-19

ter this robe of honour carefully, and twenty years later he wore it for a meeting with the Jesuit priest John Nobili at Okanagan Lake.

McDonald and Hamlyn accompanied Simpson down the Thompson River to the reunion with Yale at Kumshene and then down the last section of the Fraser to Fort Langley. When their canoes encountered the canyon rapids, Simpson's plans for using the Fraser as a transportation corridor vanished. In his journal he compared his terrifying experiences to those of Simon Fraser and John Stuart:

> I cannot however take leave of the dangerous parts of Frazers River, without saying that the great exertions and unwearied perseverance of Chief Factor John Stewart [sic] and his fellow Travellers, in the course of discovery, which enabled them in the summer of 1808 to pass from the Rocky Mountains to the Pacific Ocean by this route; a great part of which they performed on foot, carrying their provisions & Baggage on their

backs, does them infinite credit; an undertaking, compared to which, in my humble opinion, the much talked of and high sounding performances of His Majestys recent discovery Expeditions [by Sir John Franklin] in the Arctic regions were excursions of pleasure.[152]

THE CANOES ARRIVED AT FORT LANGLEY on the evening of October 10. Written reports state that Simpson's canoe included McDonald, Hamlyn and twenty men, and Yale's canoe carried "7 men from New Caledonia & Thompson's River." Nowhere is it mentioned that Simpson's wife, Margaret Taylor, was part of this expedition, but it must be assumed that she, too, experienced the terror of running the rapids of the Fraser Canyon.[153]

When planning his departure from Fort Langley to Fort Vancouver, Simpson took into account the Native unrest he might encounter near Puget Sound and decided to travel overland to Fort Vancouver from the Cowlitz Portage. He waited five days while two more canoes were built, then with one other boat he departed for the portage by water. His party included Donald Manson and Chief Factor James McMillan who had now completed their assignment to establish Fort Langley. Archibald McDonald and James Murray Yale remained as their replacements.[154]

SIMPSON AND MARGARET TAYLOR wintered with John McLoughlin at Fort Vancouver, then returned east with the 1829 spring express over Athabasca Pass, which is located at the headwaters of the Whirlpool River, a tributary of the Athabasca River, at the extreme southern tip of what is now Jasper National Park. Simpson apparently crossed the pass on snowshoes, but this must have been difficult for Margaret, who was five months pregnant with their second child, because even today physically fit hikers need a week to traverse this remote wilderness on foot.[155] On reaching Red River, Simpson left Margaret with John Stuart, now stationed at Bas de la Rivière, before going on to attend the annual council at Norway House. Margaret's sister, Mary, was Stuart's new country wife.

Margaret gave birth to John McKenzie Simpson in August while Simpson was at Lachine preparing for a trip to England to search for a wife. Without informing Stuart or Margaret of his plans, he married his cousin, Frances Simpson, in February 1830 and brought her back to reside at Red River. Stuart then had the unenviable task of finding a husband for Margaret while keeping her and the children out of sight. As Simpson provided a dowry for her, Amable Hogue came to the rescue, and the couple was married in 1831.[156]

MOST TRADERS seemed to have one extremely difficult year during their tenure at Fort St. James, and William Connolly's was clearly 1828. The loss of the three boatmen on the Columbia River, the murder of Duncan Livingston and the killing of one of the Fort George murderers were the worst of his troubles. He also had

At one of the great fishing sites on the Columbia River, the North West Company and the New Caledonia fur brigades portaged around Celilo Falls and paid the Native fishermen a tribute for passing through their territory. The falls are now submerged behind the Dalles Dam. OREGON HISTORICAL SOCIETY 373-A

difficulty obtaining leather from east of the Rockies and suffered a shortage of winter *engagés* because Simpson had commandeered some of his best men, including the interpreter Waccan Boucher, for his trip down the Fraser. Connolly complained to him in February 1829:

> The absence of our Men deranged us so much that the effects of it will be felt for the remainder of the Winter, besides subjecting the District to the immediate loss of a few Packs arising from the want of means to forward some of the Outfits at the time they were required; but the want of our Interpreter was what will be most permanently felt; after what had happened in the Spring and Summer, it would have been of the utmost consequence to have come to some understanding with the Natives, but having no Person sufficiently conversant with the language to explain matters to them this could not be effected.[157]

Then in November 1828, while en route to Fort Fraser, James Douglas encountered a group of angry Natives who threatened his life. Connolly now feared that his son-in-law did not have a safe future at Fort St. James and pleaded with Simpson to transfer him to the Columbia: "He would readily face a hundred of them, but he does not much like the idea of being assassinated; with your permission he might next year be removed to the Columbia, wherever he may be placed he can not fail of being essentially useful." His request was not formally granted until the council's meeting in June 1829.[158]

In January 1829 Natives in the vicinity of Fort Fraser killed an Iroquois employee, fifty-year-old Jacques Tranquash. He had served in New Caledonia as early as 1822 when the Fort St. James servants' account book was inscribed, "A very faithful, good man for an Iroquois." Connolly blamed clerk John McDonnell's imprudence for sending Tranquash off alone and unarmed for a sled load of fish.[159] But while John Stuart might have sought revenge for the death of a long-serving employee like Tranquash, Connolly believed it had not been caused by Native revenge and, probably wanting to avoid any more conflict with the Carrier people, he did not take any retaliatory action.

IN THE WAKE OF SIMPSON'S DEPARTURE from Fort St. James, Connolly acted on his orders to re-establish Fort George and to send George McDougall from Fort Alexandria to re-examine the possibility of a post in the Chilcotin. Connolly, accompanied by McDougall and another nine men, had reconnoitered the area in December 1825 when it was still thought possible to build a major depot near tidewater at Bella Coola.[160] But Native unrest and a shortage of personnel had permitted nothing more than a seasonal post in the Chilcotin. This proved to be still true in 1829.

After almost twenty-five years in New Caledonia, James Mc-Dougall's health had begun to fail, and in the fall of 1827 his brother George had found him confined to bed at Fort St. James, suffering from weakness in his legs and left arm. Although his Native wife nursed him carefully during that winter, he remained quite feeble, and when Connolly left with the brigade in the spring of 1828 he had put James into the care of his brother at Fort Alexandria. However, a summer away from Stuart Lake did not improve his condition and he was still unwell when the brigade returned in the fall.[161]

George Simpson must have met James McDougall on his 1828 tour through New Caledonia and agreed that he should be transferred to an easier post east of the mountains. Thus, in the spring of 1829 Connolly, accompanied by a hired Native aide, took McDougall south to Fort Vancouver. Also travelling with the brigade were an ailing John Tod and John Harriott from Fraser Lake with his wife, Elizabeth Pruden, who was suffering from bouts of mental illness, probably exacerbated by the stress of pregnancy. The Harriotts had been transferred only the previous year from Fort Assiniboine. When the brigade reached Fort Vancouver, the fort's medical doctor determined that neither McDougall nor Elizabeth were well enough to manage the trek over Athabasca Pass. They finally set out in July 1830, but while crossing the Rocky Mountains Elizabeth Pruden went missing from the campsite. The brigade searched for her without success, then carried on to Edmonton House where her baby daughter, Margaret, was handed over to the care of Chief Factor John Rowand's wife, Louise.[162]

After devoting the best years of his life to New Caledonia, James McDougall retired from service in 1831. The governor and committee made a donation of £500 sterling "that he be at liberty to draw for the same as he may consider expedient."[163] When Archibald McDonald retired to Chambly, near Montreal, in 1845, he reported on the success of former Nor'westers living there but stated that "poor James McDougald [sic] is an exception to all." McDougall apparently lived in straitened circumstances until his death in Montreal in 1851; the company agreed to pay his funeral expenses to a maximum of £10 sterling.[164] By 1831 Connolly's health was also failing and he departed New Caledonia, but by that time the tensions of the late 1820s had been resolved. He left the Native and fur trade populations in a stable relationship that lasted for another decade.

It seems Connolly had intended to be faithful to his Cree wife, Miyo Nipiy (Susanne Pas-de-Nom), who had been his country wife for twenty-eight years. But in 1832, shortly after the family arrived at Saint-Eustache, Lower Canada, he obtained a dispensation from the bishop and formally married his second cousin, Julia Woolwich.[165] With financial assistance from Connolly, Miyo Nipiy moved to Montreal and then to Red River where she went to live in the Grey Nuns convent. After Connolly's death, Julia continued to support her.

In 1864 Connolly's will, leaving everything to Julia, was challenged by Miyo Nipiy's son John, and a long court case ensued over whether his mother's marriage "in the custom of the country" was valid. When John's claim to a portion of the estate was upheld by the Superior Court, Court of Appeals and Court of Revision, Julia's heirs appealed to the Privy Council in London.

Eventually a private settlement was reached out of court. This was a significant if not a precedent-setting case because it established that some judges considered that Native women married according to the custom of the country were legal wives and they and their children were entitled to be beneficiaries of a fur trader's estate.[166]

$Chapter\ Eight$

PETER WARREN DEASE AND PETER SKENE OGDEN

FORT ST. JAMES was administered by another former Nor'wester from 1831 to 1835. Peter Warren Dease had joined the XY Company in 1801 at the age of thirteen and became a clerk following that company's amalgamation with the North West Company in 1804. He gained chief trader status after the merger of the NWC and HBC.[167]

Having served east of the Rocky Mountains until his posting to Stuart Lake in 1831, Dease was totally unfamiliar with the Columbia brigade route, and his crew suffered badly on his first trek south. At Fort George Canyon, Louis Paul, leader of the brigade and the "best *boute* in the district," was knocked into the water by the sweep oar and drowned. Returning up the Columbia in July, two more *boutes*, Augustin and J. Moreau, drowned near the Cascades.[168] The following year when the brigade reached Fort Okanagan, six of Dease's men came down with "intermittent fever" or malaria. The disease had appeared for the first time in 1830 at Fort Vancouver, taking a toll on HBC personnel and on the Natives of the district. Peter Skene Ogden and fifty-two men were stricken at that time,[169] and John McLoughlin estimated that 75 percent of the Natives had died.[170]

One of the most interesting events during Dease's administration was the arrival at Fort St. James of the Scottish botanist David Douglas. In 1823 under the auspices of the Horticultural Society of London, Douglas had collected plants in the northeastern United States and Upper Canada. When the Society sponsored a second field trip in 1824, this time in the Pacific Northwest, Douglas had relied on HBC personnel for material support. On his return to London in 1827, his collection set a record "for species introduced by an individual into Britain," and seeds from a flowering red currant shrub *(ribes sanguineum)*, native to British Columbia, produced plants so popular that the Society recouped the entire cost of the expedition. The Colonial Office subsequently sought Douglas' opinion on the US claim to Oregon, and he strongly supported British rights, urging that the Columbia River should be the boundary line west of the Rockies.[171]

Douglas returned to the Pacific Northwest in 1829, and after exploring as far afield as California and the Sandwich Islands, he decided to return to England via Alaska and Siberia—in spite of the fact that his eyesight had deteriorated to the point where he was now half–blind. He set off from Fort Vancouver on March 20, 1833, for Fort St. James, accompanied by HBC employee William Johnson. He was well equipped with food, a tent and twelve pairs of moccasins, as well as "several Indians, ten or twelve horses, and my old terrier, a most faithful and now, to judge from his long gray beard, venerable friend, who has guarded me throughout all my journies, and whom, should I live to return, I mean certainly to pension off on four pennyworth of cat's meat per day."[172] While spending the night with Samuel Black at Fort Thompson, Douglas is supposed to have disparaged the HBC by claiming it was "simply a mercenary corporation; there is not an officer in it with a soul above a beaver skin." Black instantly challenged Douglas to a duel that he managed to avoid the following morning.[173]

Douglas hoped to find guides at Fort St. James who could help him reach the Pacific Coast, and when he arrived at the fort, he learned that Simon McGillivray Jr. was about to conduct a voyage of discovery down the Babine and Simpson (Skeena) rivers. However, after duly considering the possibility that McGillivray's expedition might not reach the Pacific or any of the maritime HBC posts, Douglas changed his mind and with Johnson began retracing his route down the Fraser River.[174] On June 13 their canoe was destroyed in the rapids of Fort George Canyon and they barely survived. All Douglas's botanical notes and a 400-species plant collection vanished in the mishap. The only evidence remaining from the expedition is a set of penciled maps now preserved in the British Columbia Archives.[175] After the mishap Douglas and Johnson returned upriver to Fort George where George Linton, the clerk in charge there, helped them on their way again.

It was just as well that Douglas returned to Fort Vancouver because Simon McGillivray Jr. only explored the upper portion of the Skeena. Near Rocher de Boule where the Bulkley meets the Skeena River, he received a note dated February 7, 1833, from Peter Skene Ogden, who was stationed at Fort Simpson on the Nass River: "Reports are in circulation here that a party of whites are in quest of this place. If so, I shall be happy to see them." But McGillivray did not risk going any further down the Skeena.[176]

UNDER DEASE'S LEADERSHIP Fort St. James was a lively place. He was popular with his men and participated in musical soirees, playing the violin and flute. Feasts of "roasted bear, beaver and marmot" and games of chess, whist and backgammon helped to pass the long winter evenings. To maintain the food supply, he continued Connolly's agricultural practices,[177] although the staple food remained dried salmon. When Clerk Thomas Dears, who developed the farm at Fraser Lake, took charge of Fort St. James while Dease was absent with the brigade in the summer of 1831, he wrote to a friend that:

I was generally a slender person; what would you say if you

saw my emaciated Body now? I am every morning when dressing in danger of slipping through my breeks and falling into my boots. Many a night I go to bed hungry and craving something better than this horrid dried salmon.[178]

When Dease's contract expired in 1835, he pleaded for a furlough to recover his health. On his departure from Stuart Lake his men presented him with a musical snuff box as a token of their appreciation. But while a posting to New Caledonia was considered harsh enough, the HBC Council next assigned Dease to an Arctic expedition with Thomas Simpson, whose goal was to explore the uncharted portions of the Arctic coastline. Over three summers, 1836 to 1839, they completed the survey of the Northwest Passage across 60 degrees of latitude.[179]

Dease married his Metis wife, Elizabeth Chouinard, in 1840. Presumably, since he was by that time already a grandfather, his family of four sons and four daughters must have resided with him while he was in charge at Fort St. James from 1831 to 1835.[180]

PETER SKENE OGDEN replaced Dease in 1835—the last of the Nor'westers to manage New Caledonia. Born in Quebec City in 1790, the son of a judge, he and his close friend Samuel Black joined the North West Company in 1809 and both earned reputations for violence during the worst years of the rivalry between that company and the HBC. After a Lower Canada court drew up an indictment for murder against him in 1818, the NWC transferred him to the Columbia Department to put him out of reach of the law.

At this time he took as his country wife Julia Rivet, a Spokane Native, having left behind the Cree woman who had borne his first child, Peter Jr. Julia was the stepdaughter of François Rivet who had served under David Thompson and became one of the early settlers on French Prairie in the Willamette Valley.[181] She accompanied her husband on some of his trapping expeditions, and during their lifelong union she raised Peter Jr. and

The last ex-Nor'wester to manage New Caledonia, Peter Skene Ogden served the HBC faithfully in many difficult situations. His crowning achievement was the rescue of the Whitman massacre survivors in 1847. His portrait is by John Mix Stanley. BRITISH COLUMBIA ARCHIVES A-01813

bore seven children, including Euretta Mary and Isaac, who were born at Fort St. James.[182]

After the merger of the two companies, Ogden was sent to the mostly unmapped Snake River country, the large mountainous area south of the Columbia River between the continental divide and the Pacific Coast. There, as a deterrent to American immigrants, Simpson ordered him to trap the beaver and other fur-bearing animals to extinction to create a "barren desert" on the eastern approaches to Oregon Territory. (Ogden's exploits are documented in two HBRS publications known as *Peter Ogden's Snake Country Journals.*[183]) On his final Snake River expedition in 1830, nine of his men, 500 furs and all of his papers disappeared in the swirling waters of the Dalles on the Columbia River.

In April 1831 Ogden sailed from Fort Vancouver to establish a new post near the mouth of the Nass River on the northwest coast. From this post, originally called Fort Nass and then renamed Fort Simpson, Ogden competed with American traders and the Russian American Company based in Sitka, Alaska. In 1834 he was given command of the New Caledonia district and he arrived at Fort St. James the following summer. He was then forty-five years old and had recently achieved chief factor status. He was described by Simpson as "a keen, sharp, off-hand fellow of superior abilities to most of his colleagues, very hardy and active and not sparing of his personal labour."[184]

Ogden's new responsibilities included supporting the Natives to conserve the richest fur-bearing region in the Columbia Department, a practice that contrasted sharply with his experiences in the Snake River country. During his nine years in New Caledonia, Ogden did his best to maintain the forts as viable operations. To this end he ordered the construction of flour mills at Forts Okanagan, Alexandria and George to relieve New Caledonia's dependence on flour from Fort Colvile, the company fort built in 1825 at Kettle Falls on the Columbia River. Ogden always had one eye on the accounts and claimed he abolished the debt system. He also examined the leather distribution to employees and found that the greatest portion of dressed leather went to company servants who wasted it, "in some cases for a maiden's favour." By allowing only sufficient leather for "one pair of shoes for fifteen days," Ogden estimated that one hundred skins per year could be saved.[185]

In 1836 Ogden ordered that Fort Alexandra be relocated to the west side of the Fraser River, a move that meant Natives from the Chilcotin would not have to cross the partially frozen Fraser River in winter to bring in their furs or trespass on the Shuswap people's territory on the east side of the river. It also meant that the fort's staff could give greater support to personnel stationed in the Chilcotin, and as a result, Fort Chilcotin was built one hundred miles west of Fort Alexandria near the junction of the Chilcotin and Chilanko rivers.

Ogden also worked hard to keep his employees content, but his skillful management was hampered by the calibre of personnel at the forts. This fact was amply demonstrated at the time of the drowning deaths of George Linton, Wastayap Campbell and their families. On his first brigade trip north in 1835, Ogden had met George Linton, the clerk in charge at Fort George, and Alexander Fisher, the chief trader at Fort Alexandria, although he probably already knew of them by reputation. Simpson had transferred Fisher from east of the Rockies to Alexandria, noting in his Character Book that Fisher could "make himself agreeable to Indians until they discover his falsehood which must very soon be the case, as he is totally regardless of truth, in fact, a habitual Liar without conduct or principle, and was becoming so much addicted to liquor that I found it necessary to remove him a few years ago to one of our most Sober Stations." George Linton had joined the NWC at age nineteen and was one of the bullies who had taunted George Simpson and his men at Fort Wedderburn during the winter of 1820–21. After the merger he had continued to serve in the Athabasca region as a clerk for the HBC until he was transferred to New Caledonia in 1831. Simpson described him as a "stout, strong, square-built fellow who would have made a very good figure in the 'Prize Ring' being an excellent bruiser; has a good deal of the Manner of a man accustomed to live by his Wits, and I suspect is out of a bad nest."[186]

When Ogden arrived at Fort George in 1835, he reassigned Linton to Fort Chilcotin, replacing him with John McLean. Linton, however, delayed his departure because the leather party under the leadership of a new clerk, Alexander Caulfield Anderson, had not yet arrived from Jasper House. However, he waited too long, and ice was forming on the Fraser River when his entourage finally set out for Fort Alexandria. Their two canoes were overloaded with Linton, Campbell, two women, four children, a dog and considerable luggage. Fifteen miles downriver they had to run the ice-clogged Fort George Canyon. When Linton's dog returned to Fort George, McLean assumed that all members of the party had perished.[187]

This was the accepted conclusion until a few years later when Fisher publicly reported at Norway House that the two families had been murdered by Natives. Ogden was now duty bound to investigate and seek retribution. The report that he submitted to Simpson in early 1842 reveals his legal upbringing and his desire to be fair.

It is certainly much to be regretted that Mr. C.T. Fisher—when he saw the body of the deceased Mr. Linton recognizable from his dress, having a green blanket capot on, and not far distant from the shore, floating down on a cake of ice—that he had not sent a canoe or boat to secure it, and after on the same day when some of his Indians informed him that within two hours march of the fort, at a place called the little eddy, that the body of the Chief [George Linton] was there and that the crows had already attacked it—independent of other considerations, motives of humanity should have dictated to him the propriety of sending and ascertaining if the report was corrected or not. Had the body been seen and examined, it could soon have been ascertained if he had been killed or drowned and all doubts or surmises would have ceased. During the winter a bale and a small box containing goods and wearing apparel were found a short distance below the Fort and delivered by the Indians to Mr. Fisher. This circumstance then was considered fully convincing to Mr. F. who wrote me officially to that effect . . .

Ogden had concluded that one of the canoes had been wrecked in the Fort George Canyon and the entire party had continued down the Fraser in the other vessel.

On the following spring, on my way down to Alexandria, I saw the canoe which the party had embarked in, floating down the river about twenty miles above the fort. It had a large hole in the bow as it had been stow'ed in, either by the ice or stones. No doubt existed in the minds of any one then, nor until two years afterwards but that the unfortunate party had all but drowned and not before the spring of 1837 was there the least suspicion or even surmise that they were murdered and this entirely arose from a woman who had deserted from the village of the supposed murderers and has since connected herself with the Carrier Chief of Alexandria.

Ogden included the woman's story in his report to Simpson, but discounted it:

> Now, since the woman first made the above statement she has so far contradicted herself by stating she was absent at the time but received the accounts from another woman, and it rests solely on her information that Mr. C[hief] T[rader] Fisher has come to the conclusion the Party was murdered, and on no other, but not sufficient to convince me. And C.T. Fisher, when we conversed on the subject, was then of opinion the woman's story required further confirmation (which he never obtained and if he did never divulged it to anyone, no doubt to suit his views at a future date) ere it would be proper to take any decisive measures against the supposed murderers. It however appears both from what he has written and publicly reported at Norway House he has changed that opinion; what motive he has for so doing I shall not attempt to discover and shall leave him full liberty to enjoy it . . .
>
> In the fall of 1840 I was encamped within half a mile of Stony Island [Fort George Canyon] rapids, the water being then very low, on a sandy beach. One of the servants found a gun that was embedded in the sand, and at the very time the Father of Campbell's Wife and four other Fort George Indians were encamped with us, and after short conversation and examination, recognized the gun as belonging to Campbell, the latter having given his fine one in lieu of it prior to his separating from his father-in-law, and the old man thus remarked, "if he had not been drowned, how come the gun here?"—and a short time prior to this, near the same place, a pair of cloth leggings worked with beads were said to have belonged to Campbell's wife. The latter however I did not see, but state it on Indian report. Now as regards the gun, I am confident all those who are any ways acquainted with the character of the Carriers will agree with me in opinion, these firearms would have been the first thing secured.

I have now given all the information that has come to my knowledge relative to the melancholy affair, and will abide by the opinion of all impartial men, if in not taking decisive measures against the supposed murderers I have acted as one in my situation should have done or not.[188]

Linton left an estate valued at £338 that the HBC discharged carefully. They first ascertained that he had no aboriginal wife or children living in New Caledonia before his destitute, eighty-year-old mother in England could obtain letters of administration. Perhaps she helped her daughter who had written Linton in 1834 asking for assistance to buy a house.[189]

Insularity protected New Caledonia from the dreadful 1838 smallpox epidemic. The disease broke out along the Missouri and spread to the Plains Indians. By this time vaccine was available from England and the governor in London urged chief factors and chief traders in the Northern and Southern Departments to introduce it at the forts. When the disease reached Fort Simpson and Fort McLoughlin on the northwest coast, John McLoughlin quickly dispatched a package of vaccine, hoping that the Indians would accept it. However, smallpox did not spread to New Caledonia, and there is no record of vaccine being sent to inland forts.[190]

Ogden was a shrewd judge of character, enabling him to treat the Carriers and other First Nations people with tact, an attribute that belies the oft-quoted statement in *Notes on Western Caledonia* that he prepared for his successor, Donald Manson, that they were "a brutish, ignorant, superstitious beggarly sett of beings."[191] When the Carrier chief Qua died in 1840, Ogden noted that the funeral preparations caused "considerable commotion" amongst the Natives. The interpreter Waccan attended the funeral feast and reported that there was a great abundance of bear fat for the guests. Qua had requested burial in a coffin and Ogden hoped that the Carrier would be influenced to give up cremation practices, but this did not happen immediately.[192] After Qua's death his two sons and his brother Hoolson continued to hunt for the fort, and Hoolson, now the chief, came to Ogden to request an annual outfit of chief's clothing such as Qua had received. But Ogden gave him only a moose skin and told him he must prove himself first as neither his conduct nor his hunting had been good the previous year.[193]

Salmon were scarce in 1840, except at Fraser Lake, and both Natives and HBC servants suffered. Ogden wrote, "In years of such scarcity it cannot be expected the returns would be increased; the reverse is the case, but fortunately compared to last year only slightly affected." He was able to renew all his men's contracts so that no new servants were needed. At the same time, he took the opportunity to request leave of absence for himself as he had now worked west of the Rockies for a quarter of a century.[194]

The early 1840s were described as "the halcyon era of the Great Monopoly" in North America. In fact, by 1839 the company was already thoroughly satisfied with the fur trade west of the Rockies, and the head office in London offered no suggestions for improvement, believing that the management at each post would do its utmost to make a profit. In the years 1838 and 1839 the directors of the HBC were able to authorize dividends of 25 and 23 percent. In 1840 it was still a good 15 percent. Chief factors benefitted financially, even if they were stationed in far-flung posts, and in many cases Governor George Simpson held power of attorney to make investments on their behalf.[195]

Because of his responsibility for the Snake River brigades of the 1820s, Ogden was an old hand at managing men, horses and river travel. Nevertheless, his New Caledonia brigades occasionally ran into trouble. His old friend Samuel Black was now in charge of Fort Thompson, having been transferred by McLoughlin from Walla Walla because he was difficult to manage and did not get along with the Nez Perce. But Black also proved unpopular with the Thompson and Okanagan First Nations, and on the 1837 brigade trek through the Okanagan, his horse had been shot out from under him and two of the Natives who attacked him were killed. Thereafter, Natives seeking revenge also threatened Ogden's passage through the Okanagan.

In spite of this, Black remained at Fort Thompson for another four years with Ogden visiting his old friend there for several weeks each year. Then on February 8, 1841, Black spent the afternoon working on his correspondence, taking little notice of a young Native man resting by the sitting room fireplace. But at an opportune moment the man withdrew a concealed gun, shot and killed Black and made his escape. One motive for the murder seemed to be revenge: a few days previous to the event Black had refused to give a gun to the murderer's uncle, Chief Tranquille, and when the Chief reached his home at Pavilion he had died unexpectedly. McLoughlin immediately sent men from Fort Vancouver to search for Black's murderer, but the man eluded his captors until the fall.[196]

Following Black's death, Ogden decided that for protection the Fort Thompson and New Caledonia brigades should henceforth proceed together to and from Fort Okanagan.[197] But along with Ogden, the New Caledonia boat crews were getting on in years. In February 1841 he wrote to Simpson that, because the best boatmen were now aging, there were more accidents occurring on the Columbia River during summer transit. The HBC needed to find replacements and should offer £2 more in wages to attract good men.[198] His dire predictions for the future were realized in 1842 when five boatmen, most of them from Fort Colvile, drowned near Priest Rapids.

New Caledonia was not on George Simpson's itinerary in 1841 when he paid his last visit to the Columbia Department although he expected to rendezvous with Ogden and the inbound brigade at Fort Okanagan. He made a rapid crossing of the Prairies, breached the Rockies via the Bow River traverse, and arrived at Fort Okanagan in August, but Ogden had already departed. Because of the Native unrest following Black's murder, he had decided to personally ensure the brigade's safe passage through the

Okanagan Valley to Fort Thompson. He wrote to Simpson from there on August 6, reporting that John Tod had come from Fort Alexandria to replace Black and that Black's murderer was still at large. Possibly to prevent being short of managers in 1842, he added a postscript requesting that Tod be allowed to return to Fort Alexandria as soon as possible. He also reported that he was reluctantly preparing to continue his journey north because the surrounding countryside was on fire and there were powder kegs stored in the fort. His departing instructions to Tod were to ensure that the local Natives captured Black's murderer.

Donald Manson, who had been second-in-command to Black when he traced the Finlay River to its source, spent the winter with Tod at Fort Thompson. Manson had also helped to build Fort Langley in 1827 and Fort McLoughlin (present-day Bella Bella) in 1833 and, finding Fort Thompson in decrepit condition, set to work erecting new buildings on the west side of the North Thompson River. When these buildings were completed, the Fort Thompson site was abandoned and the new site became known as Fort Kamloops. In October 1841 Manson wrote from Fort Colvile advising Simpson that Black's murderer had been killed with the help of Natives.[199] After briefly returning to Alexandria, Tod took over management of Fort Thompson again in 1842 and Alexander Caulfield Anderson, who had

While stationed at Fort Alexandria, Alexander Caulfield Anderson explored two ancient First Nations trails through the Cascade Mountains to the Fraser Valley in 1846–47. His efforts enabled Donald Manson to reroute the New Caledonia brigade from Fort Vancouver to Fort Langley commencing in 1848.
BRITISH COLUMBIA ARCHIVES A-01076

just commanded the annual brigade to York Factory, replaced Tod at Fort Alexandria.

Simpson called Black's death "one of the most melancholy occurrences that has taken place in the country within my recollection." Until this time he had dutifully passed on to all his districts the position encouraged by head office in London that HBC personnel should act prudently. But in his report to London in November 1841 (written before he received the news of Black's murderer's death) he ventured his own opinion on how to control Native violence:

> I was concerned to learn whilst passing Okanagan, that the disaffection of the Indians between that place and New Caledonia, which has shown itself more conspicuously since the death of the late Chief Factor Black than previously, had not yet subsided, and that every plan that had been formed for apprehending the assassin had failed. This unfortunate state of affairs it is thought has arisen from an ill-judged forbearance on our part in not punishing many cases of misconduct (such as horse thieving, pilfering from encampments, etc.), which have been committed by the Natives of late years, a forbearance they ascribe to shyness or timidity, instead of the proper cause, a disinclination to have recourse to measures of severity. Presuming on this laxity of discipline, they have day by day become more daring, until now, that it is considered a service of danger even to pass through the country, and can only be attempted in strong parties. The complement of people in this district has been considerably increased with a view of restoring good order, and with the hope that more effective measures may be adopted for apprehending the murderer of Mr. Black, as if he be allowed to remain at large unpunished, the impression it could have on the minds of the Natives might prove dangerous to the peace of the country, and to the lives and property of the white population.[200]

Simpson's visit to the Columbia in 1841 confirmed for him that the United States would most likely claim Oregon Territory. He had insisted on building Fort Langley after his visit to the Columbia in 1824, and he now ordered that Fort Victoria be established on Vancouver Island.[201]

PRIOR TO THIS TIME various HBC personnel had introduced some religious ideas to the Natives, and Ogden had even taken up a collection among the New Caledonia posts to help the priests Francis Norbert Blanchet and Modeste Demers of the secular Catholic clergy, who had arrived in Oregon in 1838. Demers visited Fort Langley in 1841 and the following year accompanied Ogden to New Caledonia with the brigade. He visited Fort St. James and the Chilcotin, wintered at Fort Alexandria, and stopped briefly at Fort Thompson on his return to Oregon the following spring. John Tod, however, criticized Demers' efforts to convert the 400 starving Natives near the fort and wrote in the Fort Thompson Journal, "Poor deluded creatures, they do not know how little good he can do them." Nevertheless, Demers' attempts at proselytizing laid the foundation for the positive reception received by Jesuit priest

One large structure, built in Red River style, survived for many years at Fort Alexandria on the west side of the Fraser River. Landslides from the cut banks, remnants of a giant ancient lake that reached as far as Fort George, were a constant threat to boatmen. BRITISH COLUMBIA ARCHIVES F-05775

John Nobili when he visited New Caledonia between 1845 and 1847.[202]

Like John Stuart, Ogden was also willing to help his men with romantic problems. The 1837 brigade from Fort Vancouver included a young bride-to-be, Eliza Birnie, who was bound for Fort Fraser. Because of the Native unrest in the Okanagan, John McLoughlin waited impatiently at Fort Vancouver until he learned of her safe arrival.[203] Eliza was the fifteen-year-old daughter of a long-time HBC clerk, James Birnie, who was stationed at Fort George on the Columbia River. The intended groom, Alexander Caulfield Anderson, had met her while serving under Ogden at Fort Simpson on the northwest coast. Ogden married the couple at Fort Alexandria in 1837, using his powers as magistrate, and although the Anglican minister at Fort Vancouver, Herbert Beaver, protested that this was not a legal marriage, the union lasted a lifetime and produced a family of thirteen children. On February 12, 1844, the eve of his final departure from New Caledonia, Ogden married clerk Henry Maxwell and Betsy McIntosh at Fort St. James.[204] But Ogden's readiness to formally marry company employees did not apply to his own situation; he was perfectly happy with a country marriage.

Long due for a furlough, Ogden continued to manage the affairs of New Caledonia with firmness and common sense until 1844 when he finally went on leave for one year. Just as Peter Warren Dease had left behind a commentary on his activities for Ogden prior to his departure from New Caledonia in 1835, Ogden now prepared "Notes on Western Caledonia" for his successor, Donald Manson. It contained considerable advice on dealing with the Carriers:[205]

. . . So long as you can keep them hunting in the Fall your returns will increase, and you will also find it to your interest to persuade them to make their feasts in the month of June which does not interfere with their hunts although in some cases you may succeed still you will find it rather a difficult task, however it is from the object to be gain'd by it worth a trial.[206]

Providing salmon for the long winters was one of the chief trader's most important responsibilities. Ogden noted that payment for salmon was set "at the rate of ninety for one Beaver," and he felt that it was good policy to ensure this tariff was applied equally to all forts otherwise the Natives became discontent. As the Babine area usually provided two-thirds of the 30,000 salmon that were needed annually, Ogden had introduced carts at the portage between Babine and Stuart lakes, making it easier to transport dried salmon, provisions and furs. However, he wrote that 20,000 should also be obtained from Fraser Lake to cover emergencies. He felt the number of men should not be increased, especially since recent arrivals were "the refuse of brothels and Gaols." He then tempered the criticism with the observation that:

> The Servants of this District have almost from the first year the Country was established been represented as [a] most worthless, dishonest, dissolute sett of beings. Having been now some years with them with few exceptions they are by no means so bad as represented and when we seriously take into consideration the hard duty imposed on them, food of an indifferent quality and no variety, temptations great, it is not surprising that they should occasionally deviate from the right path and under all these circumstances some allowance ought to be made for them.[207]

He reported that men serving in the brigade received an annual allowance of provisions including one hundred pounds of flour for married men and fifty pounds for bachelors, while *engagés* remaining at Fort St. James, single or married, had twenty-five pounds credited to their accounts. Interpreters were given twenty-five pounds credited to their accounts plus twenty-five pounds more and fifteen pounds of sugar as gratuities. But Ogden singled out the interpreter Jean Baptiste Boucher (Waccan) to receive special privileges. He was given a half keg of sugar and one bag of flour as gratuity, a half keg of sugar on account, and allowed to eat at the chief trader's table. Waccan certainly deserved his rewards, having served in New Caledonia longer than any employee. Ogden noted, "In Waccan the lingist [sic] you will find most useful in settling with the Indians none more capable than himself moreover from his long experience in this quarter now forty years better acquainted with all good, bad and indifferent Indians . . ."[208]

In the spring of 1844 Ogden brought the brigade as far as Fort Okanagan, handed it over to Donald Manson, and left with the express for the east. Ogden was near the pinnacle of his career by this time and well respected when he took part in the annual council of the Northern Department at Red River. He arrived at Montreal in August and prepared to set sail for London, which he had last visited in 1823 with Samuel Black to plead for acceptance by the HBC. Julia Ogden had remained at Willamette, so he took his brother's daughter, Annie Ogden, as his traveling companion to England.

When he returned to the west in 1845, he became part of the new triumvirate of chief factors managing the Columbia Department from Fort Vancouver with James Douglas and John McLoughlin.[209] Formerly, only McLoughlin had been in charge. Within two years of his return Ogden's cumulative experience with the Natives west of the Rockies was put to the supreme test by the Whitman Massacre of November 1847. At Waiilatpu near Fort Walla Walla, Cayuse and Umatilla Natives killed missionary Dr. Marcus Whitman, his wife Narcissa, and thirteen others, and took as hostage forty-seven men, women and children, mostly Oregon Trail immigrants. On learning of the tragedy, HBC clerk William McBean at Fort Walla Walla sent an urgent message to Fort Vancouver. Ogden's prompt response resulted in the rescue of all the hostages, including Donald Manson's two sons, John and Stephen, who had been placed with the Whitmans for schooling.[210]

After Ogden's return to Fort Vancouver from London in 1844, his daughter Sarah Julia had married HBC chief trader Archibald McKinlay, who had served briefly in New Caledonia under Ogden. In the early 1860s after the McKinlays' Oregon farm was flooded by the Willamette River, the family moved north to Lac La Hache, and Julia Ogden, now widowed, accompanied them. She is buried in the Lac La Hache cemetery near Phristine Brabant, the wife of Julia's stepson, Peter. A small community of ex-Fort St. James employees eventually developed around McKinlay's Lac La Hache pre-emption.[211]

Chapter Nine

DONALD MANSON

DONALD MANSON'S ADMINISTRATION in New Caledonia commenced in 1844 and lasted more than a decade. Manson was another hardy Scot, born at Thurso, Caithness, about 1798. Until this time Simpson had chosen former Nor'westers to superintend New Caledonia, but Manson had been an HBC employee from the beginning. Red-haired and over six feet tall, he was blessed with enormous powers of endurance—John Tod called him a "ramping highlander." He had helped with the fishery during Simpson's first difficult winter at Fort Wedderburn, mapped the Bow River valley then explored the Finlay River with Samuel Black in 1824. Three years later under James McMillan's supervision he had built Fort Langley and then served on the northwest coast with Ogden, William Fraser Tolmie and Alexander Anderson at Fort McLoughlin (Bella Bella). It was Tolmie, Anderson and Manson who encouraged John McLoughlin and James Douglas to start a circulating library out of Fort Vancouver to ease the isolation of the New Caledonia forts. During leave of absence in 1840 Manson took his son William back to Scotland for education and returned to Canada with George Simpson in March 1841.[212]

Manson gained chief trader status in 1837 as the result of

his resilience, dependability and experience, traits that allowed McLoughlin to rely on him in emergency situations. Thus, it was Manson that he dispatched to Fort Thompson in 1841 to assist John Tod following Samuel Black's murder, and then two years later to Fort Simpson on the Pacific Coast after his son, John McLoughlin Jr., was murdered. Manson's correspondence with Simpson, James Douglas, and members of his family is extant in the HBC and BC archives. His well-written official letters reveal a man who was both stern and pragmatic with his employees. They make a sharp contrast with the expressions of love and concern in the personal letters that he frequently sent to his children and grandchildren.

Manson took over at Fort St. James at a most unstable period in HBC history. Although the company still followed all the old ways, change was in the air. Simpson's "barren desert" policy had held off settlement in the Columbia District for several decades, but would-be farmers from the east were now pouring into the Willamette Valley. Moreover, in Europe, beaver hats were being replaced by more fashionable black silk hats, and as a consequence the demand for prime New Caledonia beaver fur had diminished drastically. Good *engagés* were also growing scarce, and new recruits were discouraged by the fact that dried salmon continued to be the mainstay of their diet. In his letter of instruction to Manson in 1844, Simpson regretted that there was a shortage of *boutes* that he could not fill. He blamed it on the fact that there

A "ramping Highlander," Donald Manson took on the most difficult HBC assignments and served at Fort St. James between 1844 and 1857. He ensured that two of his sons, William and John, also found employment with the HBC in New Caledonia. OREGON HISTORICAL SOCIETY ORTLI 9886-A

was no longer a "nursery" for training men in Canada because, as roads and canals in eastern Canada had improved, the canoe had become obsolete. At the same time he mentioned Peter Skene Ogden's suggestion for keeping skilled employees:

> *Boutes* must therefore be made of the servants of the district, which I should consider very practicable where boat and canoe transport is so general, and where so large a proportion of Natives (half breeds) are employed, and you must use your best endeavours to train up *boutes*, it being, as I have already said, quite impossible for us to provide them from this quarter.
>
> C[hief]F[actor] Ogden last year recommended that the wife of Michel Kamanasse, one of your most efficient *boutes*, should be allowed a passage this season to join her husband, as the most effective means of securing his services in the country, and accordingly encouragement was held out to her to come up by the canoes, although much encumbered with passengers. But she positively refused to leave Canada having, I presume, in her husband's absence formed a liaison there.[213]

Simpson also advised that Peter Skene Ogden's son, Peter Ogden Jr., with his wife, Euphrosine (Phristine), and child, Peter Skene Jr., would be transferred from Fort Edmonton to Fraser Lake to fill the clerk's position there. However, the company did not see any room to extend the trade in New Caledonia and vetoed a recent proposal for a new post at Tête Jaune Cache.[214]

UNLIKE OGDEN, Manson did not have much experience commanding a brigade of horses and men, but perhaps because he was extra cautious, he did not lose men by drowning as his predecessors had. He relied on physical example rather than good rapport to maintain morale. While stationed on the northwest coast, he and his men had carried big clubs, which they called "life preservers," and as a result the HBC rule there became known as "club law."

To Simpson's repeated remonstrances to be less violent, Manson pointed out that he was expected to get the job done or London would assume he was not carrying out his orders properly.

Manson was frequently at odds with John Tod at Fort Thompson because the latter held more seniority and therefore took charge of the combined New Caledonia, Fort Thompson and Fort Colvile brigades on their way to Fort Vancouver. On the 1845 brigade's return trip up the Columbia River, the two Scots got into a disagreement that was only settled by the intervention of two Jesuit priests, Anthony Ravalli and John Nobili, who were travelling with them. When the brigade reached Fort Walla Walla, five boatmen took the opportunity to desert and this necessitated taking one whole boatload of freight overland by packhorse to Fort Colvile at Kettle Falls. When Simpson learned of the situation, he chastised both Manson and Tod: "I cannot help saying it is most discreditable to yourselves to see the business thus misconducted through quarrels for which there seems to have been no good ground."[215]

Ravalli was bound for Fort Colvile to establish a new church, but Nobili planned to continue on to New Caledonia. His superiors had encouraged him to visit the Natives there, and with McLoughlin's approval, Manson agreed to let him accompany the brigade. As they commenced their journey through the Okanagan Valley, Nobili learned that Tod was anxious to placate Chief Nicola because his eldest son, also named Nicola, had been accidentally killed by HBC clerk Patrick McKenzie that spring while he and McKenzie were taking the express to Fort Colvile. Now the brigade stopped where the young man had been buried at Priest's Prairie, an overnight camp near present-day Summerland, and Nobili set up an outdoor altar and conducted a service beside the grave. Nicola appeared to understand that the HBC had not been responsible for his son's death.[216]

That fall Nobili went as far as Fort St. James where he stayed with Manson and his wife, Felicité, the daughter of two of the earliest settlers in the Willamette Valley, Etienne Lucier and his

Nouite wife.[217] Felicité had accompanied Manson to most of his postings, and when they were transferred to New Caledonia, she found friendly support from Alexander Anderson's wife, Eliza, whose mother also had Native ancestry. Felicité Manson most likely acted as a midwife for the Anderson baby born at Fort Alexandria in 1845, and for the numerous children born to Peter Ogden Jr. and his Metis wife at Fort St. James.

Felicité Manson bore her first child, William, at Fort George on the Columbia River in 1832. She accompanied her husband, Donald, to most of his postings on the Pacific Coast and in New Caledonia. Her portrait is by John Mix Stanley, ca. 1847. OREGON HISTORICAL SOCIETY AS001194

Nobili returned downriver with the HBC express canoes to Fort Alexandria, and after resting up from his strenuous two-month journey with the brigade, decided to visit the Chilcotin people before winter set in. Prior to leaving New Caledonia in 1844 Peter Skene Ogden had closed Fort Chilcotin in favour of a small outpost at the Native village of Kluskus on the Nuxalk-Carrier Grease Trail. Nobili arrived at the abandoned site in early November to find that all the windows and doors had been removed from the main building. However, he managed to scrounge enough boards to make an altar, and during the two weeks of his mission he baptized the children and the leaders or chiefs and their wives, consecrated a cemetery and raised crosses in two villages. He considered this Chilcotin visit his first real mission in New Caledonia and thereafter referred to the Natives as his "dearest Chilcotins."[218]

When Nobili returned to Fort Alexandria at the end of November, Anderson encouraged the Natives living near the fort to help complete the church that Demers had started in 1842. By

Christmas Eve it was ready for midnight mass conducted in four languages—English, French, Chilcotin and Shuswap. Nobili wintered with the Andersons and baptized two of their children, Henry and newborn Alexander, as well as the Manson's new baby.[219]

Nobili was still with the Andersons in February 1846 when John Tod sent an urgent request for reinforcements because Chief Nicola was threatening to attack Fort Kamloops in retaliation for the death of his son. Anderson refused Nobili's plea to accompany him as a mediator and left immediately with some of the Fort Alexandria *engagés*. Nobili, however, was known for his stubborn determination, and within a few days he set off for Kamloops, accompanied only by his young novice. But the danger from a Native uprising at Kamloops had been short-lived, and at Bridge Lake Nobili met Anderson returning to Fort Alexandria. Nobili went on to Kamloops anyway, returning to Fort Alexandria in time to join Manson and the outgoing brigade in May.[220] (When John Tod related the story of Nicola's aborted attack several decades later, he mentioned neither Anderson nor Nobili.)

Nobili accompanied Manson and the brigade as far as Fort Colvile in order to report to his superiors and make a retreat at St. Ignatius Mission. A month later he joined the incoming brigade at Fort Walla Walla on the Columbia River and accompanied Manson back to Fort St. James. Donald McLean then took him to visit the Babine Nation at his winter posting at Fort Kilmaurs where he gave Nobili the use of the fort's empty fur storage room for his quarters and a chapel. Unfortunately for Nobili, McLean would not permit him to travel about the region because of the hostility of the local tribes. During his stay Nobili witnessed one call to arms where McLean and his men displayed their firepower as a means of quelling a potential squabble. At the end of November McLean ensured that the priest was returned safely with a boat crew to Fort St. James; they reached the fort just as the rapidly forming ice on Stuart Lake almost caught up to the boat.[221]

Nobili remained at Fort St. James with Manson until February 1847. Compared to his first winter at Fort Alexandria, this was a severe trial. The Metis boatmen responded arrogantly to his requests to attend church services with, "Le bon Dieu arrangera!" and he had to wait patiently until the Carriers finished their winter feasting and gambling before he could carry out his mission to them. During extremely cold weather the sacramental wine froze in its little barrel, and he had to wrap himself up well to avoid frostbite. Felicité Manson made him a pair of trousers and he fashioned his own mitts and a warm head covering.[222]

Against Manson's better judgement, Nobili departed for Fort Alexandria on snowshoes in February 1847 with two Native guides and a dogsled loaded with dried fish. He could have waited a few more months and departed with the spring brigade, but he was always conscious of using up the limited supply of HBC provisions. He also wanted to meet with the Chilcotin at Fort Alexandria before they dispersed on their seasonal rounds. The weather remained bitterly cold as his party followed the frozen Stuart and Nechako rivers to Fort George and the Fraser River to Fort Alexandria. Nobili arrived totally exhausted, and Anderson had to help him remove his tattered leggings and shoes.[223] After his difficult journey, Nobili was disappointed to find that the Chilcotin had already left for their hunting grounds, and so he continued on to Kamloops and Adams Lake to conduct missions and then to the Okanagan to meet with Chief Nicola.[224]

With the establishment in 1846 of the 49th parallel as the international border, the HBC began considering alternate brigade routes because, even though the company had retained its properties south of the border, the Americans were now charging customs duty on all goods landed at Fort Vancouver. Anderson explored two routes through the Cascades from the Nicola Valley to the lower Fraser River: one terminated at Yale and the other at Hope. From either place the furs could be transported by boat to Fort Langley. The company also contemplated opening a new route from Fort Kamloops to Kootenay Lake via either Shuswap Lake or the north end of Okanagan Lake, which would continue the company's access to the upper Columbia River and Athabasca Pass. For this reason, Manson, Anderson and Tod encouraged Nobili to accept land offered by Chief Nicola at the head of Okanagan Lake. In previous years the HBC had assisted Nicola to develop gardens in that area by providing a plough, corn and seed potatoes. Thus, by the time Nobili arrived at Talle d'Epinettes at the head of the lake, Nicola and his people had grubbed out a garden of six plots, centred with a forty-foot cross, and erected a small building to be used as a residence and church. Nicola greeted Nobili "looking like a cardinal," wearing the red cloak Simpson had given him twenty years earlier. Nobili named the rustic little building St. Joseph's and, while wintering there in 1847–48, witnessed a measles epidemic that killed many Natives in the area.[225]

Nobili reported to the father general in Rome that, during his two visits to New Caledonia, Manson and Anderson had continued to be exceedingly kind to him. He had raised crosses at all the main Native sites, including the abandoned Fort Chilcotin, and blessed cemeteries at Forts George, Kilmaurs and Chilcotin. He estimated that at this time there were 4,100 Carrier, Chilcotin and Shuswap in New Caledonia and 4,800 Shuswap in the Kamloops, Lillooet and Okanagan regions. Not realizing that a letter to Rome and a response to it might take fifteen months or more, he repeated his plea of the previous year for permission to continue his mission there.[226]

Interpreter and guide Jean Baptiste Lolo (or St. Paul) arrived at Fort Alexandria at the end of December 1847 with news that 200 Natives had died from measles at Fort Colvile and thirty-six at Fort Kamloops. By mid-January a number of young Native children had died at Fort Alexandria. At Fort St. James the disease claimed the long-lived Waccan and Baptiste Regnier, known as Tappage, and many of the Sekani living near McLeod Lake.[227]

The winter of 1847–48 was an exceptionally difficult one in New Caledonia because the salmon runs had failed the previous summer in all the rivers of the Fraser watershed. Manson could only obtain salmon for Fort St. James from Babine Lake, as there was not one fish to be had at Forts George, Alexandria or Fraser. To make matters worse, only Forts Alexandria and George had wheat and potato crops. Summer frosts had destroyed the potato crop at Stuart Lake, and by late winter Manson was forced to reduce the food allowance by one-third.[228] During the previous few years some members of his brigade crews had deserted while returning to New Caledonia, and Manson felt that the main reason for this was the bad food, not maltreatment, and he complained that there was no way to enforce punishment even when the men did desert.[229] However, in February 1848 Manson was happy to inform Simpson that "notwithstanding the majority of our men's contracts expire this year, all, with the exception of those stationed at Alexandria, have renewed their engagements for two years." This information and the fact that there was a good run of salmon in 1848 was the only positive news to report that year; otherwise it would prove to be one of the worst in Manson's New Caledonia career.[230]

As a result of the Whitman Massacre in November 1847, and the ensuing Native uprising, Fort Vancouver was no longer considered useful as the provisioning depot for the New Caledonia brigade, and for the outgoing New Caledonia brigade of 1848 Manson tried the route through the Cascades to Yale that Anderson had explored two years earlier. He was accompanied by Anderson and the Fort Colvile brigade and by Nobili, who hoped to find a letter from Rome awaiting him at Fort Langley, authorizing him to continue his mission in New Caledonia.

The new route proved to be far too difficult for both men and horses, as the trail was very rough and steep. There were only small patches of grass available for the horses and they were reduced to eating pine and cedar branches; as a result, the animals were so malnourished and weakened that 151 died either on the return journey or during the following winter. In fact, this inaugural trek was so taxing that one of Anderson's men, Jacob Ballenden, committed suicide at the Fraser River campsite near Spuzzum. Nobili conducted the burial service, and as a gesture of remembrance Anderson promised that the site of "Jacob's grave" would be preserved for posterity. It was duly noted on the lithographed Arrowsmith map that he helped prepare for the Fraser River gold rush of 1858.

When Nobili did not receive the expected letter from Rome, he returned to the Okanagan with the brigade, but because he was now suffering from scurvy, his superior recalled him to the Rocky Mountain Mission for rest and recuperation and then cancelled the New Caledonia mission, a decision that distressed Nobili greatly. The following year he was recovered enough to be assigned to California where, with the assistance of other Jesuit priests from the Willamette Valley mission, he established Santa Clara College, now Santa Clara University.

After forcing the brigade over the difficult new route to Fort Langley and returning to Fort Thompson, Manson and the brigade set off in early September 1848 from Fort Alexandria on the last leg of their return journey to Fort St. James. Tracking up the Fraser was tedious and slow, and Manson camped for several nights unaware that a Native man had joined them and for some unknown reason planned to kill him. When the brigade reached the mouth of the Quesnel River, the would-be murderer met up with his family and informed them that he had changed his mind, but they taunted him into committing the deed. However, instead of shooting Manson he shot a boatman, Alexis Belanger, who was then taken downriver to Fort Alexandria where he died eight days later.[231]

Manson could not halt the brigade to search for the murderer as he had to push on to Fort St. James and distribute provisions to all the forts before winter set in. It was not until January 2, 1849, that he dispatched Donald McLean to Fort Alexandria, where he made up a party of four gentlemen and eight labourers to search for the murderer and his accomplices. Writing in the Fort St. James journal, Manson described the venture as a "difficult but most necessary and lawful duty and may the Almighty guide and protect their steps, and grant that they may be the happy means of ridding the country of such a monster." McLean, who had already earned a reputation for viciousness when he pursued Samuel Black's murderer in 1841, returned on February 23 and reported that they had killed the murderer's accomplice and the chief of Quesnel River but the man who had actually killed Belanger had escaped. As a consequence of the disturbance, the winter fur returns were not as large as usual.[232]

Donald McLean spent over a decade in New Caledonia and served as a clerk at almost all of its posts. He came out of retirement to assist with the Chilcotin uprising and was shot and killed there in 1864. BRITISH COLUMBIA ARCHIVES A-01454

When Simpson received Manson's letter of February 28, 1849, outlining these events, he was most upset by the barbarity and wrote him immediately. He insisted on receiving the full story, and wanted the murderer taken to Victoria if and when he was captured:

It is very much regretted that the murderer was not apprehended and still more so that you should have considered it necessary to retaliate upon others, even though you state they are accomplices. It would have been satisfactory to have known the reasons you had for supposing they were accomplices as there is no proof of it in the evidence of more shots than one having been fired on the boat.

I have to beg you will transmit to me the details of this deplorable event, the cause of quarrel, if any, your reasons for supposing the two men were accomplices of the murderer; the mode of their punishment, and whether by their tribe or by the persons sent after them. Should you succeed in apprehending the murderer, I have to desire that he may be sent to Fort Victoria, there to await instructions from the Governor and Committee or from the Council as to the steps that are to be taken in regard to him. I cannot too urgently impress on you the importance of using every means of conciliation with the Natives altogether abstaining from violence unless in self-defence.[233]

Although Donald McLean had conducted the search for Belanger's murderer, Manson had to accept the blame for its resolution. By this time the pressure on HBC forts to refrain from revenge in favour of a court trial was becoming more important to London. In previous years serious offenders from east of the Rocky Mountains had been taken to England for trial, and recently law reform had been introduced at Red River. However, west of the Rocky Mountains quick retribution was still being used; when Natives murdered HBC employee Kenneth McKay near Pillar Rock in 1841, McLoughlin had informed Simpson from Fort Vancouver that "vengeance was taken immediately on the murderers and all has been quiet ever since."[234] He saw no reason to change his methods.

Immediately after completing the inaugural round trip to Fort Langley in 1848, Manson had reported on the new route to James Douglas at Fort Victoria and Peter Skene Ogden at Fort Vancouver. When Douglas suggested that Manson was exaggerating the difficulties of the route, Manson wrote to Simpson that "it is actually much worse than I have described it, and in my opinion it would be highly imprudent again to send a Brigade such as ours through that difficult and dangerous Pass." He said that he feared his men would not renew their contracts because they had been forced to make most of the return journey to Fort Kamloops on foot. Furthermore, he had not been supplied with the number of horses requested nor had the horses been equipped with *apachemons* to protect their backs and sides from the loads they carried.[235]

Then, in a rare display of solidarity, Manson, Tod and Anderson jointly prepared a letter to Henry Newsham Peers, who had accompanied the returning brigade as far as Kamloops, requesting him to open out Anderson's second, more southerly route for use in 1849. Peers, a twenty-seven-year-old Englishman who had been serving as a clerk at Fort Vancouver since 1843, set out to locate a route where elevation and lingering snow would not provide such formidable obstacles. His new trail followed the 1848 brigade trail from Kamloops through the Nicola Valley and then continued south to Otter Lake and Campement des Femmes, a mile or so below Tulameen Village. Here it met the trail that continued southeast through the Similkameen Valley to Fort Colvile. From Campement des Femmes, Peers mapped a new thirty-seven-mile trail southwest and then west following Podunk Creek through the Cascades to Campement du Chevreuil (Deer Camp) at an elevation of 6,000 feet. The final portion of the trail continued for thirty-three miles down the western slope of the Cascades around Manson Mountain to Peers Creek and then followed the Coquihalla River to Hope. It was better than the first trail but still very steep and difficult, and high winds and heavy snows caused a huge number of blowdowns, making it difficult for both men and pack animals.

Unfortunately, the following spring, deep snow in the mountains and a directive from Douglas to use the south-facing 1848 trail, on which the snow would melt earlier, forced Manson to use that route again to Fort Langley although he had already ordered Baptiste Lolo and a crew of Native labourers to clear the newer route as far as Campement du Chevreuil [Deer Camp]. He also wrote to Anderson, who was bringing a brigade from Fort Colvile up the Okanagan valley to connect with Peers' trail at Campement de Femmes, to request that he clear the westernmost portion of the new trail terminating at Hope because his brigade would be first over it. Anderson refused, forcing Manson to hire a crew of twenty Native labourers when his brigade was outbound in midsummer. They cleared the western half of the route in fifteen days.

Thereafter the New Caledonia brigade left Fort St. James a little later so that the snow would have a hard crust on top and Manson could get his horses through to Hope in better condition.[236]

Meanwhile, after two decades of James Murray Yale's management, Fort Langley had become well established; farming flourished, and most years many barrels of cranberries and salted salmon were sent off to Hawaii and California. But after the fort was designated as the new brigade terminus in 1848, Yale's pleasant routine there was abruptly shattered each spring with the arrival of Manson's and Anderson's rowdy *engagés* who commenced their usual hijinks. Arguments also broke out between the brigade leaders, and for a number of years James Douglas came from Fort Victoria to lend moral and physical support as Yale coped with the mayhem.[237] From Fort Vancouver, Peter Skene Ogden expressed his concern about the example provided by brigade leaders fighting in front of their men, and he recommended staggering the arrival of the New Caledonia and Fort Colvile brigades to avoid fisticuffs. He also denigrated Manson's complaints about the difficult route through the Cascade Mountains:

> Manson in his Report truly makes Mountains of mole hills and Anderson in his states the hordes of Indians was the only obstacle they encountered, still granting the latter to be correct, from their arrangement in traveling it is fully evident from the temptation daily thrown in their way, conducted themselves with great propriety and it is only surprising to me knowing them so well as I do, they did not steal half their property, and as for friend Manson he expected to find a Turnpike road in a Country never before travel'd over with a Brigade. As he advances in Life, experience will teach him that he will not always find a smooth path to travel on. This year another route has been explored and promises greater advantages; still both Manson and Anderson will no doubt find very many obstacles and [will be] no doubt equally contradictory in their Reports.[238]

In spite of all the difficulties, however, right up to 1849 under Ogden's and then Manson's management, New Caledonia continued to consistently produce one-third of the furs garnered from the Columbia Department. Even when the demand for beaver fur had declined in Europe in the early 1840s, Native trappers had been able to switch successfully to trapping mink and marten.[239] But the end of this trying decade for the HBC was capped by the California gold rush that began in 1849 and played havoc with the labour supply. *Engagés* and *boutes* deserted Forts Vancouver, Victoria and Langley for the lure of Eldorado. At Fort Vancouver, Ogden grumbled that gold seekers were making more money in California than he had made in his entire career. In order to keep trained employees, he devised an agreement whereby they could take leave of absence for six months, during which time he would rely on Native replacements.

ON SEPTEMBER 13, 1849, the assistant governor of Rupert's Land, Eden Colvile, arrived at Fort St. James on a fact-finding tour of HBC operations in the west. Colvile had come overland from Norway House by following the old brigade route via Athabasca and Peace River, and his boatmen had been forced to clear out the abandoned portage at Peace River Canyon. After visiting the forts in New Caledonia, he proceeded on his way to Fort Vancouver, but two days' march below Fort Alexandria, he met Manson returning with the brigade. He gave him a letter from Simpson dated June 30, 1849, that included his concerns about the Belanger incident.

From Fort Kamloops Colvile travelled to Fort Langley via the new southern brigade route through the Cascades to Hope, completing the trip in just seven days. His recommendation to the governor and committee was that the route receive further attention, with more ditching, removal of fallen timber, and the sowing of timothy grass at a number of campsites.[240] When he reached Victoria in October, he set down his observations on Manson and New Caledonia for Simpson:

The Indians, since the punishment inflicted on them for the murder of Belanger last year have evinced no disposition to commit further acts of violence. As far as I could ascertain the two Indians killed by the party under the orders of Mr. McLean were present & aiding & abetting at the time of the murder, but I think that in all cases of this kind the actual perpetrator of the deed should be the only party punished, & he should, if possible, be conveyed to the nearest establishment & a proper investigation of the circumstances gone into, before any punishment is inflicted. At the same time it must be evident that unless cold blooded & unprovoked murders, as this decidedly was, be promptly & effectually punished, it will be impossible to retain a footing in this part of the country.

Later in 1851 Colvile wrote a confidential letter to Simpson, asserting that "I certainly saw no instances of club law when I was on the West side of the Mountains, nor were any complaints made to me on the subject; but no doubt both [William Henry] McNeill & Manson are very hot tempered."[241] Colvile was definitely sympathetic to Manson's plight, especially the need for brigade animals, and he purchased horses from Fort Edmonton to be delivered to him via Fort Colvile.[242]

In 1850 Manson and Anderson's brigades were plagued by gold rush desertions as soon as they reached Fort Langley. Four of Manson's men and one of Anderson's slipped away, but the Fort Langley *engagés* quickly rounded them up and James Douglas sent them to Victoria.[243]

In 1851 Douglas replaced Richard Blanshard as governor of the Colony of Vancouver Island, an appointment that gratified George Simpson: "I am well pleased that Blanshard has left, he was no friend of the Company, & now that the office is in the hands of the Company's representative, we shall have less jawing & more work done than of late."[244] But the new position did not give Douglas greater clout, and when he complained to Simpson that the European labourers provided were not fit for work in

New Caledonia, Simpson warned him the situation was not going to improve. The California gold rush and the growing economy of eastern Canada and the United States offered abundant employment opportunities and good wages, making it increasingly impossible for the Company to obtain Canadian labourers. Simpson had already refused Anderson leave of absence from Fort Colvile over the winter of 1850–51 because he was the only officer available. He gave no further encouragement to Douglas:

> As to officers, we send you all we can, but really the service has been so drained by the Columbia within the last few years that we are sorely put to it on the East side of the mountains to find managers for the posts & districts; . . . I should be glad that the Council has it in their power to send you a more efficient officer overland this season but do not see that they have any to spare.[245]

Simpson did grant John Tod a third year's leave of absence because he planned to retire near Fort Victoria, but when Manson requested a one-year furlough to recover his health, Simpson refused because there was little chance of obtaining a replacement. However, Manson had not been well during the winter of 1850–51, and Donald McLean brought the brigade out to Fort Langley in the spring of 1851. Yale was then asked to temporarily move to New Caledonia but he refused, pleading ill health. Manson finally rescinded his request after Douglas urged him to remain at Stuart Lake because it might help towards securing chief factor status.[246]

When Manson took the brigade out in 1852, he learned that Natives near Fort Kamloops had slaughtered a number of the company's cattle and horses during the previous winter. He felt that this action threatened the safety of the brigade, and with McLean's assistance he set out to punish the culprits. Several Natives were caught and flogged, and Manson advised Simpson that, "this punishment on every occasion was witnessed by their friends and countrymen who all acknowledged the justice of their

After fifteen years of delivering furs via the Cascade Mountains, the New Caledonia brigade made its last trip to Fort Langley in 1863. Within a few years the palisade was dismantled but the fort did not close until 1886. GLENBOW ARCHIVES NA-1141-1

chastisement. This severe but salutary lesson will I trust have its desired effect."[247]

The brigade left Fort Kamloops on June 10, 1852, and reached Hope in eleven days without forcing the horses. Manson reported that this more southerly route was a decided improvement over the first one, and the brigade could travel at an earlier date than was first thought because the compacted snow at higher elevations enabled the horses to make good time.[248] But Manson risked further censure from Simpson when he rerouted the incoming recruits in the fall of 1852. Simpson had notified him earlier that, to avoid desertions to the California gold rush, most of the new men contracted for west of the Rockies would be sent via Tête Jaune Cache; only a small express party would travel via Boat Encampment on the upper Columbia and Fort Colvile. However, burdened by the added concern that a severe salmon shortage would make it impossible for Fort St. James to maintain any more *engagés* that winter, Manson dispatched an express to Jasper's House in mid-September "to prevent the expected in-coming Party from passing by the Tête Juane Cache route, as the addition of so many more mouths, had they come into this district, would have greatly helped to increase the difficulties I then anticipated." Fortunately, a late arrival of salmon at Fraser's Lake provided 43,000 fish, which was ample for the winter. Manson then requested more men for the coming year.[249]

Simpson had further reasons to chastise Manson in 1853:

There is at present here a retiring winterer from your district, one François Lacourse, who states that he was very severely beaten by Mr. P. Ogden, who knocked him down, kicked him and injured him so seriously that the man has since then been subject to epileptic fits. He states that on another occasion when angry with him you aimed a blow at him with an axe, but fortunately missed him & only cut open his coat, which he exhibited here, & he further adds that you afterwards presented him with a suit of clothes as reparation for this injury. These are the ex parte statements of Lacourse & may be in part false, but taken in connexion with other cases of late years, they afford ample evidence of the existence of a system of "club law" which must not be allowed to prevail. We duly appreciate the necessity for maintaining discipline & enforcing obedience, but that end is not to be attained by the display of violent passion and the infliction of severe & arbitrary punishment.[250]

Simpson insisted that miscreants be allowed a full hearing, and if found guilty, they be taken out of the depot, put on short rations or arrested. Knocking about or flogging would not be tolerated.

Because of his large family, Manson appears to have had no choice but to remain in charge of New Caledonia, hoping in vain for promotion. But he continued to face the recurrent problems of inadequate leather supplies and failure of the salmon run. He had not received dressed buffalo skins from Fort Colvile for four or five years and in 1853 requested twenty to twenty-five skins for horse appointments.[251] When only a small supply of moose skins was received from Dunvegan—not enough to provide all of the shoes needed for the coming year—he begged Simpson to order leather from Saskatchewan.[252] Two years later the Fraser salmon run failed completely and Fort Babine was only able to supply 8,000; this was augmented by rabbits and garden produce. The nearby Carrier people survived on rabbits, but Manson reported that "nearly all the Indians of Alexandria have been driven by starvation to Kamloops."

In 1853 the HBC separated Vancouver Island and New Caledonia—which now included all of what would become mainland British Columbia—from the Northern Department and designated them the company's new Western Department; south of the 49th parallel John Ballenden replaced Peter Skene Ogden as chief factor at Fort Vancouver in the Oregon Department. Henceforth, Manson reported to James Douglas at Fort Victoria, rather than to Fort Vancouver, but he continued to submit reports both privately and officially to Governor George Simpson.[253]

Manson's private correspondence with Simpson concerned his future and that of his children. Back in 1841 he had taken his eldest son, William, to Scotland for education, boarding him there with a relative. Two other sons, John and Stephen, had been educated by the Whitmans near Walla Walla where they had survived the massacre that took the Whitmans' lives. Like many HBC officers, Manson appealed to Simpson to help him find positions for his sons once they reached maturity. Because Peter Skene Ogden's son, Peter Jr., and two of Simpson's sons by Margaret Taylor, John and George, were already working for the HBC in New Caledonia, Simpson was sympathetic to Manson's plight. The shortage of trained men east of the Rockies was also an influencing factor, and as a result, both William and John Manson gained employment with the HBC when they were in their late teens. William served as a clerk at Fort Kamloops under Donald McLean and married McLean's daughter, Elizabeth. He took charge of Fort Alexandria in the 1860s, and both he and John served terms at Fort Fraser.

Soon after the New Caledonia brigade arrived at Fort Langley in 1855, James Murray Yale gave away his two daughters in a sensational double wedding. Attired in wedding gowns ordered from Paris, Aurelia married John Manson, and Belle married George Simpson Jr. The ceremony was conducted by James Douglas, and his daughter Agnes and Chief Justice Cameron's daughter were the attendants. Following the ceremony Peter Ogden Jr. arranged for the wedding party to be paddled in *bateaux* around McMillan's Island, while the boatmen sang voyageur songs and the fort's cannon fired a special salute. Aurelia and John Manson spent their honeymoon travelling with the brigade to their HBC posting at Fort Fraser.[254] While crossing the Cascades, the newlyweds witnessed the tragic death of chief trader Paul Fraser of Fort Thompson who was accidentally killed by a falling tree at Campement du Chevreuil.[255]

When Donald Manson went on furlough in 1857, he and his family travelled south with the brigade as a matter of convenience. They wintered either at Fort Langley or Fort Victoria and in March 1858 journeyed to Fort Vancouver on the *Otter*, en route to their new home, a 221-acre farm in the Willamette Valley.[256] When the governor and council refused to grant an extension of Manson's furlough for the following year, he resigned.[257] Despite a letter of recommendation from James Douglas, Manson had never received chief factor status, which would have greatly helped his pension income. Of small consolation was the fact that Anderson, Yale and Tod had not been promoted either, although all four had served in New Caledonia and had been HBC men from day one.

The intermarriage of HBC families continued when Manson's daughter Anna married Isaac Ogden, son of Peter Skene Ogden Sr., and they, too, went to live in the Willamette Valley. After Isaac Ogden was accidentally killed, Anna married a Mr. Tremewan. She had been born at Fort Simpson but fondly remembered her childhood at Stuart Lake where she recalled seeing fish swimming in the crystal clear waters. During her father's absence with the brigade one year her mother gave birth to a baby girl, Elizabeth, and Anna had waited impatiently to greet him with the happy news when he returned in the fall. Three boys, Donald, George and James, were also born at Fort St. James, and there was one other sister, Isabella. Another baby had died at Fort Simpson and was reinterred at Fort McLoughlin (Bella Bella).[258]

The Manson family's new life in Oregon did not go smoothly. They lost their house and barn when the Willamette River flooded in 1861. However, the Friends of Historic Champoeg have restored the replacement barn built in 1862, and it is "possibly the oldest structure in the State of Oregon from the standpoint of the materials used to construct it." Today it forms part of the Donald Manson Farmstead and is cared for by the Friends. The large box stove from the family home is displayed at the Oregon Historical Society in Portland.

Manson never returned to British Columbia, but he corresponded regularly with his sons John and William who remained there. Following Felicité's death in 1867, he shared the Oregon farm with his widowed daughter Anna Ogden and her family. He died in January 1880.[259] Donald and Felicité Manson are buried in the Champoeg cemetery.

Chapter Ten

THE GOLD RUSH YEARS

AS THE MANSON FAMILY sailed south to Oregon, thousands of men (and a few women) were heading in the opposite direction to take part in the Fraser River gold rush. New Caledonia would soon be renamed the Colony of British Columbia, and the HBC would lose its exclusive right to trade with First Nations. As many of the gold miners became the first settlers, the fur trade was no longer the main focus of commerce, but it did continue to play an important role in opening up the province for settlement well into the twentieth century.

At Fort Kamloops, chief trader Donald McLean had been quietly collecting small amounts of gold from Natives since he took charge there in 1855, but word didn't leak out to the coast until 1857. However, there was not a lot of gold in the sandbars of the Fraser Canyon and Thompson River; in the first eight months of 1858 only 1,000 ounces were produced, and it was fine flour gold.[260] Nevertheless, the heavy influx of hopefuls, many of them Americans, provided the impetus for the British Colonial Secretary, Sir Edward Bulwer Lytton, to introduce a bill creating a second crown colony on the Pacific Coast. Queen Victoria chose the new name British Columbia because there was already a French colony named New Caledonia. "Columbia" was borrowed from the HBC's Columbia District and "British" was added to reinforce the fact that this was not an American territory.[261]

Lytton also wanted to cancel the HBC's exclusive trading rights with First Nations, and James Douglas, having experienced a small gold rush on the Queen Charlotte Islands in 1852, recognized that it would be difficult to maintain the company's rights on the mainland. When the British Parliament subsequently approved cancellation of the company's trading rights, it offered Douglas the position of governor of British Columbia on condition that he sever his ties with the company. Douglas agreed to this stipulation and an installation ceremony took place on November 19, 1858, at Fort Langley.[262] At the same time a formal system of law and order was introduced, and Matthew Baillie Begbie was sworn in as the first judge in the new colony. Henceforth, all HBC criminal cases would go before British Columbia's courts.

Meanwhile, Peter Ogden, Jr. had taken over from Donald Manson as the chief trader responsible for New Caledonia, a transfer of authority to a local employee that reflected the difficult labour situation in eastern Canada. Ogden was, however, an excellent choice. He had been educated at Red River and served for a number of years as a clerk under Manson in New Caledonia. He carried on with fur-trading activities, bringing the brigade out annually, while the gold seekers pressed north up the Fraser to the mouth of the Quesnel River, where they found the sandbars streaked with coarse gold. They bought up most of Fort Alexandria's available supplies and set off to follow the Quesnel River to Quesnel Forks and Horsefly and then up the Cariboo River to Cariboo Lake on the south side of the Snowshoe Plateau. In the winter of 1860–61 greater riches were discovered on the north side of the Plateau on Antler, Lightning and Williams creeks, and intense mining activity continued in the region until 1865. Thereafter, annual gold returns dwindled gradually although hope remained that a large strike might still occur.

During the height of the gold rush Fort Alexandria clerk John

Saunders had his hands full trying to retain his employees when packers offered better wages and new strikes were occurring daily at Antler and Williams creeks, only a hundred miles away. To take advantage of the prospectors' needs, he opened a store and restaurant at the original site of Alexandria, on the east side of the river, where three free traders had already set up shop. After gold was discovered on Williams Creek, the Cariboo Road was completed as far as Soda Creek, a private company established steamship service from there to Quesnel in 1863, and the colonial government opened a trail between Quesnel and Barker-

Born in Rupert's Land while his father, Peter Skene Ogden, served with the North West Company, Peter Ogden Jr. was educated at Red River. He became a chief trader and took charge of New Caledonia from Donald Manson in 1858.
BRITISH COLUMBIA ARCHIVES A-01922

ville (Williams Creek). Saunders suggested to HBC headquarters in Victoria that the company should get involved in packing to the mines, but his idea was ignored.

Gold-seeking groups known as the Overlanders came from eastern Canada and the United States, venturing across the Prairies and down the Fraser and Thompson rivers. Some who attempted to navigate the upper Fraser by raft came to grief at Grand Rapid, forty-five miles upstream from Fort George. Three men drowned and the survivors straggled into Fort George, where the clerk, Thomas Charles, looked after them until they were ready to challenge the river again. By using the existing HBC routes, a few Cariboo miners had also tested bars on the Finlay and Peace rivers. George Simpson Jr., by now chief trader at Dunvegan, met them in September 1862 while he was travelling with the annual leather party from Fort St. James. Duplicating the 1828 route taken by his father, Governor George Simpson, he visited Forts McLeod, St. James and George, and when he arrived at Victoria the *British Colonist* published his recommendation that gold seekers use the Giscome Portage Trail rather than travel the longer route via Fort St. James to reach the Finlay and Peace rivers.[263]

Since the HBC monopoly on trading had been cancelled, merchants of all nationalities carried pack loads of provisions to the gold fields and opened stores. Most were based in Victoria or New Westminster with suppliers in San Francisco or Great Britain. In addition, American entrepreneurs brought trading goods north by pack train through the Okanagan and sold the animals locally at the end of the season. Joel Palmer from the Willamette Valley travelled as far as Fort Alexandria where Saunders bought some of his merchandise. American ranchers north of the Columbia River drove herds of beef cattle across the border at Osoyoos, wintering them in the Kamloops area before taking them on to the Cariboo. It was the progeny of these herds that eventually led to the demise of the forts' reliance on dried salmon.

Other entrepreneurs attempted to locate more efficient routes to the gold fields via Bella Coola and Bute Inlet. In 1862 Royal Engineer Lieutenant Henry Spencer Palmer investigated the possibility of a wagon road across the Chilcotin Plateau from Bella Coola to Fort Alexandria. He discovered the fort's buildings had

First stationed at the small outpost of Kluskus, Thomas Charles served for more than a decade at Fort George. BRITISH COLUMBIA ARCHIVES G-09070

degenerated to a "half wrecked cluster of log dwellings, roofed with mud, right bank of the Fraser, 50 feet above the river."

In that same year entrepreneur and grocery merchant Alfred Waddington conceived a plan to build a road from tidewater at Bute Inlet across the Plateau to Quesnel. Crews worked for two summers on the road, but Waddington had failed to negotiate passage with the Native people, and the intrusion of his workers into Chilcotin territory led to the outbreak of the Chilcotin Uprising of April 1864. Deaths included thirteen road workers murdered on the upper reaches of the Homathco River, three packers and one Chilcotin woman on the trail southwest of Nancootlem (Anaheim Lake) and one settler at Puntzi Lake. At New Westminster the colony's new governor, Frederick Seymour, who had replaced James Douglas the previous year, responded immediately by ordering Police Magistrate Chartres Brew to take an expedition by ship to Bute Inlet. Gold Commissioner William George Cox at Barkerville was instructed to gather a force of miners and proceed overland to meet Brew at Puntzi Lake.

The uprising provided a temporary reprieve for Fort Alexandria, which had suffered a loss of business when the focus of the Cariboo gold rush had changed to the north side of the Snowshoe Plateau in 1862. In fact, on his trip down to Soda Creek by steamer in September 1863, Judge Begbie had noted, "Alexandria we did not stop at. It looks as weary & forsaken as ever."[264] But in the bustling summer of 1864, under the supervision of clerk William Manson (who had replaced Saunders), the fort and its restaurant took on a new life. Gold Commissioner Cox placed large orders for everything from blotting paper to tin kettles, while the miners recruited from Barkerville to quell the uprising were boarded temporarily at the fort. William Ogilvy brought up crates of guns and ammunition from Yale, and Donald McLean, who had retired to farm at Hat Creek, came out of retirement to help with the search parties. Meanwhile, the Colonial Office sent notices to all the HBC posts in the Interior, warning them to suspend the sale of gunpowder because it might be passed on to the Chilcotin people, and HBC headquarters in Victoria cautioned Manson at Fort Alexandria to move all valuable items to the east bank of the river for storage and to take extra safety precautions.[265]

Shortly before Cox arrived, Chief Alexis of the Chilcotin people had come to the fort with news of the murder of William Manning, a settler at Puntzi Lake. When Alexis declared the intention of most of his band to assist the whites in bringing the murderers to justice, Cox subsequently used Puntzi Lake and the abandoned Fort Chilcotin site for his camps. The ancient trails across Alexis' territory connected these camps with Fort Alexandria, and his cooperation allowed couriers and packers to bring in supplies and messages safely. Manson later provided gratuities on behalf of the colonial government to Alexis and his band.[266]

By July 5 the Chilcotin expedition's indebtedness to Fort Alexandria already totalled $5,500, including a case of common Indian guns that Manson had sold to Cox for the expedition. But a feeling of apprehension was growing at the fort because it was rumoured that "old Mr. [Donald] McLean with thirty men were killed and Mr. Cox with the balance of the party [are] prisoners." Manson reported that he had "taken all possible precautions in case of an attack—there is no harm in being ready—the fact of our having ammunition here is of itself [reason] to induce the Indians to come and attack us."[267] However, the rumours were only partly true. Thirty men had not been killed, but the HBC had lost one of its former traders when, shortly before six of the guilty Chilcotin surrendered, Donald McLean had been shot in the back while out on patrol. He was buried at his death site, south of Eagle Lake, and the provincial government provided a small pension to his widow, Sophia. (McLean's primary legacy to British Columbia would turn out to be the most notorious outlaw gang, the Wild McLeans, composed of three of his sons, Allen, Archie and Charley, and their friend Alex Hare. In 1879, having shot and killed a provincial police officer, they killed another man while making their getaway. They were caught, tried, found guilty and hanged in January 1881.) While still in the Chilcotin, Cox sent word to Judge Matthew Baillie Begbie that if he conducted the trial of the Natives charged with the Chilcotin murders at "Chilco" (presumably Fort Chilcotin), it might harm the attempts to locate more of the murderers still at large. Begbie, however, preferred Quesnel, and Cox brought the prisoners there via Fort Alexandria. The formal trial that followed included a lawyer for the defence and a prosecutor. Only the previous year Begbie had sentenced two of four Shuswap Natives to death by hanging at Williams Lake after they confessed to the murder of itinerant prospectors. With this recent precedent well known throughout the Cariboo–Chilcotin region, he now sentenced five of the six Chilcotin to death by hanging because they confessed to killing Waddington's men. The executions took place at Quesnel.[268]

After the trial Cox requested an armed escort for Begbie, and precautions were taken to ensure the safety of the residents of Quesnel. For a short time volunteers kept night watches but no retaliations occurred. After the two female witnesses who testified at the trial, Il-le-dart-nell and Nancie, expressed fear that they might be killed by the Anaheim and Telloot bands, Cox requested that they be cared for at Alexandria until hostilities settled down. Nancie soon became the wife of pioneer farmer William Swanson. For her actions during the Chilcotin War and subsequent assistance to new settlers in the eastern Chilcotin, Nancie is revered as a heroine, and her grave overlooking the Fraser River has been restored by schoolteacher/historian David Falconer.[269]

By the end of 1864 the colonial government's account with Fort Alexandria had doubled to $11,012.95. This included charges for such services as recovering and burying a dead body, ranching government horses and mules, expenses for the Bute Inlet expedition and for Governor Seymour who made a tour of the region, travelling as far as Barkerville.[270] Fort Alexandria received more business in the summer of 1865 as preparations for the Collins Overland Telegraph line began with the arrival of Major Franklin L. Pope, chief of exploration for a line that would go to Alaska and then by cable under the Bering Strait and across Siberia to

Europe. Pope's twenty-four-man crew improved the transportation corridor between Quesnel, Fraser Lake and Stuart Lake by opening up ancient Native trails, bridging swamps and streams and removing timber in a fifty-foot-wide swath that would accommodate loaded pack trains. Pope next sought a route via Fort St. James to the Stikine River, relying on Carrier informants because the country north of Stuart Lake had not been thoroughly mapped. Peter Ogden Jr. brought up two boatloads of supplies from Fort Alexandria, enabling Pope and his men to winter at the north end of Takla Lake in a cabin they called Bulkley House.[271] At the same time, chief factor Joseph McKay, who was stationed at Fort Kamloops, was employed to lead a second Overland Telegraph exploration from Kamloops up the North Thompson Valley, then through a connecting mountain pass to Barkerville. He was in the field from April 7 to July 28, 1865, and purchased more than $250 worth of supplies from Fort Alexandria.[272]

When Pope's supervisor, Edward Conway, arrived at Fort Fraser in the spring of 1866, he cancelled plans for the route via Fort St. James and instead commenced work on a trail along the Bulkley River to the Skeena. Then suddenly in July 1866, in a bizarre twist of fate, the need for an overland telegraph line was ended by the successful laying of a transatlantic cable from Ireland to Newfoundland.[273] The poles and wire of the Collins line were immediately abandoned, but the cleared access allowed cattle to be driven as far as Hazelton, and most goods bound for Fort Fraser and Fort St. James could now be taken in by pack horse with little difficulty. The greater variety of food and the addition of beef gradually ended the curse of dried fish for HBC personnel, but the Carrier and Sekani people still coped with starvation in the lean years because they continued to rely on wild game and the salmon harvest.

Year by year, as the Interior became more accessible by road, trail, steamer and telegraph, the huge imprint of Hudson's Bay Company began to shrink. The brigade trail through the Cascades from Kamloops to Fort Langley was last used in 1863, and two years later the Cariboo Road was finally completed to Barkerville. The HBC turned over the transportation of furs to private companies and disposed of its pack horses at Kamloops and Alexandria, although this took some time as many of them were not in very good shape.

The HBC headquarters in Victoria closed Fort Alexandria in 1867 but leased out the farm and store for a few more years. William Manson, who had been in charge of Alexandria, was posted to Fort Simpson on the Nass River and then to Fort Fraser. He resigned his position from Fort Fraser effective June 1, 1872, but remained in charge there until mid-August because there were considerable furs and provisions on hand. When the HBC refused to reimburse him the $718 for the extra time served, he filed a suit against the company. Judge Matthew Baillie Begbie heard the case in Supreme Court in November 1877 and decided in his favour.[274] Manson and his second wife, Adelaide (the daughter of Peter and Phristine Ogden), retired to a ranch at 111 Mile House; their children married and remained in the Cariboo.[275]

The company opened a new store at Quesnel and another one at Barkerville. Aided by steamboat service from Soda Creek to Quesnel and improved transportation via the Cariboo Road to Barkerville, the Quesnel HBC store became the transshipment point for goods bound for Interior forts. Steamers initially took the cargo only as far as Fort George Canyon, where it was offloaded and transferred to scows on the north side. When more

A beloved New Caledonia matriarch and the wife of Peter Ogden Jr., Phristine gave birth to eleven children. Her seven beautiful daughters all married men connected with the Hudson's Bay Company. BRITISH COLUMBIA ARCHIVES B-01720

powerful vessels were introduced that were able to navigate the canyon, cargoes were delivered to the landing in front of Fort George. There was a hiatus in steamer service from 1886 to 1896, and during this quiet decade the HBC used its own barges. A winter sleigh road from Quesnel to Fort George was completed in 1910.[276]

The Barkerville store operated for only a short time before the disastrous fire of September 16, 1868, consumed most of the buildings in the little settlement. The HBC incurred a loss of $65,000 in building and goods, but manager John M. Wark immediately sent an order to Victoria for 30,000 pounds of merchandise in the hope that at least some of it could be freighted as far as Quesnel before winter set in. In spite of all the chaos, the store was rebuilt within a month.[277]

Though often out of order, a branch of the telegraph line was installed from Quesnel to Barkerville, connecting these two isolated HBC posts to the rest of the world. The HBC board of management in Victoria could now instantly relay news of the latest fur sales in London or warn of a local price war in flour. For the next few years the Barkerville store did a good business in gold dust and liquor, and it remained open until 1882 under the management of clerk Hugh Ross.[278]

The many changes in the delivery of provisions and the demands on the forts and stores created immense challenges for the HBC accountants in the field. After a particularly harrowing evening coping with a freight delivery by steamboat, Robert Williams wrote a letter of complaint from his post at Quesnel to Chief Factor James Allan Grahame in Victoria:

> I now beg to call your attention to the fact that the season has now commenced at Quesnelle and Williams is still alone and unassisted, and also to repeat what I wrote to you in February last that it is utterly impossible for me, individually, to attend to the removing of freight, keeping store, corresponding, etc., etc., all of which comes in a lump during the few hours

the steamer remains here. As instance this night steamer arrived at 6 pm. I have been receiving freight until nearly nine o'clock, store closed and several customers gone unsupplied from the door and now I sit down to write to yourself, Yale & Barkerville. You left instructions for me to keep copies of my letters. Had you not have locked up the copying materials I should certainly have done so, but as the steamer leaves again at daylight and the post closes in half an hour I have merely time to write the letters and dispatch them.[279]

HBC headquarters at Victoria sent Grahame to Quesnel in April 1868 to take temporary charge of the New Caledonia and Cariboo districts. On his way up the Cariboo Road he stopped at Lac La Hache to arrange for Archibald McKinlay to lease the Fort Alexandria property. In addition, Grahame was charged with disposal of the cattle at Alexandria and the horses at Fort Kamloops. Victoria also notified him that a group of white trappers on the upper Peace River had collected a large number of furs and that they might bypass Fort Grahame, built on the Finlay in 1867, and turn up at Quesnel to sell them.[280]

The son of Donald Manson, William (left) served for twenty years in New Caledonia and became a chief trader. After many years with the HBC in the Columbia District, Archibald McKinlay settled at Lac La Hache in the 1860s, forming the nucleus of an HBC enclave that eventually included William and his family. BRITISH COLUMBIA ARCHIVES E-02730

James Allan Grahame, born in Edinburgh, had joined the HBC as an apprentice clerk in 1843 and was promoted rapidly during the 1850s. He was placed in charge of Fort Vancouver in 1853, became a chief trader the following year and became administrator of the company's Oregon Department in 1858. On June 14, 1860, Grahame handed Fort Vancouver over to American authorities and transferred himself and everything of value to Fort Victoria where he gained chief factor status in 1861. He subsequently served at Lower Fort Garry and Norway House before returning to the Western Department in 1867 where he was assigned to prepare a report on operations in the Interior.[281]

Grahame had the experience to deal with directives from W.F. Tolmie in Victoria that made no sense in the Cariboo, such as the order in May 1868 that Sunday trading was forbidden throughout the department. He immediately wrote to Tolmie, pointing out that business would suffer because Sunday trading was "the confirmed custom of the country, especially amongst the Jews and Chinese."[282] After spending May and June at Quesnel, Grahame and his family moved to Fort St. James and remained there for the winter.[283] When Grahame returned to Quesnel in the spring of 1869, Peter Ogden resumed charge of Fort St. James and J.M. Lindsay Alexander took over management of Fort George.[284]

Upon receipt of Grahame's report, the company's London council questioned a number of items. In view of the recent Barkerville fire they were not pleased to learn that the Quesnel storehouse for New Caledonia goods was situated between two saloons. Had this storage been improved, they asked. They also questioned accountant Robert Williams' qualifications to be manager at Quesnel and wanted to know if the failure of the salmon run in 1867 indicated an ongoing problem. If so, "In the opinion of the Board the establishments of New Caledonia would require to be considerably reduced if by the failure of the fisheries the Servants of the Company have to live upon imported provisions such as bacon and flour."[285]

On June 1, 1870, Grahame returned to Victoria and assumed joint charge of the Western Department with his brother-in-law Roderick Finlayson. The following February Robert Williams received a letter from Finlayson advising that the Quesnel store would be kept open for one more year on a trial basis, "under you or some other officer." In fact, the store remained open until after 1900. James Grahame went on to greater fame, succeeding Donald Alexander Smith in 1874 as chief commissioner of the HBC.[286]

Chapter Eleven

THE COMPANY IN SLOW DECLINE

PETER OGDEN JR. AND PHRISTINE BRABANT had four sons and seven daughters. One son, Charles, served intermittently as a clerk at Fort George from the 1870s until 1902. Another son, Peter Skene, was stationed at Fort Fraser[287] where in October 1870 he over-exerted himself while bear hunting and succumbed to influenza. Six days later his father died from the same illness at Fort St. James. Peter Ogden Jr. had served New Caledonia as faithfully as his own father, Peter Skene Ogden, had in the 1830s, and Roderick Finlayson praised him as "an old and efficient officer . . . The want of his intimate knowledge of the language, trade and of the hunters of New Caledonia will, I fear, prove a serious injury to the trade of that valuable district, as it is difficult to replace him."[288]

One of Peter Ogden Jr.'s daughters, Margaret Julia, had married HBC clerk Gavin Hamilton, who witnessed her father's hastily made will just before his death and immediately assumed management of Fort St. James. He also built a small house within the fort's boundaries for Phristine Brabant. Hamilton, born in the Orkneys, had begun his service with the company in 1853 as an apprentice clerk at Fort Langley under James Murray Yale. After leaving Fort Langley in 1857, he worked as a clerk at Babine and

McLeod lakes before being transferred to Fort St. James. After his father-in-law's death in 1870, he served as "clerk in charge of the district" for two years and as factor until 1878. He helped to establish the Fort St. James school district in 1877, volunteering one of the fort's buildings for the school. Until this time the traders' male children had usually been educated elsewhere. In 1860 Peter Ogden's young sons, Peter Skene Jr. and Charles, had attended the Colonial School in Victoria with former New Caledonia fur traders' children James Douglas Jr. and Isaac Tod. Thomas Charles at Fort George had also sent his son to boarding school, and in the 1870s James Alexander attended St. Joseph's Mission School at Williams Lake.[289]

Hamilton's first year in charge of Fort St. James was highlighted by the gold rush to the Omineca River, one of the headwaters of the Peace. Prospectors arrived at Fort St. James on foot or horseback, making the fort their supply depot before pushing northward. If they returned empty-handed at the end of the mining season, both the Fort St. James and Quesnel stores gave them free assistance.[290] Another trail from the Skeena River to the Omineca district brought business to Fort Babine. Barkerville, on the other hand, was drained of miners, and Clerk Hugh Ross at the Barkerville store complained that their outstanding debts amounted to almost $20,000.[291]

Pioneer road builder Gustavus Blinn Wright, who had built sections of the Cariboo Wagon Road and ran steamboats on both the upper and lower Fraser, hoped to employ his steamboat *Enterprise* on Stuart and Takla lakes to transport miners and supplies. Built and launched at Soda Creek in 1863, this boat had the lightest draft of any British Columbia steamer and a carrying capacity of seventy-five tons. In June 1871 it took on a full load of passengers and freight, including flour from the Collins Mill at Soda Creek, and proceeded up the Fraser to Fort George. It then navigated the rapids of the Nechako and Stuart rivers to reach Stuart Lake, went up Tachie River to Trembleur Lake and finally to Takla Lake. Although this was an incredible accomplishment, the service was not financially viable, and when the provincial Lands and Works Department provided $5,800 to open a road from Fort St. James to the Omineca mines, the *Enterprise* was abandoned at Trembleur Lake, its funnel recycled for smoking fish.[292]

The promise of a transcontinental railway brought British Columbia into confederation in 1871. Surveys for a route across British Columbia commenced the next year and resulted in some interesting customers from eastern Canada requesting assistance at Fort St. James. Following orders from CPR surveyor Sandford Fleming, in September 1872 photographer Charles Horetzky and botanist John Macoun set out from Edmonton with ten horses to reconnoitre the Peace River and Pine Pass routes through the Rocky Mountains. They met trapper Pete Toy and his partner Bill Southcombe near the junction of the Finlay and Parsnip rivers and accompanied them to Fort McLeod. The clerk at the fort, William Sinclair, guided Macoun and Horetzky overland to Fort St. James where Gavin Hamilton arranged for Macoun to go on to Victoria via Quesnel. Horetzky enjoyed a convivial evening with Hamilton and reported that Hamilton had set up a saloon operated by his brother, Thomas, "where brandy-smashes, cocktails, and three card monte helped to ease the reckless miner of his hard-earned gains."[293] Horetzky continued his survey to the Pacific Coast, trekking through the snow via Fort Babine where he found the clerk absent and helped himself to bacon, beans, flour, tea and sugar. He returned to Ottawa convinced that Pine Pass was the best route for the new railway and waged a futile campaign against the federal government's decision to use the pass through the Selkirk Mountains.[294] Adventure traveller and writer William Francis Butler arrived in 1873 via the Peace River. He, too, met trapper Pete Toy and continued south to Fort St. James where he obtained transportation to Quesnel.[295]

From Montreal came George Mercer Dawson, eager to assist with the Canadian Pacific Railway survey. A recent graduate of the London School of Mines, he had been hired by the Geological Survey of Canada to map the mineral deposits of British

Columbia. Only the province's coal deposits had been seriously examined and he was about to discover that the cordillera was a crazy quilt of subducted and faulted terranes reaching north into Alaska. Dawson crossed the southern half of British Columbia numerous times under a unique agreement with the CPR that allowed him freedom to leave the company's camps and—at the company's expense—examine mineral regions not included in the railway's survey plans. His interest in fossil collecting, ethnology and photography added excitement to his field work.

Gavin Hamilton took charge of Fort St. James when Peter Ogden Jr. died suddenly of influenza in 1870. BRITISH COLUMBIA ARCHIVES G-00396

In 1875 Dawson visited Fort George where he found "a tumbled down looking place like Hudson Bay Posts generally, & surrounded by a number of shanties belonging to Indians who are now nearly all absent hunting." He found a good showing of colours when panning for gold, and en route down the Fraser to Quesnel, his canoe passed a large number of Chinese prospectors near the mouth of Cottonwood River.[296] The following year Dawson headed for Stuart Lake and spent the afternoon of his arrival gathering fossils from the limestone formation on Mount Pope. When a strong wind made it difficult to return across the lake by canoe, Gavin Hamilton invited him to spend the night at Fort St. James. After dining on roast beaver, Dawson spent a friendly evening with Hamilton, his brother and two clerks named Hall and Weaver. The next morning he browsed through the fort's extensive garden while waiting for his Native boatmen to complete their devotions at the Catholic mission. He noted "cabbages, cauliflowers, turnips, beets, carrots, onions &c. grow easily & well. Cabbages and cauliflower not forced in spring but sometimes attain very great size. Cucumbers grown in frame. Barley & potatoes grown in some quantity for use at fort. In Garden notwithstanding frosts (pretty severe one last night) Mallow, mignonette, mesembryanthemum, Portulacca & sweet pea."[297]

In his journal Dawson described Fort St. James as a collection of a "few dilapidated shanties" but "probably about as good a sample of a H.B. post as now extant, & the most important post in B. Columbia." The buildings in the quadrangle were certainly old and neglected, but in the kitchen the elderly French Canadian cook cheerfully shared his warm, comfortable space with the fort employees.[298]

Dawson visited Fort George a second time in October 1876. Assisted by a boat crew of three Fort Fraser Natives, he canoed down the Nechako River and portaged around Isle Pierre Rapids but ran the White Mud (Chala-oo-chick) Rapids that Simon Fraser and John Stuart had considered too dangerous. While waiting at Fort George for his pack train to arrive, Dawson explored the area on horseback with Charles Ogden. He visited the Catholic Church on the Native reserve and took photographs from the high bank opposite the fort. These photographs are some of the earliest taken of New Caledonia HBC sites. Gavin Hamilton and his wife, Margaret Ogden, had sixteen children, and when he resigned from HBC service in 1878, he moved his family south to a ranch purchased from A.S. Bates at 150 Mile House. Once again, he was instrumental in establishing the first public school in the region. In 1883 the family moved to the HBC enclave at Lac La Hache, where many of Peter Ogden Jr.'s children and their mother, Phristine, had settled.[299]

JAMES M. LINDSAY ALEXANDER joined the HBC in Saskatchewan in 1863 and transferred to New Caledonia in 1868. He served at Fort George and Fort Fraser and married Peter Ogden's daughter Sarah. When he replaced Gavin Hamilton at Fort St. James in 1878, the fort itself had deteriorated badly, and the slump in the general economy of North America meant that the focus at most forts was simply to make a profit one way or another. However, Fort St. James was still supplying provisions to the placer miners in the Omineca region, where in the year following his arrival fifty-seven white men and twenty Chinese produced $36,000 in gold there. This compared favourably with the first year of mining, 1874, when seventy-four white men had produced $38,000.[300]

The Catholic Church had arrived at Fort St. James in 1873 when Oblate missionary Father Jean Marie LeJacq and Brother Georges Blanchet began a mission to the 1,000 Carrier people and 150 to 200 Sekani in the region. In time they built Our Lady of Good Hope Church near the fort on the shores of Stuart Lake. But the friendly cooperation they fostered with the HBC changed after August 1885 when Father Adrian Gabriel Morice was transferred from the Chilcotin to Stuart Lake, in a move made by his bishop as a "desperate expedient" to deal with his difficult personality. He was twenty-six years old, headstrong and ambitious; more importantly, however, he was a keen linguist and, while stationed at the Cariboo Mission near Williams Lake, had begun learning the Carrier language with help from James Alexander's young son who boarded there.[301] This ability to communicate with the Carrier in their own language gave Morice an advantage over the HBC whenever there were problems with the Natives. In his 1885 report, James Alexander believed that the Carrier were negatively influenced by the priests:

> Formerly the Indians were tractable & easily dealt with. Now they are bad and very troublesome. This is to be attributed more to the Priests than the miners with whom the intercourse has always been very limited. The Priests have no scruple in using every means in their power to curry favour with the Indians and undermine any influence we traders may have among them.[302]

James Alexander apparently transferred from Fort St. James to Quesnel in 1886 and the following year was promoted to chief factor. That same year his wife, Sarah, died at age 40, leaving nine children. He remarried and briefly served at Masset in the Queen Charlotte Islands before resigning from the HBC to move to Port Simpson, where he was collector of customs and a civil magistrate until his death in 1901.[303]

About the same time as James Lindsay Alexander was posted to Fort St. James, Alexander Campbell Murray, son of HBC chief trader Alexander Hunter Murray, was hired as a clerk for Fort Fraser. He set to work moving the old fort to the north side of the Nautley River and in 1878 built Stony Creek Post, about thirty miles south of present-day Vanderhoof. He next reconnoitred a new outpost near the site of the abandoned Fort Grahame, about sixty miles north of the junction of the Peace and Finlay rivers, re-naming it Bear Lake Outpost, and remained in charge there for the next three winters. But in June 1883, after Murray had returned to Fort Fraser to marry Mary Bird of Fort Connolly,[304] much against chief trader James Lindsay Alexander's wishes, HBC headquarters in Victoria ordered the closing of both Bear Lake Outpost and Fort Fraser as cost-cutting measures. Alexander complained that "they were the only posts in the Dist. which never failed to show a good profit"; he re-established Fort Fraser a year later with a small out-fit, but Bear Lake Outpost was not reopened until 1891.[305]

Chief factor Roderick MacFarlane took charge of Fort St. James in 1886. Born in Stornaway, Scotland, MacFarlane had entered the service at age nineteen and was posted the following year to Fort Good Hope in the Mackenzie River region. In 1857 he led a voyage of discovery down the Beghula River, northeast of Fort Good Hope, and renamed it Anderson River in honour of chief factor James Anderson. Like many HBC personnel, he was a keen naturalist and later published his notes on mammals and birds of the lower Mackenzie River. But he was also concerned about the future of First Nations people, and in 1880, at a time when the federal government practised a policy of "no treaty, no help," MacFarlane chastised David Laird, lieutenant-governor of the North-West Territories, for not doing more. He wrote from Fort Chipewyan:

> It strikes me very forcibly that something must be done and that speedily to help these poor people. Confining my remarks as applicable to the District of Peace River, Athabasca, English River, and the Mackenzie, I am really unaware of anything that has yet been accomplished by our rulers . . . since the territory was transferred to Canada.[306]

For the fur-trading year 1886–87 there was an apparent deficit of $7,548 in the district of New Caledonia; although Fort St. James had brought in $16,431 and Fort George $11,891, both posted losses for the year. The traders blamed an outbreak of measles, the HBC headquarters decision to change the tariff (the price the company would pay for furs) and competition from free trader Frank Guy, a Frenchman who, after years of operating a stopping house and ranch east of 150 Mile House, had turned to fur trading. In order to eliminate him, the Company bought up all his furs. However, the HBC loss that year did not deter Roderick MacFarlane from his decision to renovate Fort St. James, and he brought Murray from Fraser Lake to help replace some of the most decrepit buildings. The fourteen-foot-high stockade, two bastions, and all the old houses from Donald Manson's time were pulled down and all the salvageable filling logs reused in the new structures. Only the house built by Peter Ogden in 1867 and the dwelling house, forty by thirty-one feet, erected three years earlier remained because they were still in good condition. Over the course of the next three years, MacFarlane supervised construction of a general warehouse and fur store, salmon storage building, small dwelling house and workshop at the fort and a warehouse at the northwest end of Babine Portage. The cost of all the repairs and improvements between 1887 and 1889 amounted to $3,000, but they provided a footprint for a Parks Canada restoration seventy years later.

By 1887 HBC headquarters in Victoria was facing American competition for furs, mainly from New York agents who outbid the highest prices the HBC traders were authorized to pay. In an effort to improve management, Victoria recommended that the Quesnel District, which had been operating as a separate unit, be amalgamated with New Caledonia and placed under MacFarlane's administration.[307] The good news that year was that Fort George's returns had improved, even though the post had problems, losing two hunters through illness and "one first class Indian" by drowning. At the same time, the independent trader Twelve Foot Davis—famous for staking a rich, twelve-foot-wide gold claim at Barkerville—was intercepting Natives on the Giscome Portage, thirty miles upriver from Fort George, paying high prices for certain skins and promising to have a trader there to meet them the following winter.[308]

In 1888 the HBC assistant manager at Victoria reported even more competition and a continued lack of profits:

> We have to compete with several merchants who, with commendable enterprise, have taken hold of industries which help to a very large extent their commercial business. They own and run lumber mills, flour mills, mines and canneries, and associate themselves with every enterprise which they think will increase their trade. There is also increasing competition from the East, caused by large Firms there sending travelers to all parts of this Colony, who in order to open up a business, cut prices very fine.[309]

In July MacFarlane advised Victoria that the number of beaver pelts had been declining for the past ten years "at an alarming rate" and blamed it on the virtual abandonment of Fort Fraser as well as the outposts at Stony Creek and Connolly's Lake. He also pointed out that the posts' annual orders for supplies were never completely filled, so they seldom had enough trading goods on hand, the fur tariffs were too low, and there had been increased

The HBC moved to this location near the outlet of Babine Lake from the abandoned Fort Kilmaurs (Old Fort). BRITISH COLUMBIA ARCHIVES D-06446

opposition and over-hunting by the Natives.[310] That year for the first time supplies for New Caledonia, with the exception of provisions for Fort George, were shipped to Stuart Lake via the Skeena River to Hazelton rather than via the Cariboo Road. From Hazelton a pack train operated by entrepreneurs George Adolphus Vieth and Robert Borland took the freight to Babine Lake, where HBC schooners transported it to the Babine Portage and from the portage to the fort. This was an immense undertaking as the outfit included up to seventy tons of flour and all manner of dry goods including overalls, underwear and mining shovels. Furs were shipped out by the same route in time to reach Victoria by August.

During that first season using the new route, the scows were delayed by difficulties created by Natives on the Upper Skeena in an episode known as the "Skeena Uprising," sparked by the shooting of a Gitksan man. The Natives had also suffered from a shortage of food during the previous long winter and a measles epidemic that had taken 240 lives, many of them children. The white residents of Hazelton, fearing an outbreak of violence, wrote to the Attorney General requesting assistance, and packer Robert Borland volunteered to personally deliver their letter to Victoria. It was anticipated that his pack trains would be attacked as he was transporting HBC goods to Babine that summer, but the Natives allowed his canoe to pass down the Skeena unharmed. Arriving in Victoria, he strode into a sitting of the legislature to startle the members with the question, "Gentlemen, do you know there is a war on?" Subsequently he met with the executive council several times to formulate a plan of action, and eighty men of "C" Battery, Royal Garrison Artillery, and a contingent of police constables led by Superintendent Herbert Roycraft were soon dispatched. But Roycraft had the sense to leave the artillery at the mouth of the river while he and his constables went up the Skeena and met with thirteen chiefs to work out a peace settlement.[311]

Although Fort St. James' returns dropped to $14,165 in 1888–89, the fort actually posted a profit of $3,380. MacFarlane reported that fur returns had been low because of a mild winter and the absence of the rabbits that normally attracted lynx and foxes, and he suggested that beaver numbers be given a chance to recoup the following year when rabbits were expected to return. By this time he had completed the improvements at Fort St. James, and he turned his attention to upgrading the region's pack trails. Only $500 had been authorized for this purpose, but he spent $1,153 to improve the route to McLeod Lake, make a new wagon road across Babine Portage and open a horse track from Hazelton to Babine. The fort had a further debt of $4,032 on its books caused by supplying provisions to Superintendent Roycraft to put down the Skeena Uprising, but this amount had to be collected by the HBC commissioner in Winnipeg who dealt with all matters relating to the Indian Affairs Department. Because of the dearth of salmon that year, MacFarlane also spent $1,355 on provisions for destitute Natives, an amount that he hoped the HBC would recover from the federal government, but he had taken care to write to BC Premier Alexander E.B. Davie about this relief in order to ensure compensation.[312]

McFarlane remained in charge of Fort St. James until 1889, when he was posted to the Cumberland District. In 1902 he received Queen Victoria's Arctic Medal for his discovery of the Beghula River in 1857.

Chapter Twelve

THE DEPRESSION YEARS OF THE 1890s

THE 1890S WAS A CRUCIAL TIME in HBC history as the company faced more and more competition from free traders. Extremely skilled managers were needed to keep the forts viable and increase the quota of furs, and to this end, the company began recruiting experienced men from Rupert's Land. Among them was William Edward Traill, who became the next chief factor at Fort St. James. Traill was the son of Upper Canada pioneer author Catherine Parr Traill, and his wife, Harriet, was the daughter of HBC Chief Factor William McKay. The Traills eventually had a family of twelve children. At the time of their transfer to Fort St. James three had died and two of their boys were living on their own, but five girls—Ethel, Jessie, Mary, Maria and Harriet—travelled west with their parents. Two more girls would be born at Stuart Lake.

The Traills were veterans of numerous transfers between posts east of the Rocky Mountains, but the move from Fort Vermilion to Fort St. James involved a challenging eighty-eight-day trek by way of Fort Chipewyan, Athabasca Landing and Edmonton to reach Calgary. There they took the train to Ashcroft and then the stage to Quesnel, where Traill met former trader Gavin Hamilton at a stopping house. Hamilton, who had been drinking, offered profuse advice on how to manage Fort St. James—which Traill said he ignored. At Quesnel the family transferred to a riverboat for the final leg of the journey up the Fraser, Nechako and Stuart rivers. By now Harriet was six months pregnant and she endured part of it crammed into the hold with her daughters. Traill wrote to his mother:

> As you may suppose Harriet was heartily tired of the trip as we were cramped up in a space about 6 ft. square. To keep off the rain we had the tent pitched over our nest in which H. & the children were cooped up night & day . . . We ate on shore when the weather would permit, but where it rained too hard H. & children ate in the hold. The river is very rapid with the exception of 30 or 40 miles on the Stewart River. There are several dangerous rapids but the men are very expert and we had no accident whatever.[313]

When the family arrived at Fort St. James, they were delighted with the beautiful setting of lake and mountains but especially with the many new buildings that MacFarlane had built in the fort compound. At several of their previous postings they had been forced to camp out while William renovated and enlarged shabby dwelling houses. Traill immediately threw himself into the fort's routine. In deference to most of his employees, who were Roman Catholic, he allowed time off for their church holidays such as All Saints Day, but he read the Protestant service on Sundays and observed a day of rest. The family had a Christmas tree and continued the old tradition of a New Year's Day *regale* for fort employees and nearby Carrier families.

An adequate diet with a good variety of food was no longer a challenge at Fort St. James. With the improvements to the transportation service, provisions were delivered more frequently, and roast beef had replaced the dreary winter diet of dried salmon.

The two youngest girls of the William Edward Traill family, Annie and Catherine Barbara (front row), were born at Fort St. James. GLENBOW ARCHIVES NA-741-5

Both Traill and Alexander Murray, who had stayed on to serve as accountant, were excellent outdoorsmen who enjoyed supplementing the improved fare with ducks, geese and rabbits.

Despite his cooperation with the local Roman Catholic mission, Traill had difficulty coping with Father Morice. His agreement with the wily priest included the proviso that the mission would get free mail delivery if the priest encouraged the Natives to sell their furs at Fort St. James and not at Quesnel. However, Morice, who was loath to pay Natives to bring his copious mail and extra supplies from Quesnel, used the scare tactic that he would allow the Natives to take their furs to independent traders if the HBC did not oblige him. Another major issue was the Oblate missionaries' practice of whipping penitents. Along with other well-known merchants, such as F.W. Foster at Clinton and Robert McLeese at Soda Creek, Traill publicly expressed his abhorrence of physical punishment, believing that moral suasion was sufficient. In 1892 Father Chirouse, an Oblate priest stationed in the southern Cariboo, was imprisoned for sanctioning the whipping of a Lillooet Native girl. Morice responded that, if the courts of Canada could order whipping as a punishment, why couldn't his church? He believed incorrectly that North American Native peoples had employed whipping as a deterrent and that, therefore, the Oblates were following established Native practices. Eventually, Traill had to back down, and it remained for Alexander C. McNab, chief trader at Fort St. James from 1899 to 1901, to put further pressure on Morice in this regard, thereby helping to end the practice in the early 1900s.[314]

In 1891 Robert Hall, the HBC superintendent for New Caledonia in the 1890s, carried out the commissioner's decision to reduce working expenses in the Western Department by lowering tariffs, discontinuing boarding allowances and restructuring the districts. Stony Creek Post and Fort Connolly were permanently closed, Fort George became part of the Cariboo District under the management of the post at Quesnel, and Fort Babine became part of the Simpson District under the management of Hazelton. Hall advised Traill that these new arrangements should reduce his long hours of accounting, and because he would have time for more personal contact with his customers in the shop, he could discharge his Native interpreters. The HBC even considered abandoning the "made beaver" tariff.[315]

Hall's deputy, Inspecting Officer J. McDougall, made the annual inspection trip to the New Caledonia forts in the summer of 1891, and his report throws much interesting light on the economic and social climate at Fort St. James during this period. According to McDougall's report, the gross profit on furs for 1890 had been $5,739 or about 100 percent, and the gross profit on cash sales was equal to 54 percent. He noted that Traill's accounts "were kept carefully" but inventory showed a loss of $1,790 for the year. In order to reduce expenses, he recommended that the officer and clerks' mess could be trimmed, especially the wine and spirits allowance of $125, which included eight gallons of brandy, seven gallons of Jamaican rum, seven gallons of port wine and four gallons of sherry. Travelling expenses included an annual trip to Victoria that he thought unnecessary. Even the wages for the fort's Chinese cook Kin Foo came under scrutiny; McDougall thought he was overpaid at $30 a month, although he did not criticize the £50 annual pension given to former clerk Ferdinand McKenzie, the son of chief factor Roderick McKenzie of Red River. The younger McKenzie had been educated in England for a medical career, and after serving at most of the forts in New Caledonia, he had retired in 1886 because of failing eyesight but had continued to live at Stuart Lake with his wife, Catherine. McDougall noted, "He has considerable influence with the Indians of the District and is still zealous in using it for the Company's interest." A year later Hall suggested that a second elderly employee, James Boucher, son of Waccan, should be allowed to retire on a pension of £10 annually.

Rachel Sarah Ogden rose from humble beginnings at Fort St. James to become the wife of HBC Commissioner Robert Hanley Hall. They lived in Fort Simpson and Victoria before being transferred to the Saskatchewan district in 1902.
BRITISH COLUMBIA ARCHIVES G-09385

Robert Hall made annual summer inspection trips to New Caledonia between 1892 and 1895. As he had served as a clerk at Fort St. James from 1873 to 1877 and married Peter Ogden Jr.'s daughter, Rachel Sarah, he should have been sympathetic to the plight of the fur traders there, but in his reports he showed no mercy. Although fluctuations in fur prices and the varying abilities of the clerks to keep accurate accounts underlay most of the discrepancies in their reports, he flayed post personnel for the long hours he had to spend poring over their ledgers. He was also responsible for hiring permanent employees, preferring local people because "outsiders" tended to learn the business and then become competitors.

Traill's responsibilities at this time included Bear Lake Outpost, which had been reopened, and McLeod Lake. He made long trips to visit all the posts under his supervision, leaving Harriet to cope with the family for weeks at a time. Communication was still difficult in winter when mail was received only twice a month from Quesnel. (The mail carrier took 14 days to make the round trip from Quesnel via the Telegraph Trail to Fort Fraser and the pack trail to Fort St. James and return to Quesnel.) However, much of Traill's time was taken up with the transportation of supplies because most of the goods for New Caledonia were now shipped up the Skeena River on the new HBC steamer *Caledonia*. All freight had to be checked carefully on arrival at Fort Babine, at Babine Portage and again at Stuart Lake to ensure that no pilfering had taken place. In addition, Traill had to supervise the building and outfitting of two new schooners, one for Babine Lake and the other for Stuart Lake, and he spent many hours writing letters to order everything from oar locks to sailcloth from Victoria. Each schooner could deliver 3,000 pounds of freight per trip to HBC warehouses at the ends of the Babine/Stuart Lake portage. Horses and carts brought the goods over the portage, and at the end of the season Traill ensured that the boats were safely stored and the horses brought back to Fort St. James for the winter. In cooperation with Alexander McNab at the Quesnel HBC store, he also supervised pack train operators Joseph Aguayo, another man known only as Sanchez, Jean Caux—otherwise known as Cataline—and Vieth and Borland, who brought flour from the Soda Creek mill and other supplies from Quesnel. Vieth and Borland also provided the fort with cattle from their extensive ranch at 150 Mile House.[316]

Sanchez and Aguayo were most likely members of a group of Mexican packers who came north from California at the time of the Cariboo gold rush and remained in the country to make their living by operating pack trains in the spring and summer. They wintered their mules and horses on the grasslands of the southern Cariboo and Chilcotin. The most dependable pack train operators were Cataline, a native of France, George Vieth from Nova Scotia and his partner Robert Borland from Ontario. All three men had arrived during the Cariboo gold rush and their exploits were deeply woven into the history of New Caledonia. Cataline's annual routine in the 1890s began in the spring when he took his mules from their winter quarters to Ashcroft to pick up a full load of freight and then brought them up the Cariboo Road and over the Telegraph Trail to Fort Fraser and Fort St. James before carrying on to McLeod Lake. He then made several trips to Quesnel during the summer. Over the years he walked or rode on horseback for thousands of miles, from Yale to Barkerville, Quesnel to Hazelton and Hazelton to Babine Lake, servicing gold rush merchants, fur traders and railway contractors. After the HBC began using the Skeena for freight shipments, he operated from Hazelton and died there in 1922, aged 93. Vieth and Borland's partnership ended with Vieth's death in 1906, but Borland remained active in Cariboo business until his death at 83 in 1923.[317]

After four years at Fort St. James, Traill, who had served with

A legend in his own time, Cataline employed a number of First Nations packers annually to help him manage his pack trains. BRITISH COLUMBIA ARCHIVES I-51525

In the early 1900s most supplies for Fort St. James were transported via steamboat on the Skeena River to Hazelton, by pack train to Babine Lake, then by schooners equipped with sails on Babine and Stuart lakes. Only durable items survived. BRITISH COLUMBIA ARCHIVES I-33272

the HBC since 1864, grew discouraged when he couldn't improve the annual number of fur packs; he was convinced that the region had been trapped out. By the time his contract came up for renewal in 1893 his family had increased by two more daughters, Annie and Catherine Barbara, and he had become most concerned about his children's education. He chose to farm in Saskatchewan rather than continue with the company, and the Traill family departed Fort St. James in May 1893, travelling by riverboat. At Fort George they were joined by Charles Ogden who was leaving the service to become a free trader. When they reached Fort George Canyon, Ogden guided Harriet and the children over the portage trail while William helped take the boat through the rapids. Although the steersman was knocked overboard and nearly drowned, they eventually arrived safely at Soda Creek, where they switched to horse and buggy transportation in order to reach Ashcroft and the eastbound train.[318]

That September, Alexander Murray, who had taken over the administration of Fort St. James, wrote a friendly letter to the Traills, advising that the district had made a profit of $6,117.07 because of the cost-cutting measures. He went on to say that he and his wife missed the happy chatter of the Traill children, and a new schooner would be named "Jessie" in honour of one of the girls.

With sixteen years of experience in New Caledonia, Alexander Murray managed well as the administrator at Fort St. James. His letterbooks reveal that he was a good communicator, adapting easily to changes in personnel and responsibilities, which included maintaining morale at outlying posts, the boom and bust demands on HBC merchandise by surveyors and miners, and the distressing treatment of the Natives by the HBC and federal governments. Although Quesnel and Fort St. James were now in separate districts, the mail and certain provisions such as flour and livestock were delivered over the Telegraph Trail between the two posts. For these reasons Murray maintained regular contact with Alexander McNab, the manager of the HBC store at Quesnel.

Before his transfer to Quesnel in 1894, McNab had served at Lac La Pluie, Ontario. His father, Robert, operated a small store on Snowshoe Creek for Vieth and Borland and was a well-known gold miner in the Keithley Creek and Barkerville areas. When McNab first took over at Quesnel, he found the HBC's cost-cutting measures too restrictive. At Lac La Pluie he had been able to adjust the tariff to suit current circumstances, but Victoria insisted that he follow their tariff prices to the letter. To establish a friendly atmosphere, he liked to give the Natives some tobacco when they first arrived at the store, but this, too, was forbidden. Nevertheless, while he was in charge of Quesnel, he showed his mettle in dealing with New Caledonia's problems.

McNab used considerable foresight in arranging for a large supply of provisions early in 1898 after the *Ashcroft Mining Journal* irresponsibly promoted the use of the interior route via the Cariboo Road and Telegraph Trail to reach the Klondike. This was followed by a flurry of mail inquiries about the cost of prospecting outfits, and he did his best to send the miners off with as much equipment as they could afford. But many of them were not prepared for wilderness conditions, and when English adventurer Sir Arthur Curtis went missing, the HBC commissioner in Winnipeg requested McNab's help. He in turn asked Charles Ogden to send out a search party of five trustworthy Natives from Fort George, but they were unsuccessful in locating any trace of Curtis.

With completion of the CPR railway in 1885, Ashcroft had become the transfer centre for goods bound for the Interior. It was now easy to obtain almost any kind of material item, especially mining and agricultural machinery, from suppliers in eastern Canada or the United States and almost as easy to have them delivered by train to Ashcroft and then hauled by mule, ox or horse team over the Cariboo Road as far as Quesnel. As the road between Quesnel and Soda Creek could be very muddy in wet weather, perishable goods, especially flour from the local mill, were generally shipped farther north by steamer. But a general depression in the early 1890s slowed business to a standstill in the Interior. Most steamer transport on the upper Fraser ceased, and it was not until the launching of Senator James Reid's sternwheeler *Charlotte* at Quesnel in August 1896 that a slow revival began.[319] After that, goods bound for Forts George, McLeod and Grahame via Giscome Portage could go by steamer, although the steamboats had to be tied up from November until breakup in April.

It was cheaper, however, for goods bound for Fraser and Stuart lakes to be taken from Quesnel over the Telegraph Trail, but moving goods this way was an immense challenge for HBC personnel. Some of the heavy drinking packers demanded credit to cover the cost of their provisions for the summer with the promise of payment at the end of the season. For example, in the HBC's contract for the 1898 season with the packer Sanchez, the company advanced more than $200 to replace horses that had died in the Chilcotin during the previous winter. But when Sanchez arrived at Quesnel with his outfit, Alexander McNab, the manager of the

HBC store there, discovered that he had lied about the number of animals he had available for use. McNab then had to arrange a further outlay for more horses and saddles, and by the time all the costs were added up, he figured the HBC owned the pack train. Eventually he managed to get Sanchez' rig ferried across the Fraser River in readiness for the long trip via the Telegraph Trail to Fort St. James and McLeod Lake. But the old packer was getting on in years and in the days prior to his departure he over-indulged in alcohol. He was taken to a hotel and lingered there a month before he died. Fortunately, before Sanchez died, McNab persuaded him to sign a bill of sale for his pack train, then scrambling to get this first train of the season off on time, he convinced packer Joseph Aguayo to assume Sanchez' contract, a risky arrangement because a few years previously the HBC had to forgive Aguayo's debt of $463.[320] Aguayo later had the nerve to try to claim that he had been in partnership with Sanchez and owned half of the old man's pack train.

MEANWHILE, HBC AND GOVERNMENT POLICIES were continuing to affect the Natives in negative ways. When the HBC closed the Stony Creek outpost in 1891, the trappers of the Cheslatta band refused to trade at Fort Fraser. Instead they sold their furs to an independent trader named Price who promised high values, then took their furs to the Coast but never sent any payment.[321]

Four years later, in order to cut costs, the federal Department of Indian Affairs ceased assisting Natives with medicine, seeds and farming implements. HBC superintendent Robert Hall, recognizing the damage that this policy would cause, quickly duplicated the government's previous year's order at HBC headquarters in Victoria and sent it off along with two ploughs to Fort St. James. He requested that Murray ask the Native people for only a small amount for the seeds and only the actual cost for the ploughs.[322] At Fort Fraser, William Sinclair reported that in May and June 1895 a bad flu virus prevented many Natives from trading furs. When a number of children at Stony Creek died from it, he ordered their coffins to be made out of the lumber from the abandoned trading post.[323]

Little is written about the wives of HBC managers, except for the odd mention in the post's daily journal. Presumably many of them were called on to assist with menial chores when there was not enough staff. However, Mrs. Murray's activities were noted in her husband's journals, and we learn that, besides entertaining the local priests, she helped her husband by cleaning out the men's living quarters and the store, milking the cows, feeding the chickens and caring for the garden. As Mrs. Murray was a Catholic, her husband seems to have been on a better footing than Traill with the Roman Catholic mission, and Fathers Blanchet and Morice frequently dined with them. One of the few bright spots in the lives of the women at the forts was the arrival of the HBC catalogues. From 1881 to 1913 the women could order the latest fashions in hats, dresses and underwear for themselves and their children, and the men could order the finest suits, choosing their preferred fabric from swatches glued to the pages. Everything from household furnishings to children's toys, patent medicines, harnesses, saddles and English marmalade could be delivered to the nearest railway station, and small parcels were sent by mail. There was even a Christmas catalogue. The company's operating policy of "Goods satisfactory or money refunded" included the mailing charges.[324]

The clerks who managed Fort George, McLeod Lake and its outlying post of Bear Lake had the most difficult time with isolation but only one clerk was lured away by gold mining. Robert Tibbet Alexander at McLeod Lake advised Murray in January 1895 that he would be leaving to go placer mining when his first contract was finished in May.[325] However, his replacement, William Ware, proved to be a long-time, reliable employee in the north, serving at Forts McLeod and Babine, Telegraph Creek and Hazelton. He then became inspector and assistant district manager at HBC Vancouver. By the time he retired in 1932 he had received the Company's long service silver medal and two bars in

1920, the gold medal in 1925, and gold bar in 1930. (Fort Ware, a small HBC outpost on the Finlay River, which operated between 1938 and 1953, seventy-five miles above Fort Grahame, is not named for him, but for James Ware.)[326]

The journals of other men in the outlying posts reveal more of the hardships and isolation. Ernest Sturrock Peters, who was born in Abroath, Scotland, had been a cowboy in Texas and Montana before he entered HBC service in September 1888 as an apprentice clerk at Fort McLeod and served as the clerk at Bear Lake Outpost from 1891 to 1893. Here the ordinary routine of Sekani Natives bringing in furs from the Nation River area and the odd prospector passing by was only broken by occasional visits from Father Morice and federal geologist R.C. McConnell who was exploring the Liard River region for the Geological Survey of Canada. But Peters also experienced the sadness of watching the Natives cope with illness, noting in his journal how difficult it was for the Native women to care for sick children when their husbands were away hunting. Four children died in one year, and in the following year two children died of whooping cough. One woman, Old Ahkin-ah, remained near the fort, and when her children died, Peters helped to build their coffins and bury them.[327] On December 25, 1892, he wrote in the post journal, "Christmas Day spent in camp, feast of Bacon, dried peaches and bread. No one appeared. I hope this will be the last Xmas day I will have to spend in this country with which I cannot describe my disgust."[328] Before Christmas 1893 the HBC granted Peters a transfer to Fort George. Except that he was no longer completely isolated, conditions there were probably not much better as the fort still had the same buildings that had been described by George Dawson in 1875 and they were now badly in need of repair.

When William Fox, a young Metis from Manitoba, replaced Peters at Fort Grahame in the spring of 1894, his abilities were tested almost immediately. Warm weather and heavy rains exacerbated the Finlay River's abnormally high runoff, and on May 26 Fox noted in the journal that "if the water continues to raise for a few days more I am afraid the buildings will go and it is utterly impossible for one man to manage a canoe in this strong current." Two days later the water had risen another three feet and Fox built a large fire on a nearby hill to summon help. The river soon overflowed it banks, flooding the store to a depth of two feet. Natives finally arrived to remove the goods and place them upstairs in Fox's house, but he could not re-enter the store until June 11 to clean up the mud and replace the merchandise.[329] In the latter part of 1895 Fox erected a new store and house in a secure location farther up the Finlay. Despite the distraction of miners making $100 a day placer mining in the nearby Omineca region, he remained faithfully at his post. When a long winter loomed, he begged Murray to send him lots of reading material and some rum. "I think if I have nothing to read this winter I will go crazy." To reinforce his request, he wrote again in September to ask Murray to order $5 worth of novels.[330]

In January 1898 five members of the North West Mounted Police found their way to Fort Grahame. Inspector J.D. Moodie and a party of four constables and two guides had left Edmonton on September 4, 1897, with orders to determine whether a wagon road and cattle trail could be opened to the headwaters of the Pelly River in the Yukon. They arrived at Fort St. John on November 1 and spent several weeks preparing themselves and their twenty-four pack horses and six saddle horses for winter travel. Unfortunately, in late December they lost their way, only managing to find Fort Grahame on January 18, and here they spent the remainder of the winter as William Fox's guests. By March supplies were running low and Moodie, together with three constables, trekked south to Fort St. James and on to Quesnel in search of more provisions. They enjoyed fishing and hunting at Fort St. James and bought nine horses from W.E. Camsell before returning to Fort Grahame via Manson Creek. They finally set out again in July, blazed a trail beyond the Finlay River and reached the Yukon on October 24.[331]

Seven years after Moodie's heroic efforts, the Royal [added in

Located near the Fraser River, the HBC store at Quesnel was the distribution centre for supplies sent upriver by steamer to Fort George, by pack horse over the Telegraph Trail, or by sleigh and wagon to the mining community of Barkerville. VANCOUVER PUBLIC LIBRARY 13550

1905] North West Mounted Police were ordered a second time to open up 750 miles of trail from Fort St. John to Teslin Lake. They did not use Moodie's route but instead charted a difficult trail directly west from Fort Grahame, across the mountains to Bear Lake and onward to the Telegraph Trail north of Hazelton. This seemed a futile exercise because the Klondike rush had died down by this time, and access to the Yukon by the coastal route was well-established as steamers connected Seattle and Vancouver with Skagway and the White Pass and Yukon Railway. Nevertheless, the RNWMP obeyed the order, but when they called for tenders to deliver twenty tons of goods to Peace River, Fort St. John and Fort Grahame, the HBC at Edmonton hesitated to deliver to the third site: "We have no men to send and it would require both Pack Train and men to build boats to get it in from this side." The HBC in Victoria submitted an offer of twenty cents a pound but it was apparently not accepted.[332]

Superintendent Charles Constantine and Inspector J. Richards set out with a contingent of six non-commissioned officers, twenty-two constables, two special constables and sixty horses. An advance party under Corporal McLeod wintered with Fox, but the trail was not completed to Fort Grahame until August 1906, and it ended at the Telegraph Trail, 104 miles north of Hazelton, in 1907. HBC Manager James Thomson spent the next year chasing down payment for bank-refused cheques written by the two special constables who had since left the force.[333]

Meanwhile, the increasing white population in the region was putting pressure on the Carrier people to adapt while at the same time creating a greater need for law and order. The economy was still depressed, however, so the provincial government was operating on a reactive basis where policing was concerned. There was only a scattering of law enforcement officers in rural areas of the province, most of them located in the mining centres. For example, the village of Quesnel, where there were saloons for white people and the Natives could obtain liquor from Chinese bootleggers, had telegraph service, a jail, and a resident magistrate, W.A. Johnston. Tax collector and road superintendent Joseph St. Laurent acted as special constable if he was available, but in the

HBC clerk William Fox stands with his Sekani wife, children and sister-in-law at Fort Grahame. Three Royal North West Mounted Police from the second Yukon trail project are seated in front. GLENBOW ARCHIVES NA-494-39

summertime he was generally absent looking after road repairs. The nearest senior policeman, William Stephenson, resided at Quesnel Forks at the junction of the Cariboo and Quesnel rivers, sixty miles east of 150 Mile House, but his main occupation was government agent and mining recorder for a district currently undergoing a hydraulic mining boom. Two constables assisted him: James Bain, who looked after the mining district, and William Parker, who patrolled the Cariboo Road. When not on duty, Parker lived on his ranch at Big Lake, thirty miles east of the Cariboo Road. Stephenson had no telegraph or telephone connection with the outside world; messages were delivered on horseback, a two-day ride from 150 Mile House.

At Fort George, seventy miles upriver from Quesnel, Ernest Peters, the HBC officer in charge, was expected to deal with law and order although there was no bridge across the Fraser River or wagon road south and no telegraph connection to the outside world to get help if the need arose. Peters spent a quiet winter there in 1894–95, broken only by a ten-day trip to Quesnel in January, but things changed abruptly as spring turned into summer. With all the problems created by mining activity in the Quesnel area, Stephenson did not need the added responsibility of maintaining law and order at Fort George, but on July 27, 1895, he had no choice but to respond when he received a message from Robert Hall, who had been inspecting operations at the Quesnel HBC store. It seems that a man named Louis Stoehr had arrived from Fort George and presented Hall with a letter from Ernest Peters:

> I send you this down by Louis Stoehr who goes down to see if we cannot be protected against drunken Indians. Yesterday some of the Indians arrived from Quesnelle with a supply of liquor. They came down to the fort in the afternoon and tried to assault me. Being unable to cope with these men I managed to get way from them and left the house securely locked. They immediately proceeded to break in all the doors, bursting the locks, also broke one window in each of the end rooms and

generally did all the damage they could inside the house. After they left I returned to the house and in the evening they again returned and commenced again, but as I am quite unable to handle any of these men and knowing that if they got hold of me I would be severely handled, I took to my heels and got out of the way.

Jack Devereux seized the man who was after me and he got badly mauled by the whole band who immediately jumped him. I have therefore sent down to inform you of this that you may take what steps you think necessary for the proper protection of the company's property and their agents. It is impossible for me as I have said to stand off the whole band, and I have therefore either to get out of the way or else resort to firearms to protect myself and the Coy's property. And were I to resort to the latter, the law might not uphold me.[334]

Stoehr, a prospector working in the vicinity of Fort George, provided a witness statement, implicating Carrier Natives John Quaw and Jimmie Bird:

What I really lost was not of very much value but having to go to Quesnell to replace the artickles I wished to consult a Justice of the peace in regard to protecting myself in another case similar hereafter but not getting my satisfactory answer I am as much advanced as before leaving Ft. George. I think had Mr. Peters been alone he would have met with serious punishment if not kicked and beaten to death for so long as a white man is down they don't appear to try to pull the Indians off but are very ready to part them when the Indian is under.[335]

Stephenson sent word immediately to Parker to proceed to Quesnel and went ahead to organize a river party. He then wrote to his superior, Police Superintendent Frederick Hussey, in Victoria:

Two of the specials going with Parker are Stoehr & Deveraux. Both of those men were in trouble and they claim they know the Indians wanted and also know the country up there. Mr. Hall of the HBC will lend us firearms and also hire us canoes at light expense, and as we get supplies from the Coy. They will take back anything that is left off our hands at cost price.[336]

After seeing Parker off for Fort George with four special constables and two Native canoemen, Hall returned to HBC headquarters at Victoria and Stephenson to Quesnel Forks. But after two weeks had passed without word from Parker, Stephenson began to worry about mounting government expenses. He rode horseback to 150 Mile House only to find no messages waiting for him. However, a few days later Parker arrived at Quesnel with the culprits, and W.A. Johnston held court, then reported to Stephenson on August 30:

Re the Fort George trouble

No doubt you have heard the particulars from Mr. Parker. I was completely disgusted with the business. There being no evidence whatever of felonious intent when the charges came up for examination and it meant a very heavy expense in getting witnesses, etc. to the supreme court if we committed the prisoners for trial. I therefore thought that justice could be done by punishing them as severely as possible in the way of costs which have been secured by the HB Co. to the amount of two hundred and thirty dollars, and we also succeeded in convicting a Chinaman for supplying them with the liquor, fining him $50 costs and costs of court, $15 of which had to be paid for witnesses.

It was very evident that the informant was under influence to prevent him to tell all he knew about the affair, which made it very unpleasant for me. P.S. Will you be up to square up the business?[337]

This expensive exercise influenced Hussey and the provincial government to station police constable David Anderson at Quesnel on a permanent basis after 1896. His area of responsibility included Forts George, St. James and Fraser. A few years later Alexander C. Murray, HBC post manager at Fort St. James, was made a justice of the peace for that area, and Indian Agent R.E. Loring at Hazelton designated a number of Native peacekeepers for some of the reserves.[338]

THROUGHOUT THIS PERIOD competition from private merchants continued full bore, and in Victoria Robert Hall instituted a policy of eliminating the free traders who hovered around the forts by matching the prices they were offering for furs. At Quesnel in 1895 Wah Lee and Telesphore Marion both traded in furs, Senator James Reid built a new store near the HBC store and invested in a pack train, and James Deacon established a trading store at Hixon, north of Quesnel.[339] When in 1895 Charles Ogden, who had left the company's service two years earlier, returned to the Fort George area to buy furs independently, Ernest Peters spent the remainder of the year trying to outbid him. Hall and Alexander McNab became obsessed with eliminating Ogden's venture. "Crush the opposition," Hall ordered from Victoria, and McNab sent off a message from Quesnel to Peters saying that "it will be better to lose money this year if our object can be gained, and I would leave no stone unturned to accomplish it."[340] When Ogden purchased a stock of goods and prepared to trade at Giscome during the winter of 1895–96, McNab took an even bolder step. With Hall's permission, he got Ogden to agree to return to the service and take charge of Fort George, starting November 1. McNab then dismissed Peters in mid-October, giving him one month's extra pay in lieu of the short notice.[341]

Under McNab's supervision Ogden did his best in spite of low fur tariffs and continuing problems with security. Thieves broke in and stole a large number of furs, but Victoria headquarters allowed him to rebuild the store and order a new stock of provisions. His 1897 grocery list suggests why Ogden was a big man: besides basics such as 2,000 pounds of bacon, 20,000 pounds of flour, 10,000 pounds of sugar and 150 pounds of candles, he ordered 200 pounds of candy and 600 pounds of lard as well as 500 pounds of tobacco, twenty-five pounds of red paint, ten cases of coal oil and two dozen horseshoes.[342]

IN THE LATE 1890s the winters at Fort St. James were just as quiet as they had ever been, except for mid-winter celebrations when lavish preparations were made. For example, two men were employed during the last two days of 1896 just to bake bread for the New Year's Day *regale*. The journal entry for January 1, 1897, reads, "All the Indians around the lake at fort today. After greetings, Dancing was kept up till late in evening."[343] But the summer months were filled with Chinese miners driving cattle to Manson Creek, Sanchez and Joseph Aguayo packing to McLeod Lake, and surveyors, Indian agents and the North West Mounted Police coming and going. In 1895 Frank Devereaux formally surveyed the sites of the HBC forts and Native reserves in New Caledonia, accompanied by Indian agent R.E. Loring.[344] Meanwhile, the resident blacksmith coped with all manner of broken ironworks, although specialized items such as guns and watches had to be sent to Victoria or Winnipeg for repairs. Once, when Hall couldn't understand Murray's description of a certain wagon part that was beyond repair, he found a wagon at Yale and had it repaired and shipped north by steamer. Two new wagons were also sent down from the HBC's short-lived post at Glenora (1897–1909) near Telegraph Creek on the Stikine River for use on the Babine portage.

When the Murrays transferred to Port Simpson in 1897 they were replaced by W.E. Camsell until October 1898, then by Alexander C. McNab.

In his 1898 report to the commissioner, Robert Hall claimed

that he visited the main posts in New Caledonia annually between 1892 and 1895:

> I virtually assumed the active charge of its affairs, taking
> stock, making up the accounts and giving every clerk his in-
> structions in writing on the spot, and the following results im-
> mediately followed, viz.: Outfit 1892, net gain, $5,494; 1893,
> $5,885; 1894, $8,167; 1895, $664. The reduced profit of Outfit
> 1895 was due to a heavy falling off of $8,000 along with a
> serious drop in the value of Furs.
>
> Since 1895 New Caledonia has not been visited until this
> Summer, my time having been given to Cassiar District where
> we had a problem to solve even more difficult than New Cal-
> edonia presented in 1892, and the latter District under inef-
> ficient management, has gone backwards rapidly.
>
> Mr. McNab is an indefatigable worker, and I have very
> great confidence that the affairs of his own Post will be
> managed with good sense and economy. I have strong
> hopes that he will also prove big enough to be thoroughly
> master of his men and to control the management of the
> three Outposts.[345]

In 1899 HBC headquarters in Winnipeg merged the Yukon and
Cassiar districts into one and then combined it with the Port Simpson, Cariboo and New Caledonia districts in the Western Department. All four districts now reported to the manager in Victoria.
But there were more changes ahead. After almost one hundred
years of using the "made beaver" system of trading, in June 1899
Fort St. James and Fort Fraser switched to currency as McNab felt
that the local Carrier people were familiar with dollars and he did
not anticipate any objections: "Considerable cash found its way
into the District last year . . . I am sure most of it could have been
spent here had goods been sold at a more reasonable figure." The
cash flow increased the following year because of work on the

Dominion Telegraph line. Then Carrier boatmen began asking to be paid in cash, and McNab expected a good part of this would be spent locally.[346]

McNab spent a good year at Fort St. James with his wife, Annabella, before a number of tragedies occurred. The first happened on October 31, 1899, when William Sinclair, who was in charge at Fort Fraser, committed suicide—one of the rare instances of suicide in HBC service. Sinclair was a third-generation HBC employee, both his father and grandfather having been chief factors,[347] but the decline in his management abilities had come to Hall's attention in the summer of 1899. Hall noted that the trader was seventy-one years old and throughout his forty years with the HBC his honesty had been beyond suspicion, but there were now deficits in Sinclair's accounts, clearly indicating that:

> his faculties are failing fast . . . He is still physically vigorous but his private account shows that he is being victimized by the Native women, as an old man, living at Fraser's Lake without wife or family, could have no need for the innumerable shawls, silk handkerchiefs, &ct. with which he has charged himself. During the last two years I am informed that his personal appearance has given him much concern, and he now dyes his grey hair and whiskers black."[348]

Hall then sent a scathing letter to Sinclair on September 30, 1899, demanding an explanation for the deficits:

> If you have ordinary intelligence, the information contained in the above figures is not news to you and I am therefore the more surprised that you have not hastened to explain the cause of the alarming deficit.
>
> Either your accounts are a farce or the Company's Post at Fraser's Lake has been systematically robbed and you will at the earliest date possible report at Stuart's Lake to Mr. McNab,

bringing with you all the accounts which are likely to throw light on this subject. Your character is at stake and upon the solution of the causes of the deficit depends whether you can any longer be entrusted with the shares of the Post.[349]

Sinclair was buried at Fort Fraser and McNab arranged for H.A. Greenwood, an apprentice clerk, to remain at the fort temporarily while a frantic search was made for a replacement. Later, after Ernest Peters took charge there, he sent a box of Sinclair's personal belongings to Mrs. Sinclair, who lived in Victoria. When Sinclair's daughter complained that some items such as his gold-rimmed glasses and his watch were missing and she asked for an explanation, McNab cautioned that "it would be as well for the late Mr. Sinclair's relatives not to enquire too closely."[350]

Personal tragedy then struck the McNab family. Annabella had travelled to Quesnel in October to be under the care of a doctor during the latter months of her pregnancy. Their baby son, Hugh James, was born in November but only lived until January 5, 1900. McNab brought Annabella back to Fort St. James where she became seriously ill and she died on August 6; the cause of death was listed as diabetes. As the fort's graveyard was in a "disreputable condition," McNab arranged for his wife and child to be interred in the Quesnel pioneer cemetery where their graves were marked by tombstones and enclosed by an iron fence ordered from Victoria.[351]

Later in the year McNab wrote to Hall:

I would have asked for a transfer this fall but I knew that would be impossible. This place since my wife's death is unbearable, and I know I have a most miserable winter ahead, but there is no getting out of it.

It requires a man here who is content with the society of the Siwashes and the others around here. I have never been intimate with Indians anywhere and I cannot bring myself down to their level and associate with them for company, consequently the place in winter is very lonely.[352]

But at the turn of the century, HBC Inspector E.K. Beeston's report ended on an optimistic note:

> The passing of miners, government officials and prospectors has had some effect upon the Indians, and they are getting more independent and tricky and exorbitant in their demands. By abolishing the Made Beaver Tariff and if possible the Indian debts the trade can be better watched so as to obtain better results. I understand that the local Legislature have passed an act enforcing a close season for beaver. This will have a bad effect if strictly carried out, as the beaver is the principal fur and a large article of food. Instructions how to act should be sent to the Clerk in Charge of the District. The name of the Post should be changed to Fort St. James, the Postal and Telegraphic address. As already suggested, it would be well for Mr. McNab to visit Victoria and Vancouver and make a selection of some new goods. With careful management the Post should still be a profitable one.[353]

A short time later Victoria headquarters requested McNab to repair the Fort St. James cemetery then transferred him to Hazelton. He retired from the HBC in 1903, returned to Ontario and then rejoined the Company in 1907. After service at Fort Smith, Edmonton and James Bay, he retired as a district manager in 1913.[354]

Chapter Thirteen

THE NEW CENTURY

WHEN ALEXANDER MCNAB was transferred to Hazelton in late 1901, Alexander Murray returned once again to Fort St. James and he remained in charge there until his retirement in 1913. Looming on the horizon were major changes to transportation systems and to government legislation restricting access to fish and game resources, especially beaver. As increasing numbers of settlers and developers arrived, more responsibilities were added to the post manager's job—justice of the peace, sub-mining recorder, post office manager and supervisor of road and trail development—and the volume of correspondence increased dramatically. Murray continued to write all his reports and letters by hand, while at Fort Fraser Ernest Peters had acquired a typewriter. Their jobs were complicated by the fact that requests for payment of some accounts, especially those from the federal and provincial governments, had to be approved by the HBC commissioner in Winnipeg before being sent on for processing. Any challenges delayed payment for up to a year. Meanwhile, over the next decade all the post managers would doggedly pursue the need for the provincial and federal governments to take over responsibility for

Alexander and Mary Murray, with daughter Annie, enjoy a summer sports day at Fort St. James. BRITISH COLUMBIA ARCHIVES I-33127

improvement of services that the NWC and HBC had maintained for almost one hundred years.

Fort George

Relations between the HBC staff at Fort George and the local Carrier people remained unstable in the early years of the century, and in March 1902 clerk E.L. Kepner complained to Constable David Anderson at Quesnel that his life had been threatened by a Native man named Charles Williams. In addition, Louis Tsan, the murderer of Chinese prospector Ah Mook near Quesnel in 1901, was thought to be hiding out in the area. Using the cover of an assistant HBC clerk, special constable William McLaren joined Kepner at the fort and soon arrested Tsan. He set out for Quesnel with his prisoner in a canoe supplied by Kepner, who was the only person at Fort George who would provide one, but it was wrecked while being lined through Fort George Canyon. With considerable difficulty, McLaren managed to return upriver with his prisoner to get another canoe from the fort. This time he reached Quesnel safely, but at the fall assizes in Clinton in October 1902 Tsan was found not guilty.[355] A short time later Kepner moved to Quesnel to operate the Occidental Hotel, and by 1906 Fort George's next clerk in charge, Joseph Reid, had apparently "calmed things down considerably."[356]

In May and June 1903 Father Adrian Morice wrote a series of letters to the Indian Superintendent in Victoria protesting the wanton slaughter of beaver by white men. Many of the Sekanis and the Fort George Carrier had starved the previous winter because they had no furs to trade, and Morice enclosed a petition from the chiefs and heads of families of the Fort George band, reiterating his concerns and protesting the white man's use of poisoned bait. The petition requested that whites be forbidden to trap on Native lands and that the Natives receive "periodical annuities or rations from the Government in compensation for the furs taken from our preserves and to prevent us, our wives and children from starving to death."[357]

Besides letters from Natives and missionaries, Sidney Williams at Quesnel, the organizer of the Game Protection Society, encouraged the Cariboo District's Conservatives to demand a law protecting the beaver for a number of years in order to allow the population to recover. As a result, in January 1905 the provincial government passed an amendment to the Provincial Game Act, prohibiting the trapping of beaver for six years, effective February 1, 1905. The law applied to all residents of the province; no one was allowed to have untanned pelts in their possession during that time period.[358]

Lobbying began immediately to exempt the Carrier and Sekani because they still relied on beaver for income and food. Advocates pointed out that the law was a second assault on their traditional way of food gathering because the fishing industry had already succeeded in getting the federal government to amend the Fisheries Act to prohibit dams and weirs on tributaries of the Skeena and the Fraser.[359] Reports from W. Fleet Robertson, provincial mineralogist, and HBC manager James Thomson pressed for an amendment to the Game Act to exclude the Carrier and Sekani. Their actions were successful and an Order-in-Council on November 2, 1905, provided an exemption between November 1 and April 1 for two years for Natives living north of the junction of the Blackwater River and the Fraser between latitudes 53° and 54°. Thereafter, regular lobbying by Carrier chiefs, Indian agents, missionaries and HBC personnel managed to keep the exemption in place for all six years of the government order. However, in 1912 Premier Richard McBride and Attorney General W.J. Bowser refused any further appeals.[360]

When the closure was first introduced in 1905, Constable David Anderson requested clarification from Police Superintendent F.S. Hussey whether the Quesnel HBC store and other traders south of the Blackwater River could legally trade in furs. Hussey replied:

> I am instructed to say that inasmuch as the order in council of the 2nd of November, 1905, was passed for the benefit of the said Indians, it would appear to be contrary to the intention of the Order if these Indians were prohibited from disposing of beaver pelts to the best advantage and forbidden to trade with a dealer in skins because he happens to reside south of the Blackwater River. These dealers must be aware, and the Indians will in time understand, that the object aimed at in proclaiming a close[d] season is the preservation of the beaver, and it will be to their mutual advantage in the end to abide faithfully by the provisions of the order. It is not expected that any trader of repute will knowingly infringe the law by purchasing pelts of beaver killed south of the Blackwater River within the time limited.[361]

CONSTRUCTION OF THE SECTION of Grand Trunk Pacific Railway between Edmonton and Prince Rupert between 1906 and 1914 put immense demands on the HBC for supplies, efficient delivery and especially credit. A new trader's house complete with a picket fence had been built in 1904 at Fort George but the company was hesitant to enlarge the store (or the one at Quesnel) even though they faced increasing competition from merchants eager to get in on the new market. The Cassiar and Klondike gold excitement had completely faded by this time, and the HBC appeared reluctant to be involved so soon again in a boom or bust situation. With all the promotional activity, HBC district manager James Thomson claimed it was difficult to determine where the centre of commerce might develop. He wrote from Victoria to W.L. Collins in Quesnel in December 1908:

> I have just returned from the East after discussing affairs generally with the Commissioner and I am to point out to you that business contingent upon development in the Northwest and British Columbia is receiving the serious attention of those charged with the administration of the Company's affairs. The capital already employed or which might be invested in the future is, or will be, very large and it is a question whether adequate profit will be made on it. I note what you say in regard to instances where you have exceeded the rules and regulations, but it will be an easy matter for you to communicate with this office before committing the Company.[362]

Two years later Collins received another cautious reply to his query about prospects for business:

> Until a definite policy has been decided upon I do not feel justified in adding materially to the capital at present employed at either Quesnel or Fort George. To hold the trade it must advance with the growth of the country or retire. Experience has shown that it is not desirable for the Company to embark in mercantile business at points where only a comparatively limited volume of trade is possible . . . In the meantime it is desirable to know just what we are leading up to and for this

reason I am anxiously waiting a decision in regard to Fort George and one or two other points.[363]

When hotel keepers, packers, surveyors and labourers demanded a certain amount of credit, Thomson set $100 as a limit for known customers. Letters of credit could only be obtained through the Vancouver or Victoria HBC offices with a cash deposit. He was, therefore, not pleased when James Cowie at Fort George required power of attorney from Grand Trunk Pacific employees to ensure that their debts were paid; Thomson suspected that Cowie was advancing money and paying men's wages in situations where the company would not be reimbursed for three months. He wrote Cowie:

> If my surmise is correct, I am not prepared to authorize the continuance of such an arrangement . . . Bearing the above circumstances in mind I am therefore to ask you to rigidly adhere to the instructions concerning credit. If as a result the Company does less business, there will be infinitely less risk run.

HBC Victoria kept a close eye on outstanding debts and regularly urged store managers to collect them. In one instance at Quesnel, storekeeper Collins decided to accept a few pack horses or a barrel of port wine as final payment from steamboat captain A.D. Foster because he "thought it better to take them over than run any further chances on the account."[364]

The coming of the Grand Trunk Pacific Railway (GTP) transformed Fort George into a city within a few short years. The process was accelerated when the GTP purchased Fort George Indian Reserve No. 1 in November 1911 in exchange for building a new Native village farther up the Fraser River at Shelley. The houses on Reserve No. 1 were burned down in 1913, and the railway formally arrived on January 27, 1914. By that time the lands belonging to the fort were already surrounded by the speculative townsites of South Fort George and Fort George. A former HBC clerk, John Daniell, remembered that even the food changed at the fort. "The beaver stews that used to delight Jim Cowie and myself, the moose and bear roasts, venison and caribou joints, gave way to butcher's beef."[365]

James Cowie and a Mr. Armstrong were the last fort managers. Cowie had signed on with the company in the Shetland Islands and began his service at York Factory in 1876. He moved from Ontario to Fort George in 1907 and in addition to managing the fort he served on the school board that established the first school in South Fort George. He died there in 1913, one year after retirement. As Armstrong had a wife and family, he modernized the manager's house after he took over from Cowie in 1912. But the trading post was torn down about 1914–15, and the factor's residence was rented out to Constable W. Dunwoodie of the Provincial Police until 1916 when it burned to the ground. Meanwhile, the business district had developed too far from the site of the old fort and the land and railway boom had died down, so the HBC did not rebuild on the original site. (An HBC department store was built in the downtown area in the 1950s.) One by one, the paddlewheel steamers were taken out of service and beached at South Fort George and on the Nechako River. For many years until they were eventually demolished, children played pirates and families enjoyed Sunday picnics on their decks.[366]

The provincial government and the GTP argued back and forth over the legal name for the new town that had replaced the old fort. Provincial archivist R.E. Gosnell defended the historical name: "Fort George is one of the most historic points of the northern interior." GTP President Charles M. Hays preferred Prince George because it sounded more distinguished and matched the name of the railway's terminal city, Prince Rupert, and his opinion won out over history when Fort George became Prince George in the spring of 1914.[367] Because the name Fort George had not been used until shortly after the fort was permanently established in 1820 and John Stuart had wanted to cement good relations with the new HBC Governor, George Simpson, it seems logical that the fort was named for him and not for any other reason. However, Simpson would have approved his promotion to royal status.

Fort Fraser

During the frantic search for a clerk to fill the vacancy caused by the death of William Sinclair at Fort Fraser in the fall of 1899, Robert Hall wrote the HBC commissioner that he did not know of anyone who would accept charge of the fort at the current annual rate of £100 and board:

> Clerks at the Northern Salmon Canneries, at all of which some Indian trade is done, get as much as $75 per month and board, but these men would not accept employment at such a place as Fraser's Lake unless paid very much higher wages.[368]

However, Ernest Peters, who had been fired from his post at Fort George in 1895 in order to make way for the hiring of Charles Ogden, and who was by this time employed as a clerk with a mining company near Quesnel, expressed a desire to return to the company's service. He had served at Forts Grahame, McLeod and George, and although Hall did not think highly of his record at Fort George, the company was desperate. But Peters proved to be an energetic manager at Fort Fraser and remained there from 1901 to 1910. He married Louise Betsy Rois of Fort George and they had several children, one of whom died in June 1904 and was buried in the HBC cemetery at Fort St. James.[369]

In 1900 as a direct result of the Klondike gold rush the federal government had begun the restoration of the former Collins Telegraph line as the Dominion Government Telegraph Service (DGTS), extending it to Dawson City and Atlin. Under an agreement with the supervisor of construction, J.B. Charlson, the HBC at Fort St. James paid for local freight and labour costs, which the HBC in Victoria then recovered from the DGTS. That summer two scows manned by Carrier boatmen brought seventeen tons of copper wire from Quesnel to Fort St. James, and by the end of the year the DGTS had an outstanding debt of $7,100 on the Fort St. James account books, although initially the line did not reach to Stuart Lake—messages were sent there from Fraser Lake until a branch line to Manson Creek was installed in 1901.[370] As a result of the growth in mining, fishing and timber industries after the turn of the century, provincial revenues doubled between 1904 and 1906 to $3,250,000, and in the run-up to the election of 1907 the provincial government used this surplus to bolster its popularity, building roads, trails, schools and other public buildings.[371] Ernest Peters took advantage of this situation to circulate and present a petition for a subsidy to provide ferry service across the Nechako River near Fort Fraser. In 1906 the government granted former gold miner Vital LaForce $100 to complete the construction of a scow and buy 600 feet of wire cable to guide the scow across the river; once in operation he was allowed to collect a small toll from his passengers.[372]

The Fort Fraser journal for the years 1907 to 1910 records the exciting push to open up the country for settlement and transportation in that area. Engineers and surveyors working for the GTP passed constantly to and fro during the summer months while they laid out the route; they built a warehouse near the HBC store, and at first they ordered their provisions through the HBC. Unfortunately, when construction got underway, they changed their source of supply, leaving the HBC store overstocked and Peters' profit and loss statement badly skewed.

The Fraser Lake HBC store remained open on Sundays because it was the only day off for surveyors and GTP men. As the railway required increasingly larger amounts of provisions, more and more pack trains made the long trek from Quesnel and Hazelton to Fort Fraser. The packer Cataline with the aid of his Chinese assistant, Joe Fook, operated a mule train and a horse pack train from Hazelton where he connected with steamers on the Skeena River. Chief John at Quesnel also had a pack team, and the fort itself had two teams so that on a busy summer day up to 250 mules and horses grazed in the vicinity of the fort.

Construction of the railway made it imperative to have rapid connection with Quesnel in order to bring in freight and mail,[373] and in 1908 Peters circulated a petition for a sleigh road between Fraser Lake and Quesnel. The government agreed to provide $400 and the road was built following the telegraph line and the Blackwater trail. There was considerable criticism from residents of Quesnel, but Peters defended the work: "So far as I can make out, any proposal to open up this northern country is always opposed by the would-be politicians of Quesnel as they think it will interfere with their interests." The HBC store became a voting station for the federal election in 1908 when seven votes were cast, and in December of that year the community felt confident enough to form a settlers' association. Under Peters' leadership they petitioned for a doctor and a school.[374]

Despite all the activity Peters also maintained a large garden. In 1905 provincial mineralogist William Fleet Robertson visited Fort Fraser in late summer and took away samples of Peters' ripened oats, barley, timothy and wheat that he entered in the Dominion Exhibition in New Westminster. As a result, Peters received a diploma of merit. Two years later he harvested 5,000 pounds of turnips, 447 pounds of cabbage, 342 pounds of onions, 100 pounds of leeks, 200 pounds of beets, 660 pounds of carrots, and 16,399 pounds of potatoes. The following year he tried to improve the management of the farm by ordering a fanning mill, horse rake and disc harrow through the HBC, but the equipment was delivered with so many missing parts that the company refused to handle any more orders for agricultural machinery.[375]

Meanwhile, developers were plotting out the Fort Fraser townsite and advertising lots for sale. Speculators arrived, accessing the district via the trail from Hazelton and the Telegraph Trail, to look for possible investment land, and as a result, more surveyors were needed to map pre-emptions before prospective settlers could register their properties. All this activity was aided by the telegraph conveniently housed in the warehouse at the HBC post.

Soon Peters was overwhelmed with work and in 1908 Thomson in Victoria granted permission to hire the telegraph operator, G.W. Proctor, as a part-time assistant at $25 a month. Peters also managed to get a raise in pay for the fort's cook, Ah Chow, from $30 to $35.[376]

With people arriving from all points of the compass, the post manager had to be prepared for anything, including tragedy. When Walter Groneweg from Council Bluffs, Iowa, drowned in a rafting accident on the Nechako River, Peters hired four Carrier men to search for his body. Groneweg was buried next to William Sinclair in the Fort Fraser cemetery and the funeral account for $106.75 was paid by an Iowa relative.[377]

Another transportation milestone occurred in May 1909 when W. L. Collins, the manager of the HBC store at Quesnel, forwarded 10,000 pounds of freight on the recently launched *Nechacco* for Fraser Lake and 2,000 pounds for Fort St. James. In mid-June Captain J.H. Bonser guided the little steamer from Quesnel all the way up the Fraser and Nechako rivers to Fort Fraser. Built by the Fort George L. & N. Company, the steamer had a draft of just thirteen inches, so that even when heavily loaded, it could still reach the first or second canyon on the upper Nechako River. On this inaugural trip Bonser invited Peters and his family and a few other residents on board for a trip to the west end of Fraser Lake, returning the same evening. Soon afterwards, Bonser pioneered a second trip with the *Nechacco* as far as Tête Jaune Cache on the Fraser River, but the little steamer, renamed the *Chilco* in 1910, sank in Cottonwood Canyon the following year.[378]

For reasons that are not clear, the HBC discharged Peters after a visit by James Thomson at the end of December 1910. He moved his family to his ranch, then later to Prince George where he became a sheriff. He remained involved in the community until his death in 1933. William Bunting transferred from Quesnel to man the Fort Fraser store and remained until it was closed in 1914. In April of that year the local population turned out to celebrate the pounding of the last spike to mark the completion of the Grand

Trunk Pacific Railway, and the first passenger train bound from Edmonton to Prince Rupert passed through a few months later.

Fort Babine

The returns for Fort Babine from 1889 to 1915 ranged from a low of 349 furs in 1889 to a high of 983 in 1905. Silver fox commanded the highest tariff of $188.55 in 1899 and then for the next two decades ranged from $30 to $300, depending on the quality of the pelt. Although of the same species as the red fox (*Vulupus fulvus*), silver foxes have white guard hairs over black under-fur, which gives them a beautiful sheen, but the one in twenty odds of trapping one contributed to their allure in high fashion circles where fur muffs were in vogue, and two pelts would make a long, wide scarf. As a result, Thomson requested that all posts send their silver fox pelts to Victoria by mail as soon as acquired.

Besides fur trading, after the turn of the century Fort Babine remained a transshipment point for goods entering the north country via the Skeena River and bound for Forts St. James, Fraser, Grahame and McLeod. It was an expensive system, however, because by the time this freight reached Fort St. James, it had been handled at least six times. Furs were shipped out via the same route.[379]

Another of the advantages of the HBC having a post on Babine Lake was that salmon were available a month earlier there than at the Fraser River posts. But in 1903 Fisheries Commissioner John Pease Babcock blamed the failure of that year's Fraser River salmon run on interception by North Coast fishermen because by this time there were eleven canneries at the mouth of the Skeena and three more on the Nass. Babcock also noted that there were First Nations fishing sites on most of the lakes, and to deal with the problem, the provincial government installed hatcheries at Anderson and Babine lakes and began enforcing the laws forbidding the use of weirs and dams on the Babine River. Henceforth all fishing at lake outlets was to be done with nets. (Initially, weirs on Fraser and Stuart lakes were not affected because they were part of the Fraser River system.) This prohibition put even greater stress on Babine Lake Natives to secure adequate supplies of salmon for the winter, and the HBC posts at Babine, Fraser and Stuart lakes had to give out larger and larger quantities of provisions to starving Native families.[380] An HBC store operated at the northwest exit of Babine Lake until 1971.[381]

Fort Grahame (Bear Lake Outpost) and Fort McLeod

At Fort Grahame (the official name of Bear Lake Outpost after 1900) manager William Fox got himself in trouble with District Manager James Thomson during the Klondike gold rush by accepting mining equipment in exchange for provisions. This misstep and a few more blunders provoked Thomson to the point where he wanted to fire Fox, but it was very difficult to find a replacement for this isolated post. HBC Victoria even requested London to recruit three young men from northern Scotland for the district but there were no takers. Then they considered hiring a young clerk named H.A. Greenwood, but when he insisted on marrying Alexander Murray's sister-in-law before making the transfer, HBC superintendent Robert Hall rejected him. Greenwood resigned and left with the young lady for Wyoming.

By 1900 Fox was facing stiff competition from Telesphore Marion, who had been a successful fur trader at Quesnel for a few years and had recently extended his business to include a summer trading post at Giscome Portage. HBC Inspector Beeston wanted Marion vigorously opposed:

> I will be much pleased if Marion's fur-trading venture ends in disaster for him. It will be unwise, however, to make little of his opposition. He is a keen Indian Trader, and will quickly realise the difficulties in transportation, etc., and just as quickly remedy any mistakes he has made through ignorance.

The following year Marion caved in, accepting the HBC offer of $135 for his Fort Grahame stock and $185 for that at Finlay Forks, but he continued to prosper at Quesnel and in 1909 launched the *Quesnel*, a coal-burning steamboat.[382]

A CONSTANT THEME over almost one hundred years of management in New Caledonia was that post managers were allowing the Carrier and Sekani people too much credit or "jawbone." Almost every post manager since the time of John Stuart had been ordered to cut or eliminate the practice. Superintendent Robert Hall wrote to Alexander McNab at Fort St. James in February 1899, laying down the law:

> .There are instances where Indians cannot go hunting without some ammunition, etc., but where anything but the most trifling amounts are given on credit, security for payment should be obtained. At Hazelton debt is only given on the security of Blankets, Rifles or Gold or Silver Jewelry deposited, and there are absolutely no losses from Indian Debts there. This general principle must now govern you at all your Posts and the Indians must and will accept our terms of prompt grading. "Goods in exchange for Furs."[383]

However, any number of factors could affect a winter hunt—harsh winters, mild winters, measles, influenza, failure of the salmon run and lack of game—and post journals frequently recorded the traders' concern that some Natives would not make it through to spring. Between 1900 and 1910 a series of harsh winters compounded by lack of salmon and the provincial prohibition on beaver trapping caused considerable havoc among the Carrier and Sekani, and McNab sent the first warning to Hall in September 1900. It was a warning that was repeated almost every year for the next dozen years by Alexander Murray, who replaced McNab at Fort St. James at the end of 1901.

In 1903 C.C. Chipman, the HBC commissioner, requested comments from Murray and the clerks at Forts McLeod and Grahame about reducing debts. Clerk Thomas Hammett at McLeod

Lake wrote an impassioned three-page response urging that a reduction in credit be introduced gradually:

> Here at McLeod's Lake the Siccanies, a small band, and about the last to come in contact with civilised life, a people who retained the bow and arrow for hunting, when all around them had firearms, the Coy. is looked to with a feeling of reverence which no Government ever could be . . . the Company has lost very little by these people, unless death or sickness intervened and therefore they are entitled to all the latitude that the Company can possibly give . . . I feel that an abrupt termination of what has grown to be part of the Indian's existence would not be of any service to either, but rather hurry forward what is a sure thing in the near future, the extinction of the McLeod's Lake Indians.[384]

On receipt of Hammett's letter the commissioner wrote to Hall that "there is perhaps as much of sentiment as of interest in Mr. Hammett's letter, and sentiment in Indian trade is answerable for many an unpaid debt. It is perhaps invariably the trader that gives way to sentiment. This is not an Indian weakness." But Chipman agreed that it would be "a gross injustice" and poor business policy to stop credit suddenly. "The worst feature of the Indian debt question has been that advances have but too frequently been given beyond what the Indian has earning capacity to pay." Thomson relayed the commissioner's decision to Murray, advising that, "the way should gradually be paved" for reduction.[385] But it was the fish and game laws introduced by the provincial government in 1905 that really hampered the commissioner's long-range plan to eliminate "jawbone."

Until 1900, under an arrangement with the provincial Indian Affairs Department (IAD), the HBC had only provided assistance to widows, children and the extremely destitute, but as the need gradually increased in the next decade, the HBC seems to have made a concerted effort to shift more responsibility to the IAD.

Fortunately, whenever HBC requests for reimbursement were queried by A.W. Vowell, the superintendent of Indian Affairs for BC, they were approved by the local Indian agent, a man named Loring.

As the result of their isolation, the Sekani in the area of Forts Grahame and McLeod were most adversely affected by the 1905 province-wide ban on beaver trapping because they set out for their winter hunts before the annual amending Order-in-Council came out permitting them to hunt between November 1 and April 1. Once out on the hunt there was no way to communicate the good news to them. When in May 1908 the Department of Indian Affairs challenged an invoice for $638 that Fox submitted to Thomson in Victoria for aid to destitute Natives, Thomson wrote to Murray, requesting comments from the clerks at Forts McLeod and Grahame. Murray, replying in November, explained that it would be the end of March before he could expect to hear from Hammett and sometime in June before he could have a reply from Fox. He then continued:

> Regarding the prices for Flour, Bacon, etc., which are considered exorbitant, I might say that they are quite reasonable and the charges made are in perfect order. The people of Ottawa have no idea of the difficulties met with in transporting supplies to these distant inland Posts.
>
> Those inquiring about our charges might possibly find out right in Ottawa what it cost to ship supplies to Grahame for a contingent of the Royal North West Mounted Police which wintered there two years ago. The freight or cost handed on their supplies must have been very high, and I heard that a large portion of the Police Supplies were spoilt in transit and had to be thrown away.
>
> The clerks in this District do not care to give goods to the Indians for nothing, as we are afraid that it might tend to make them expect it all the time, and might make them stay around near the Posts.

Looking ahead, I have to say that this winter now setting in is going to be another hard one on the Indians and I am certain we will be obliged to furnish relief again to the sick and destitute this season.[386]

After consulting again with Murray, Thomson reported to the commissioner in Winnipeg:

Hitherto these Indians (who are named Siccanies) have been able to "extract" a living out of the country from the proceeds of Furs and Game. In recent years, Moose has become scarce and the introduction by the Provincial Government of a Statute prohibiting the killing of Beaver has materially restricted the natural resources. While it is quite true that largely upon the representations of the Hudson's Bay Company the Provincial Government has, during the past three years, by

One of the most important mainstays of the New Caledonia fur trade, Carrier women and children enjoy Dominion Day celebrations outside the palisaded walls of Fort St. James. The HBC fish storage house is in the background. BRITISH COLUMBIA ARCHIVES D-06397

Order-in-Council, excepted the Indians in the Northern part of British Columbia from the [restrictions] of the Act in regard to Beaver, the decision was arrived at in each year too late to be of much service, as the Indians had gone out to hunt and could not be communicated with. While at Hazelton I met parties who had come from the neighborhood of Fort Grahame and they informed me that there would be much destitution among the Indians in that section and considerable relief would have to be afforded. This report is confirmed by Mr. Murray and it would be well to advise the Department accordingly. A fairly substantial outfit has been provided for McLeod's Lake and Fort Grahame this season, as that there will be sufficient food on hand to avert starvations. I would add that I have communicated the above circumstances to Mr. A.W. Vowell, Superintendent of Indian Affairs for British Columbia.[387]

Neither the HBC nor the Department of Indian Affairs wanted the negative publicity of Native deaths from starvation.

When Premier Bowser refused to extend the exemption for Sekani and Carrier hunters after 1911, Indian Agents Loring at Hazelton and W.J. McAllan at Fraser Lake pleaded with provincial and federal Indian Affairs to get approval from the provincial government for them to trap beaver north of the GTP Railway line. This, too, was refused. (By this time Babine First Nations were also coping with the loss of their weirs and dams.) In January 1913 Father Nicolas Coccola at Hazelton received a telegram from J.D. McLean of the federal Indian Affairs Department, giving him permission to aid the most serious cases, but he was warned to be "very economical."[388]

When provincial government surveyor Frank Swannell and his crew arrived at Fort Grahame in July 1914, postmaster C. Ross—the only person on duty there at that time—was absent downriver. A number of Sekani were camped nearby, and Swannell noted in his diary, "Seven are sick, five already dead. Disease unknown,

On a cold, wintery day HBC blankets make warm capots for Frank Swannell's jolly surveying crew. They are heading home on the Telegraph Trail after working all summer near Fraser Lake. British Columbia Archives I-58387

probably largely starvation. Although they can see food on the shelves they are too honest to break in and are amazed that I dare break the flimsy lock and serve them out supplies." Swannell's field assistant, George Copely, boiled wild strawberry leaves and added maple syrup. "This cured the Indians of dysentery caused by starvation and the boiled flour gruel they had been living on.[389]

The store at Fort Grahame appears to have continued operation until 1949; on a summer canoe trip that year R.M. Patterson found the buildings extant and noted that they had only been abandoned two months previously after operating for sixty years. The site was covered by the waters of Williston Lake in the late 1960s after the W.A.C. Bennett Dam was built at Rocky Mountain Portage.[390]

The HBC store at Fort McLeod remained open until 1968.[391]

Fort St. James

The New Year's Day *regale* at Fort St. James, a century-old custom dating back to the days of the Nor'westers, did not sit well with Father Adrian Morice, and in 1900 he complained to BC

Indian Affairs superintendent A.W. Vowell that HBC personnel were giving liquor to Carrier Natives. Vowell relayed his concerns to Thomson, who wrote to McNab. Thomson accepted McNab's explanation that this was definitely not the case, but he asked that in future liquor not be given to Metis employees because it "might be misconstrued." He then went one step further and suggested cancelling any future *regales*:

> I should be personally sorry to discontinue any old time custom of this nature, but I fear it is not now possible to keep it within reasonable bounds, and it involves an expense for which there is really no return. If, therefore, it could be discontinued without loss of trade or prestige, it would be well to do so.[392]

Alexander Murray was less successful than Ernest Peters had been in gaining government grants to improve transportation corridors in his area. In 1902 he requested that James Thomson contact the provincial government for aid to improve the McLeod Lake to Fort St. James trail as it was used not only by HBC packers but also by prospectors, and no work had been done on it by the government since the Klondike gold rush. He thought $300 would be enough to replace the rotten corduroy bridges that had become so dangerous for pack animals. Thomson replied in January 1903 that the provincial government had refused assistance even though the company was one of the largest taxpayers in BC and deserved some consideration. Murray then tried for a grant to improve the Babine Portage, but this, too, was denied.[393]

During McNab's brief management of Fort St. James from 1899 to 1901, he'd had to compete with opposition practically on his doorstep because the local Carrier people had supported an independent trader named Joseph Castillion from the Nicola Valley by intermittently selling a few furs to him. When Castillion set up business on the reserve, Robert Hall contacted Indian Affairs, and local agent R.E. Loring ordered him to leave. Hall then warned

McNab not to let Castillion get a foothold, but it was about this time that Alexander Murray took over from McNab, and the wily trader built a shack on a corner of the fort's property, claiming that it was Crown land. Murray wrote to Hall for advice and even discussed the situation with the HBC commissioner while on a visit to Winnipeg.[394]

Hall responded by contacting lawyer H. Dallas Helmcken in Victoria, who recommended that Castillion be warned to leave, and if he refused, Murray was within his rights to remove his possessions and take down his shack. Murray gave Castillion two months' warning, then in June 1902 assembled a group of men to dismantle the shack. When Castillion made a move to grab a shotgun, Murray used his status as a justice of the peace to arrest him. The next day he sent Castillion to Quesnel with an escort to hand him over to HBC clerk J.C. Boyd. Before laying a charge, Boyd asked Judge Clement Francis Cornwall of Ashcroft to review the papers and the information Murray had provided. Cornwall's opinion was very important as he was not only a Cambridge graduate and a barrister of the Inner Temple, but he had served as British Columbia's lieutenant-governor from 1881 to 1886 and now sat in the Senate as a representative for British Columbia. Unfortunately, Cornwall felt there was not enough proof that Castillion was trespassing on HBC property or that he intended to use the gun on anyone, and when the case was laid before a magistrate, it was dismissed.[395]

Castillion then consulted the well-known lawyer Denis Murphy at Ashcroft to demand reparation. As the HBC was reluctant to get embroiled in court proceedings, after considerable negotiations Castillion settled for $300 and the return of his furs. He went back to Fort St. James to retrieve them in November 1902, then built another shack on land just beyond the boundaries of the fort property before leaving again for the winter.[396]

HBC personnel in Victoria continued their policy of prudence whenever minor crimes were committed at Fort St. James. In 1903 Murray wanted to exercise his position as justice of the peace to deal with a robbery. He did not think it right to refuse a hearing if someone laid a complaint, "and it is in the hope of lessening the chances of such cases of complaint that I now write the Superintendent of Police [F.S. Hussey] in this strain." He asked the HBC Manager to pass on a letter to Hussey, but Thomson refused:

> I realize certain obligations are imposed upon you as a Justice of the Peace, but as you know crimes of the nature indicated can only be summarily dealt with by a Stipendiary or Police Magistrate. It is not competent for one Justice of the Peace to try such cases. Besides, I fear it would only create trouble both for the Company and yourself with the religious orders— something that, at the present time, we must endeavour to avoid. I may say that personally I sympathize with your views and appreciate the stand you have taken.[397]

Even Judge Cornwall took a moderate view of a robbery committed by a seventeen-year-old Carrier in 1904. In this instance Murray had gone to great lengths to obtain justice, personally taking the suspect to Quesnel to lay a complaint. The Fraser River was high and the two men nearly drowned when their canoe capsized at Cottonwood Canyon. But Cornwall let the young man off, binding him over to keep the peace for two years because he had confessed, returned most of the stolen goods, and was of good character. Murray then returned with him to Fort St. James by way of the Telegraph Trail.[398]

That same year a more positive response came from Victoria after Thomson supported a petition from residents at Stuart Lake for a government school to be ready for classes at Fort St. James by the end of August 1904. Then, at the request of the Superintendent of Education, he arranged for five cases of school supplies and books to be shipped by express from Victoria without delay. He also provided a letter of introduction for the teacher, Harold B. Marchant, requesting a one-third reduction in steamer fare (the same as for missionaries), free lodging with the HBC at

Hazelton and free passage with HBC freighters from Fort Babine to Stuart Lake. Alexander Murray, James Alexander and Joseph Prince formed the new school board.[399]

When provincial librarian E.O. Scholefield passed through the Interior in 1913, gathering up historical papers, he visited Forts Fraser, George and St. James. Alexander and Mary Murray treated him to all the local delicacies: salmon and potatoes for breakfast, sturgeon for lunch, and roast bear for dinner with white currants and cream for dessert. Murray explained that all the old journals had been sent to Victoria after Father Adrian Morice had published his history of New Caledonia, but Scholefield spent a busy afternoon going through the dusty papers in the post's attic and secured a few more items for the Provincial Archives.[400]

By 1912 the Fisheries and Game Department of the provincial government was well entrenched, and a deputy game warden had even been stationed at Fort George. The department's annual report confidently noted that First Nations people now understood the Game Laws and that the fur trade of the province was worth between $300,000 and $500,000.[401] Although beaver could now only be trapped by licence, poaching was rampant, and in 1918 a second province-wide closed season was ordered. Within a few years, however, the settlers in the Nechako Valley found the beaver population had already rebounded. (Each beaver pair has two to eight kittens in the spring.) Earl S. Baity, who as a teenager, trapped with his father in the upper Mud (Chilako) River Valley to augment the family's meagre farm income, claimed, "By that spring of 1922 all the creeks, ponds, lakes and even rivers in central BC were well-stocked with beaver." When the provincial government declared an open beaver season, Baity remembered the excitement:

At that moment those same words were probably being shouted from one end of Mud River to the other—even from one corner of Central British Columbia to the other. They were being shouted from trapper to trapper, from Indian camp to Indian camp. From fur buyer to fur buyer. Telegraph keys at every station along the Yukon Telegraph Line between Ashcroft and Telegraph Creek were clicking out the same message. Messengers on horseback, messengers with dog teams were being dispatched from Prince George, from Quesnel, from Hudson's Hope, from Vanderhoof and Fort St. James to carry the tidings back to isolated trading posts and to individual fur buyers circulating among the trappers and Indians.[402]

Just as the upper Mud River Valley had nurtured beaver for Chala-oo-chick Natives a hundred years earlier, now it was producing beaver for struggling pioneer farmers needing extra income to get them through to harvest time. Province-wide, the number of beaver pelts harvested increased from a mere 527 in 1920–21 to 30,914 in 1921–22.[403]

When Vancouver journalist Lukin Johnston visited Fort St. James in the early 1920s, he stayed at the old factor's house where he was hosted by Mr. and Mrs. W.R. Fraser. Later he wrote:

> The peaceful beauty of the place and the historic atmosphere which surrounded one there made me oblivious of the absence of hot and cold running water and electric light . . . In a country so new as British Columbia, one seldom thinks of ghosts of the past, but in my old room, with the solid square chimney which passed up through the centre of it, casting weird shadows across the floor, one might perhaps be forgiven for pondering on the great figures of British Columbia's romantic past who made history on this very ground.

During his three-day visit Johnston spent "a fascinating evening" with Alexander Murray and one morning witnessed a fur-buying session between Carrier Natives and traders. He also admired the Native women's skill in cutting narrow snowshoe lacing from caribou hides. After viewing furs worth thousands of dollars he concluded that Fort St. James was still "one of the chief fur-buying centres of all British Columbia."[404]

Although he retired from the company in 1913, Alexander Murray, dressed in his Scottish tam and fur trade clothes, was present in September 1928 when the local community celebrated the centennial of George Simpson's visit to Fort St. James. Locals portrayed Archibald McDonald and James Douglas, young Carrier men toted baled provisions through the gates, and Charles H. French, once a lowly clerk-in-charge at Fort Babine but now fur trade commissioner at Winnipeg, addressed the crowd as Governor Simpson. The ceremony has since been criticized as reinforcing the patriarchal attitude towards First Nations people, but photographs taken at the time suggest that it was an enjoyable occasion for everyone.[405]

After the trade store at Fort St. James was destroyed by fire in 1919, it was rebuilt at a new location near the highway. The HBC

At the 100th Anniversary celebrations of Governor George Simpson's visit to Fort St. James in September 1928, Chief Charles Martin and a group of Nak'azdli men greet HBC Commissioner Charles H. French (formerly a clerk at Fort Babine) who is acting the role of Simpson. GLENBOW ARCHIVES NA 3164-358

subdivided the post property in the 1940s and '50s but continued to use the warehouse for storage until 1953. Although so much of British Columbia's fur-trading history took place in isolated, rural areas of the province where a sparse population had little time or finances to preserve their heritage in later years, the Fort St. James Historical Society was able to care for the warehouse, fish cache and men's house there until the federal government acquired the buildings in the 1960s. Under Parks Canada, Fort St. James was eventually restored to what it had looked like during Alexander C. Murray's first period of administration in the 1890s, although it lacks the bustle of earlier times. There are no berry-picking forays to Tache in late August, no Chief Qua demanding greater satisfaction for his furs, and no clamour of brigades arriving and departing. Fortunately, the Parks Canada Master Plan for Fort St. James seeks to address this disparity.[406]

THE NEW CALEDONIA FORTS

Fort McLeod (Trout Lake Post, Fort Simpson)

Simon Fraser, James McDougall, and interpreter La Malice (Paul Bouché) established Fort McLeod at the foot of McLeod (Trout) Lake in the fall of 1805 and named it for Fraser's superior at Dunvegan, Archibald Norman McLeod. Until 1821 it was used as a final collection point for furs shipped to Fort William and between 1821 and 1826 to York Factory. For its first two decades this fort was also the major distribution centre for provisions brought from the east each fall by the incoming brigade.

Because the fort was located in the Arctic watershed, there were no salmon in the lakes and rivers, and the residents relied primarily on dried salmon brought overland from Forts St. James, Fraser and Babine and on game supplied by the local Sekani people. The poor food and near-starvation existence at times generated its nickname of "Fort Misery."

In the fall of 1823 the original buildings were washed into the Pack River, and chief trader John Stuart, who rebuilt the store and dwelling house, renamed the site Fort Simpson, presumably after Governor George Simpson. This name lasted only a few years before reverting to Fort McLeod.

Fort McLeod was abandoned in 1885 but reopened in 1889. By 1895 most of the buildings had to be replaced. The HBC acquired a Crown grant of ninety-nine acres surrounding the fort in 1899. When the Hart Highway was built in 1953, the store was moved across the lake to be more accessible, and it was not closed until January 31, 1968.[407]

Fort St. James (*Nak'azdli*)

Fort St. James was named Stuart Lake Post when it was established in July 1806 by Simon Fraser and John Stuart close to several Carrier villages and the outlet of Nak'azdli (Sturgeon, Stuart) Lake. The original post lasted for fifteen years before James McDougall erected a new fort with bastion and stockade near the old site. It was called Fort St. James after 1821, but the source of the name is uncertain. Donald Manson replaced the buildings between 1848–1852, and they lasted until 1889–1890 when Roderick MacFarlane, assisted by A.C. Murray and William Traill, rebuilt most of the structures. In 1899 the 212-acre Crown grant for this site consisted of two parcels of land, one of which included the fort site of one hundred acres. In 1919 the store burned down and was replaced by a larger building on a nearby site.[408]

The chief trader at Fort St. James supervised satellite posts at Forts Fraser, Alexandria, Babine, Connolly, George, Chilcotin, McLeod, and Grahame (Bear Lake Outpost). Short-term outposts were also built at Chala-oo-chick, Manson Creek, Stoney Creek, Kluskus and Giscome Portage.

The Fort St. James Historical Society took over the care of the remaining buildings until it was declared a national historic site in 1948. Although title transferred to the Government of Canada in 1952, Parks Canada did not commence restoration of the fort until 1972, and it was formally opened to the public in 1977. Considerable archaeological work has been carried out by Parks Canada and published as Manuscript Reports Nos. 77 and 228. Historian Jamie Morton produced a study for the Canadian Park

Service in 1988 entitled *Fort St. James 1806–1914: A Century of Fur Trade on Stuart Lake.*

Fort Fraser (*Natleh*)

Simon Fraser established Fort Fraser at the outlet of Fraser Lake in September 1806 because the annual salmon run to Stuart Lake had failed and his men faced starvation. The fort's main purpose after that was to supply salmon in the lean years to Forts St. James, McLeod and George. Fur trading was also important here as the region to the south and west of Fraser Lake was rich in beaver.

Fort Fraser gained more importance when it was linked to Quesnel by the Telegraph Trail in 1865. Packers, cattle drovers and gold miners heading to the Omineca region were frequent customers during the summer months. The HBC closed the fort as a cost-cutting measure in 1883 but it reopened the following year. In 1900 the HBC received a Crown grant of one hundred acres around the site of the fort.[409]

In the early 1900s construction of the Grand Trunk Pacific Railway attracted land speculators, surveyors and prospective settlers, all of whom required services from the HBC store. A telegraph line from Quesnel went into operation just before 1900. The fort was closed in April 1914 shortly after the formal ceremony there connecting the east-west rails of the Grand Trunk Pacific.

Fort Thompson (Kamloops)

In early 1812 David Stuart and Alexander Ross of John Jacob Astor's Pacific Fur Company established a fort at the junction of the North and South Thompson rivers. This was the farthest extension of the company's fur-trading efforts from their base at Fort Astoria at the mouth of the Columbia River. In November of the same year Joseph Larocque of the North West Company built a fort at the northeast junction of the river, but a year later, after the two companies amalgamated, the first fort was abandoned and

Larocque's fort was used thereafter, supervised by the Columbia River headquarters.

The area did not produce a large number of furs, but once the New Caledonia fur brigade was firmly established in 1826, the fort became an important stopping place on the journey overland from Fort Alexandria to Fort Okanagan. Potatoes grew well in the hot, dry climate, and dried salmon were readily traded at Native sites on the Thompson and Fraser rivers. Of greatest importance was the large horse-rearing program here, which provided stock for the brigade and replenished Fort Alexandria's herd when it did not survive a harsh winter.[410] When Donald Manson spent the winter of 1841–42 at the fort, he found the buildings in dilapidated shape and set about constructing new ones on the west side of the North Thompson River. The old fort was subsequently abandoned and the new one was named Fort Kamloops. In 1848 when the New Caledonia brigade switched to the route through the Cascade Mountains to Fort Langley, Fort Kamloops became more important as a depot. A few years later while Donald McLean was in charge there, he obtained some of the earliest gold samples from the Fraser River, igniting the Fraser River and Cariboo gold rushes of 1858 and 1859. At the request of Victoria, McLean supervised two temporary outposts, Fort Berens, built opposite present-day Lillooet, and Fort Dallas, built near the mouth of the Nicomen River, to take advantage of the influx of prospectors. These forts were closed within a year because they weren't profitable.

Fort Kamloops was moved to the south bank of the Thompson River in 1862. With the arrival of the Canadian Pacific Railway in 1886, the old buildings were abandoned for a series of stores closer to the townsite, where the HBC's business continued until 1956.[411]

Fort George (*Lheidli*)

In 1807 Hugh Faries supervised a small, temporary outpost at Lheidli at the forks of the Nechako and Fraser rivers; the following year it served as a canoe-building site and supply base to launch Simon Fraser's party on their epic voyage of discovery to the Pacific Ocean, but it was abandoned shortly after Fraser returned safely with his men that August. In October 1820 George McDougall established a trading post at the forks, and the following spring John Stuart ordered James Murray Yale to move anything portable from the outpost of Chala-oo-chick at the mouth of the Chilako (Mud) River to the rejuvenated site at Lheidli and the post was renamed Fort George. Furs came from the Chilako River and Kluskus areas to the southwest as well as from Natives to the north and east. Jesuit priest John Nobili visited the fort four times between 1845–47, consecrating the cemetery and raising a large cross in the centre of the Native village adjacent to the fort.

In August 1823 Carrier Natives murdered two HBC employees while trader James Murray Yale was absent; in April 1824 Stuart closed the fort as a retaliatory measure. It was not reopened until after Governor George Simpson's visit to New Caledonia in 1828. After Simpson encouraged the forts to become self-reliant, John McLean introduced farming in 1836. Archibald McKinlay reported to James Hargrave in 1838 that the goal to supply the district with flour had failed because frost killed the wheat, but potatoes, turnips and common vegetables grew well. The fort also tended a herd of fifteen cattle, including five milk cows.[412]

The one-hundred-acre fort site was Crown granted to the HBC in 1900, but the fort was dismantled in 1914–15. The manager's house burned down in 1916, and the property was sold by 1939.

Fort Alexandria (*Stella-yeh*)

On orders from John Stuart, Fort Alexandria was built by George McDougall in the fall of 1821 at the site where Hugh Faries had stored his canoes and transferred to horses on his 1820 trip to the Columbia River. It was named in honour of Alexander Mackenzie as it also marks the farthest point of exploration on his 1793 expedition. Pleasantly located on a bench above flood level on the east side of the Fraser, the new fort's main purpose was to serve as a terminus for the Columbia River–New Caledonia brigade system as navigation below this point on the river was too hazardous. Large meadows provided ample pasture for wintering the brigade horses and good soil made it suitable for agricultural purposes. Samuel Black's map, prepared in the 1830s, indicates Native trails leading east from Fort Alexandria to an abundance of beaver sites and to marmot habitat in the Siffleur (whistling marmot) Mountains. To the west lay the Chilcotin Plateau, which was also considered a prime location for furs, so in order to be more accessible to Chilcotin trappers, the fort was moved to the west side of the Fraser in 1836. A small flour mill was installed and agriculture flourished. To accommodate gold seekers during the Cariboo gold rush (1859–1865), new buildings, including a restaurant, were built on the east side of the Fraser River, at the original site of the fort. When the store closed in 1866, two new HBC outlets were opened in Quesnel and Barkerville. W.P. Trounce managed the Alexandria farm from July to December 1867 for $50 per month plus board; he was followed by Archibald McKinlay in 1868.

At 3,400 acres, Fort Alexandria was the largest HBC site in New Caledonia. The HBC executed a quit claim on the site in 1895, and John S. Twan acquired a Crown grant of 109.5 acres on the original fort site. Twan razed the buildings in 1922. Across the Fraser River, the 400-acre Hudson's Bay Meadows was acquired privately via another Crown grant in 1902.[413]

Fort Babine (*Kilmaurs*)

William Brown established Fort Kilmaurs in 1822 at the point between the two northerly arms of Babine Lake to prevent furs being traded to middlemen from the Pacific Coast, especially the Russians operating in Alaska. One of the advantages of the Babine post was that salmon arrived there via the Skeena River system in July, a month ahead of the Fraser River runs.

Beginning with the Omineca gold rush, Fort Kilmaurs supervised an outpost at the northern outlet of the lake where Fort Babine was built in the 1880s. Fort Kilmaurs was then abandoned and its site became known as Old Fort. The HBC was Crown granted ninety-nine acres at Fort Babine in 1899, and the fort remained open until 1971.[414]

Fort Connolly

On orders from chief factor William Connolly, James Douglas established this small outpost on Bear Lake, north of Takla Lake, in the winter of 1826–27 to trade furs with the Sekani people. Living conditions were harsh for HBC clerks at this post as they received only small supplies of dried salmon and were expected to secure their own fish from the lake to survive the winter. The fort was operated intermittently, closed entirely during the 1880s, reopened briefly, then permanently closed in 1891. Apparently no Crown grant was issued for the land surrounding it.

Fort Chilcotin

Governor George Simpson wanted Fort Chilcotin established soon after the merger of the NWC and the HBC to prevent furs being traded on the Pacific Coast. However, ongoing skirmishes between the Chilcotin and Shuswap people prevented George McDougall at Fort Alexandria from building a temporary post there until October 1829. It was situated one hundred miles west of Fort Alexandria near the junction of the Chilcotin and Chilanko rivers and near the crossroads of several Native trails. It was abandoned in 1844 in favour of a post farther north at Kluskus on the Blackwater River.

Fort Grahame/Bear Lake Outpost

Fort Grahame was established in 1867 and named for James A. Grahame, sub-commissioner of the HBC. Located approximately sixty miles north of the junction of the Peace and Finlay rivers, it was one of the most isolated posts trading with the Sekani people. When Alexander Murray rebuilt the post in 1880 he renamed it Bear Lake Outpost, but at the request of the HBC commissioner the name reverted to Fort Grahame in 1900. Its site is now beneath the waters of Lake Williston.

Quesnel

The HBC opened a store in Quesnel following the closure of Fort Alexandria in 1866. Located near the bank of the Fraser River and the steamer terminal, this depot transshipped provisions to the northern forts and to Barkerville, sixty miles to the east, where a sub-store operated from 1867 to 1882. HBC headquarters in Victoria threatened to close the Quesnel store in the 1890s, but it remained open until 1919.

Appendix 2

NATIVE LANGUAGES IN
BRITISH COLUMBIA

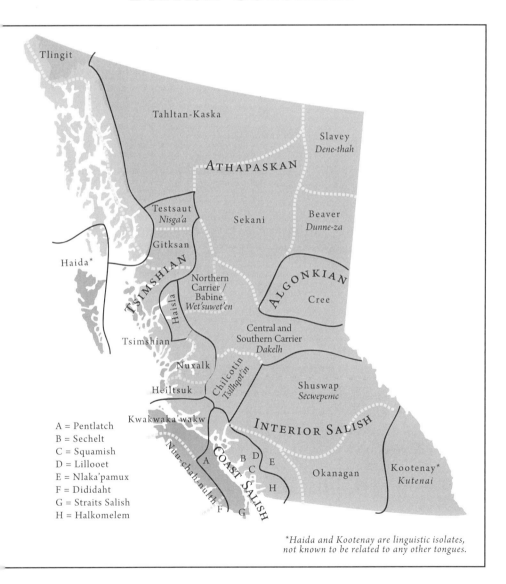

Tlingit

Tahltan-Kaska

Slavey
Dene-thah

ATHAPASKAN

Testsaut
Nisga'a

Sekani

Beaver
Dunne-za

Gitksan

Haida*

ALGONKIAN

Northern
Carrier /
Babine
Wet'suwet'en

Cree

TSIMSHIAN

Haisla

Central and
Southern Carrier
Dakelh

Tsimshian

Nuxalk

Heiltsuk

Chilcotin
Tsilhqot'in

Shuswap
Secwepemc

Kwakwaka'wakw

INTERIOR SALISH

A = Pentlatch
B = Sechelt
C = Squamish
D = Lillooet
E = Nlaka'pamux
F = Dididaht
G = Straits Salish
H = Halkomelem

Nuu-chah-nulth

COAST SALISH

A
B
C
D
E
H

F
G

Okanagan

Kootenay*
Kutenai

*Haida and Kootenay are linguistic isolates,
not known to be related to any other tongues.*

FRENCH-CANADIAN DEFINITIONS

apachemons—saddle blankets made from hides of buffalo or other large animals

au facon du pay—"in the fashion of the country." Used to describe the union of a fur trader and a native or Metis woman

babiche—rawhide lacing used for snowshoes and tying fur bundles

boute—boatman
    avant—the boatman who paddled at the rear
    governail—the steersman at the front
    milieux—the boatman in the middle

barder—dried salmon resembling a board or shingle and tough to eat. Possibly derived from *ça bard*, "it's tough going," and from *bardeau*, "shingle"

batteaux—lightweight boats similar to the York boat, made of lapped cedar strips, that were easily portaged. Used west of the Rockies, mainly on the Columbia, but there were a few on the Fraser and Stuart/Nechako rivers

canot du maître—the largest freight canoe used by the North West Company and the Hudson's Bay Company, capable of travelling over rough bodies of water such as the Great Lakes and the rapids of large rivers. They were up to forty feet in length and six feet wide, and carried up to four tons. They carried a crew of eight to ten men

canot du nord—canoe used west of the Rockies. Twenty-five feet long, four and a half feet wide, and carried 3,000 pounds

échelons—(Stuart uses "echantillions") likely means the ribs of the canoe

en derouine—leaving the fort to trade furs at native villages

engagé—paid labourers and boatmen of the NWC or HBC

livre—a French coin in circulation in Lower Canada in the early nineteenth century, probably worth 11 pence. Coin expert Wayne Jacobs believes they disappeared from circulation some time before 1842

parfleche—provision wrappings made from hides

pièce—bales of furs weighing eighty to ninety pounds

portage—a connecting land link between two important rivers or lakes over which canoes and goods were transported

raquet—snowshoes

regale—rejoicing, pleasure, merry-making

siffleux—whistling marmots that were trapped for their fur

traineaux—dogsleds that were used for moving provisions during the winter. Each dog team could pull 300 pounds on one of these sleds

varveaux—conical fish baskets that were set into a weir to catch salmon

BIBLIOGRAPHY

ARSI—Archivum Romanum Societatis Iesu, Rome
BCA—British Columbia Archives
HBCA—Hudson's Bay Company Archives, Archives of Manitoba
HBR—Hudson's Bay Record Service

Adams, John. *Old Square-Toes and His Lady, The Life of James and Amelia Douglas.* Victoria: Horsdal & Schubart, 2001.

Baity, Earl S. *I Remember Chilako*. Prince George: Prince George Printers Ltd., 1974.

Barker, Burt Brown, ed. *Letters of Dr. John McLoughlin Written at Fort Vancouver 1829–1832.* Portland, OR: Binfords & Mort, 1948.

Balf, Mary. *Kamloops: A History of the District up to 1914.* Kamloops: Thompson Valley Museum and Historical Society, n.d.

Belyk, Robert C. *John Tod, Rebel in the Ranks.* Victoria: Horsdal & Schubart, 1995.

Bishop, Charles A. "Kwah: A Carrier Chief." In *Old Trails and New Directions: Papers of the Third North American Fur Trade Conference.* Eds. Carol M. Judd and Arthur J. Ray. Toronto: University of Toronto Press, 1978.

Bowes, Gordon E, ed. *Peace River Chronicles*. Vancouver: Prescott Publishing, 1963.

British Columbia. *Our Native People.* Series 1. British Columbia Heritage Series. Victoria: Queens Printer, n.d.

Brown, Jennifer S.H. *Strangers in Blood*. Vancouver: UBC Press, 1980.

Burley, David V., Scott Hamilton and Knut R. Fladmark. *Prophecy of the Swan: The Upper Peace River Fur Trade of 1794–1823*. Vancouver: UBC Press, 1996.

Butler, William Francis. *The Wild North Land*. New York: Allerton Book Co., 1922.

Cline, Gloria Griffen. *Peter Skene Ogden and the Hudson's Bay Company*. Norman, Oklahoma: University of Oklahoma Press, 1974.

Cole, Douglas and Bradley Lockner, eds. *The Journals of George M. Dawson: British Columbia, 1875–1878*. Vol. I and Vol. II. Vancouver: UBC Press, 1989.

Cole, Jean Murray. *This Blessed Wilderness: Archibald McDonald's Letters from the Columbia, 1822–44*. Vancouver: UBC Press, 2001.

Christensen, Bev. *Prince George: Rivers, Railways, and Timber*. Windsor Publications, 1989.

Coues, Elliott, ed. *The Manuscript Journals of Alexander Henry and of David Thompson 1799–1814*. Minneapolis: Ross & Haines, 1897. (Reprint 1965)

Cox, Ross. *The Columbia River*. Edited by Edgar I. Stewart and Jane R. Stewart. Norman: The University of Oklahoma Press, 1957.

Cree, Muriel R. "Three Simpson Letters, 1815–1820." *BC Historical Quarterly*, Vol. 1, 1937, pp. 116, 120–121.

Cullen, Mary. "Outfitting New Caledonia." In *Old Trails and New Directions: Papers of the Third North American Fur Trade Conference*. Eds. Carol M. Judd and Arthur J. Ray. Toronto: University of Toronto Press, 1978.

De Aguayo, Anna. "Breaking the Competition: early Nineteenth-Century Fur Trade and Fort Kilmaurs." In *Papers of the Rupert's Land Colloquium 1994*. Winnipeg: Rupert's Land Research Centre, 1994.

Downs, Art. *Paddlewheels on the Frontier*. Sidney: Gray's Publishing Ltd., 1972.

Elliott, Gordon R. *Quesnel: Commercial Centre of the Cariboo Gold Rush*. Quesnel: Cariboo Historical Society, 1958.

Elliott, Marie. *Gold and Grand Dreams*. Victoria: Horsdal & Schubart Publishers Ltd., 2000.

_____. "Mission to New Caledonia, 1845–1848, The Letters of Father John Nobili, S.J." Unpublished manuscript.

_____. "Robert Borland," *Dictionary of Canadian Biography, 1920–29*.

Fleming, R. Harvey, ed. *Minutes of Council, Northern Department of Rupert Land, 1821–31*. London: Champlain Society for HBRS, 1940. [HBRS 3]

Forbes, Milly. *Lac La Hache*. Quesnel: Big Country Printers, n.d.

Forsythe, Mark and Greg Dickson. *The Trails of 1858*. Madeira Park: Harbour Publishing, 2007.

Friends of the Fort St. James National Historic Site Society. *A Walk Through Time*. Fort St. James: Friends of the Fort St. James National Historic Site Society, 2006.

Furniss, Elizabeth. *Changing Ways: Southern Carrier History, 1793–1940*. Quesnel: Quesnel School District (#28), 1993.

Gates, Charles M., ed. *Five Fur Traders of the Northwest.* Toronto: The Ryerson Press, 1933.

Gibson, James R. *The Lifeline of the Oregon Country: The Fraser-Columbia Brigade System, 1811–47.* Vancouver: UBC Press, 1997.

Glazebrook, G.P. De T., ed. *The Hargrave Correspondence 1821–1843.* Toronto: The Champlain Society, 1938.

Grant, J.C. Bolleau. *Bulletin No. 81: Anthropometry of the Beaver, Sekani and Carrier Indians.* Ottawa: Dept. of Mines, 1936.

Greene, Ronald. "'C' Battery and the Skeena Incident." In *British Columbia History*, Vol. 40, 1, pp. 2–6.

Hall, Lizette. *The Carrier, My People.* Cloverdale: Friesen Printers, 1992.

Hammond, Lorne Foster. *"Any Ordinary Degree of System," The Columbia Department of the Hudson's Bay Company and the Harvesting of Wildlife, 1825–1849.* Master of Arts Thesis, University of Victoria, 1988.

Harris, Cole. *The Resettlement of British Columbia.* Vancouver: UBC Press, 1997.

Harris, Donald A. *Manuscript Report Number 228: The Archaeological Excavations at the Site of Fort St. James, British Columbia, 1972.* Ottawa: Parks Canada, 1974.

Harris, Douglas. *Fish, Law and Colonialism.* Toronto: University of Toronto Press, 2001.

Harris, R.C., H.R. Hatfield and Peter Tassie. *The Okanagan Brigade Trail in the South Okanagan 1811 to 1849.* Vancouver: Wayside Press, 1989.

Harris, R.C. and H.R. Hatfield. *Old Pack Trails in the Proposed Cascade Wilderness.* Vancouver: The Okanagan Similkameen Parks Society, 1978.

Hayes, Derek. *First Crossing: Alexander Mackenzie, His Expedition Across North America, and the Opening of the Continent.* Vancouver: Douglas & McIntyre, 2001.

Holmgren, Eric J. *"Fort Dunvegan and the Fur Trade on the Upper Peace River" In Rendezvous: Selected Papers of the Fourth North American Fur Trade Conference, 1981.* Ed. Thomas C. Buckley. St. Paul, Minn. The North American Fur Trade Conference, 1984.

Innis, Harold A. *The Fur Trade in Canada.* Toronto: University of Toronto Press, 1973 (reprint).

Johnston, Lukin. *Beyond the Rockies.* Toronto: J.M. Dent & Sons Limited.

Kerr, D.G.G., ed., *A Historical Atlas of Canada.* Toronto: Thomas Nelson & Sons (Canada) Limited, 1961.

Klippenstein, Frieda. "Constructing Reality: An Example from the Fur Trade at Fort St. James, 1929." Paper, Fifth Biennial Rupert's Land Colloquium, Winnipeg, February 1992.

Laing, F.W. "Hudson's Bay Lands on the Mainland." *BCHQ*, Vol. 3, 1939, pp. 96–97.

Lamb, W. Kaye, ed. *The Letters and Journals of Simon Fraser 1806–1808.* Toronto: Macmillan, 1957.

_____, "Alexander Caulfield Anderson," DCB, XI.

_____, ed. *Sixteen Years in the Indian Country: The Journal of Daniel William Harmon 1800–1816.* Toronto: Macmillan, 1957.

Large, R. Geddes. *The Skeena, River of Destiny.* Vancouver: Mitchell Press, 1958.

Leonard, Frank. *A Thousand Blunders.* Vancouver: UBC Press, 1996.

_____, "Grand Trunk Pacific and the Establishent of the City of Prince George, 1911-1915," *BC Studies* LXIII, p. 32.

L'Heureux, Audrey Smedley. *From Trail to Rail.* Vanderhoof: Northern BC Book Publishing, 1990.

Lower, J. Arthur. *Western Canada: An Outline History.* Vancouver: Douglas & McIntyre, 1983.

Lugrin, N. de Bertrand. *The Pioneer Women of Vancouver Island 1843–1866.* John Hosie, ed. Victoria: The Women's Canadian Club of Victoria, Vancouver Island, 1928.

MacGregor, J.G. *John Rowand, Czar of the Prairies.* Saskatoon: Western Producer Prairie Books, 1978.

Mackie, Richard. *Trading Beyond the Mountains.* Vancouver: UBC Press, 1997.

MacLeod, Margaret A., ed. *The Letters of Letita Hargrave.* Toronto: Champlain Society, XXVIII (1947).

McKelvie, B.A. *Fort Langley, Outpost of Empire.* Toronto: Thomas Nelson and Sons, 1957.

_____. *Tales of Conflict.* Vancouver: The *Vancouver Daily Province*, 1949.

McLeod, Malcolm. *Peace River: A Canoe Voyage from Hudson's Bay to Pacific.* Ottawa: J. Durie & Son, 1872.

Merk, Frederick, ed. *Fur Trade and Empire, George Simpson's Journal.* Cambridge, Mass. The Belknap Press of Harvard University Press, 1968.

Milliken, A.C. "*Jean Caux—The man they called "Cataline."* In *Canada West Magazine*, Vol. 3.4 (Winter 1971)

Morice, Adrian Gabriel. *The History of the Northern Interior of British Columbia.* Smithers: Interior Stationery (1900) Ltd., 1978. Reprint.

Morse, Eric W. *Fur Trade Canoe Routes of Canada, Then and Now.* Toronto: University of Toronto Press, 1979.

Morton, Arthur S. *A History of the Canadian West to 1870–71.* Thomas Nelson and Sons, 1939.

Mulhall, David. *Will to Power: The Missionary Career of Father Morice.* Vancouver: UBC Press, 1986.

Munro, K. Douglas. *Fur Trade Letters of Willie Traill 1864–1894.* Edmonton: University of Alberta Press, 2006.

Munro, W.T. and Murray Fyfe. *Preliminary Beaver Management Plan for British Columbia.* Victoria: Ministry of Environment, 1979.

Nak'azdli Elders Society. *Nak'azdli t'enne Yahulduk; Nak'azdli Elders Speak.* Penticton: Theytus Books, 2001.

Neering, Rosemary. *Continental Dash: The Russian-American Telegraph.* Ganges: Horsdal & Schubart Publishers, 1989.

Nicks, Trudy. "The Iroquois and the Fur Trade in Western Canada." In *Old Trails and New Directions: Papers of the Third North American Fur Trade Conference.* Eds. Carol M. Judd and Arthur J. Ray. Toronto: University of Toronto Press 1978.

Ogden, Peter Skene. *Traits of American Indian Life & Character by a Fur Trader.* San Francisco: The Grabhorn Press, 1933.

O'Neill, Wiggs. *Steamboat Days on the Skeena River.* Kitimat: Northern Sentinel Press, 1961.

Ormsby, Margaret. *British Columbia: a History.* Toronto: The Macmillan in Canada, 1958.

Patterson, R.M. *Finlay's River.* New York: William Morrow & Company, Inc., 1968.

Parks Canada. *Fort St. James Management Plan.* Ottawa: Canada, 2002.

Quackenbush, William. " Tastes of Canadians and Dogs: The History and Archaeology of McLeod's Lake Post, British Columbia, GfRs–2. M.A. thesis, Department of Archaeology, Simon Fraser University, Burnaby.

Prince George Free Press, "Paddlewheel Playgrounds," September 23, 2001, p. B3.

Ramsey, Bruce and Dan Murray. *The Big Dam Country.* North Vancouver: In Focus Publications, 1969.

Rich, E.E., ed. *Colin Robertson's Correspondence Book, Sept. 1817 to Sept. 1822.* London: Champlain Society for HBRS, 1939. [HBRS 2].

_____, ed. *Journal of A Voyage From Rocky Mountain Portage in Peace River To the Sources of Finlays Branch And North West Ward in Summer 1824.* London: HBRS, 1955. [HBRS 18].

_____, ed. *Journal of Occurrences in the Athabaska Department by George Simpson, 1820 and 1821, And Report.* London: Champlain Society for HBRS, 1938. [HBRS 1].

_____, ed. *The Letters of John McLoughlin from Fort Vancouver to the Governor and Committee, Second Series, 1839–44.* London: HBRS, 1943 [HBRS 6].

_____, ed. *London Correspondence Inward from Eden Colvile, 1849–1852.* London: HBRS, 1956 [HBRS 19].

Robin, Martin. *The Rush for Spoils.* Toronto: McClelland and Stewart Limited, 1972.

Rothenburger, Mel. *The Chilcotin War.* Langley: Mr. Paperback, 1978.

_____. *We've Killed Johnny Usher!* Vancouver: Mitchell Press, 1973.

Sherwood, Ja. *Surveying Northern British Columbia, A Photojournal of Frank Swannell.* Prince George: Caitlin Press Inc., 2004.

Stangoe, Irene. Cariboo-Chilcotin, Pioneer Places and People. Surrey: Heritage House Publishing Company, 1994.

Stump, Violet and Stump, Sharon. *The People of Alexandria.* Quesnel: Spartan Printing & Advertising Ltd., n.d.

Swannell, F.S. "Ninety Years Later," The Beaver, Spring 1956, p. 33.

Tanner, Ogden. *The Canadians.* Alexandria, Va.: Time-Life Books, 1977.

Van Kirk, Sylvia. "Many Tender Ties," Women in Fur-Trade Society, 1670–1870. Winnipeg: Watson & Dwyer Publishing Ltd., 1980.

_____. "Fur Trade Social History: Some Recent Trends." In *Old Trails and New Directions: Papers of the Third North American Fur Trade Conference.* Eds. Carol M. Judd and Arthur J. Ray. Toronto: University of Toronto Press, 1978.

Walker, Russell R. *Bacon, Beans 'N Brave Hearts.* Lillooet: Lillooet Publishers Ltd., 1972.

Wallace, J.N. *The Wintering Partners on Peace River.* Ottawa: Thorburn and Abbott, 1929.

Wallace, W. Stewart, ed. *Documents Relating to the North West Company.* Toronto: The Champlain Society, 1934.

Wallace, W.S. *John McLean's Notes of a Twenty-Five Year's Service in the Hudson's Bay Territory.* Toronto: Champlain Society, 1932.

Whitehead, Margaret. *The Cariboo Mission, A History of the Oblates.* Victoria: Sono Nis Press, 1981.

_____, ed. *They Call Me Father: Memoirs of Father Nicolas Coccola.* Vancouver: UBC Press, 1988.

Williams, Glyndwr. *Hudson's Bay Miscellany.* Winnipeg: Hudson's Bay Record Society, 1975. [HBRS 30].

Wolfenden, Madge. "John Tod: "Career of a Scotch Boy." *BCHQ* XVIII (July–Oct. 1954)

Wright, Richard and Wright, Rochelle. *Canoe Routes in British Columbia.* Vancouver: Douglas & McIntyre, 1980.

NOTES

Introduction

1. *A Walk Through Time*, Friends of the Fort St. James National Historic Site Society (Fort St. James, undated), p. 21; Bob Harris, Harley Hatfield, Peter Tassie, *The Okanagan Brigade Trail in the South Okanagan* (Vancouver: Privately published, 1989).

2. A.G. Morice, *The History of the Northern Interior of British Columbia* (Smithers, BC: Interior Stationery, 1978, first published 1904); Victoria *Times Colonist*, November 24, 2007.

3. Mary Cullen, "Outfitting New Caledonia 1821–58," *Old Trails and New Directions*, Carol M. Judd and Arthur J. Ray. eds, (Toronto: University of Toronto Press, 1978), pp. 231–251.

4. "Surrey cracks down on beaver population," *Vancouver Sun*, June 14, 2008, p. A3.

Chapter One: "What cannot be cured must be endured."

5. Burley, David, J. Scott Hamilton, and Knut R. Fladmark. *Prophecy of the Swan: The Upper Peace River Fur Trade of 1794–1823* (Vancouver, UBC Press, 1996), p. 50.

6. W. Stewart Wallace, ed., *Documents Relating to the North West Company* (Toronto: The Champlain Society, 1934), p. 199.

7. Ibid, p. 60; Joyce and Peter McCart, *On the Road with David Thompson* (Calgary: Fifth House Ltd., 2000), p. 246.

8. HBCA, B.119/a/3, f. 50.

9. Lizette Hall, *The Carrier, My People*. (Cloverdale: Friesen Printers, 1992), p. 63.

10. J.N. Wallace, *The Wintering Partners on Peace River* (Ottawa: Thorburn and Abbott, 1929), p.69.

11. HBCA, B.188/d/ f. 12.

12. W. Kaye Lamb, ed. *Sixteen Years in the Indian Country: The Journal of Daniel Williams Harmon, 1800–1816* (Toronto: The Macmillan Company of Canada Limited 1957), p. 55.

13. John Nobili to Father General Roothan, December 1845. Archivum Romanum Societatis Iesu, Rome, Missio ad Montes Saxosos [Rocky Mountain Mission Correspondence], Volume 1, Section VI; HBCA, D.5/16, f. 467.

14. HBCA, B.119//a/1, f. 17; Burley, et al., *Prophecy*, p. 65.

15. W. Kaye Lamb, ed. *The Letters and Journals of Simon Fraser, 1806–1808* (Toronto: The Macmillan Company of Canada Limited, reprint 1966), p16–17.

16. Ibid., p. 16, 181–182, 184.

17. "Ancient words link Siberia, Canada," *Vancouver Sun*, April 3, 2008, p. A11. Western Washington University professor Edward Vajda discovered that the few remaining speakers of the Ket language, living in Russia's Yenisei River region, "use almost identical words for canoe and such component parts as prow and cross-piece."

18. Lamb, *Letters and Journals*, p. 19; Hall, *The Carrier*, p. 46.

19. Lamb, *Letters and Journals*, pp. 21–22.

20. Ibid., p. 21.

21. Ibid., p. 22.

22. Ibid., p. 82.

23. Ibid., p. 233.

24. Ibid., pp. 234–255.

25. Wallace, *Documents*, p. 262; Lamb, *Letters and Journals*, p. 248. Fraser also acquired a rash that he called "come riddle, come raddle," the name for the Scottish shepherd's practice of marking mated ewes with red paint. *British Columbia Historical News*, Vol. 33, No. 2.

26. Jennifer Brown, *Strangers in Blood* (Vancouver: UBC Press, 1980), pp. 96–98; Wallace, *Documents*, p. 262.

27. HBC, B.188/b/3, f. 49.

28. Wilson Duff, *The Impact of the White Man*, Vol. 1, The Indian History of British Columbia (Province of BC, Victoria, 1987), p. 60; Grant, *Anthropometry*, pp. 2–3; A.G. Morice, *The History of the Northern Interior of British Columbia*, notes that even at the turn of the century, ". . . hardly a summer now passes without some parties of the Western Denes running home with the intelligence that bodies of Beaver Indians are lurking in the woods, evidently bent on slaughter." p. 30.

29. Lamb, *Sixteen Years*, pp. 143–145, p. 190.

Chapter Two: The Tacouche Tess
30. HBCA, B.119/e1, f. 458.

31. HBCA B.119/a/3, f. 39.

32. Lamb, *Letters and Journals*, pp. 76–77.

33. Ibid., p. 87, 94.

34. Ibid., p. 109.

35. "Simon Fraser's Latitudes, 1808," by Nick Doe, *BCHN*, Vol. 33, No. 2, pp. 2–4.

36. Lamb, *Letters and Journals*, pp. 44, 47, 51.

37. HBRS X, pp. 25–26.

38. HBCA, B.188/b/1.

39. Lamb, *Sixteen Years*, p. 122, 124.

40. Ibid., p. 40, 59.

41. Ibid., pp. 127–133.

42. Ibid., pp. 134–136.

43. Ibid., p. 136.

44. Peter Deslauriers, "Jules-Maurice Quesnel," *Dictionary of Canadian Biography*, VII.

45. Lamb, *Sixteen Years*, pp. 165–166.

Chapter Three: The Price of Advancement

46. Ibid., p. 155; Wallace, ed., *Documents*, pp. 271–272.

47. Lamb, *Sixteen Years*, p. 159.

48. Richard Mackie, *Trading Beyond the Mountains* (Vancouver: UBC Press, 1997), p. 17.

49. Elliott Coues, ed., *The Manuscript Journals of Alexander Henry and of David Thompson, 1799–1814* (Minneapolis: Ross & Haines, Inc, 1965 reprint), p. 784, 830.

50. H. Lloyd Keith, "The North West Company's 'Adventure to the Columbia': A Reassessment of Financial Failure," *Paper of the Rupert's Land Symposium*.

51. Lamb, *Sixteen Years*, pp. 171–72.

52. Ross Cox. *The Columbia River,* Edgar J. Stewart and Jane R. Stewart, eds. (Norman: University of Oklahoma Press, 1957), p. 217.

53. Lamb, *Sixteen Years*, p. 185.

54. Ibid., p. 186; HBRS XXX, p. 219; X, p. 450.

55. Lamb, *Sixteen Years*, p. 195.

Chapter Four: The Invasion

56. Arthur S. Morton, *A History of the Canadian West to 1870–71* (London: Thomas Nelson & Sons. Ltd., 1939), p. 531.

57. Ibid., p. 532.

58. Gloria Griffin Cline, *Peter Skene Ogden and the Hudson's Bay Company* (Norman, Oklahoma: University of Oklahoma Press, 1974), pp. 13–25.

59. HBRS I, pp. 46–47, 123–4, 320.

60. HBRS II, p. 214.

61. Ibid., pp. 261–262.

62. HBRS I, p. 134.

63. Muriel R. Cree, "Three Simpson Letters, 1815–1820," *BCHQ,* Vol. 1, 1937, pp. 116, 120–212.

64. HBRS I, pp. 388–389.

65. Ibid., p. 391.

66. Lamb, *Sixteen Years*, p. 193.

67. HBRS I, p. 391.

68. Ibid., p. 392.

69. Ibid.

70. Ibid., p. 338.

Chapter Five: Defending New Caledonia

71. HBCA, B.188/a/1, f. 6–7.

72. Calverley, D. Samuel Black: the Unknown Explorer of the Finlay River, City of Dawson Creek Collection.

73. HBCA, B.188/a/1, f. 10, 13, 21.

74. Elliott, *Quesnel*, p. 137.

75. HBC I, p. 94; HBCA, B.188/a/1, f. 27, 34; Wallace, *Wintering Partners,* pp. 112–113.

76. HBCA B.188/a/1, f. 27.

77. Ibid, f. 33.

78. HBCA, B.188/a/1, 34–35.

79. Ibid.

80. HBCA B.188/a/1, f. 41.

81. Faries was made a chief trader after coalition, served in the Athabasca and Kenogamissie Districts, and was promoted to chief factor in 1838. He retired from service in 1840. Wallace, *Documents,* p. 439.

82. HBCA, B.188/a/1, f. 49.

83. HBCA, B.188/a/1, f. 28, 50, 53, 56.

84. Wallace, ed., *Documents*, pp. 28–29.

85. HBRS III, p. 301.

86. Ibid., pp. 304–05.

87. "Chala-oo-chick" by Yvonne Klan, *BCHN,* Vol. 38, No. 2, pp. 19–20; HBCA B.188/d/3.

88. HBRS III, pp. 302–03.

89. HBCA, AM E.24/1, f. 68–68d, Fort St. James Private Records (MF Reel 4M129).

90. HBCA, B.11/a/1, f. 33.

91. HBRS III, p. 17; Anna de Aguayo, "Breaking The Competition: Early Nineteenth-Century Fur Trade and Fort Kilmaurs," *Papers of the Rupert's Land Colloquium, 1994*, p. 86.

92. HBCA, B.11/a/1, f. 17.

93. de Aguayo, "Breaking the Competition," pp. 92–93.

94. HBCA, E.24/1, letter 20.

95. HBRS I, pp. 227–228.

96. HBCA, B.11/a/1, unpaginated last pages.

97. HBRS III, pp. 172–173.

Chapter Six: "The Blood of My Children"

98. HBCA, B.188/d/2, Fort St. James Accounts, 1821–37.

99. HBCA, B.188/a/2, f. 32.

100. HBCA, B.188/a/2, Letter 73; HBRS III, p. 27, 59.

101. HBCA, B.119/a/2, f. 70.

102. Malcolm McLeod, *Peace River: A Canoe Voyage from Hudson's Bay to Pacific, by the Late Sir George Simpson (Governor, Hon. Hudson's Bay Company) in 1828 Journal of the Late Chief Factor Archibald McDonald (Hon. Hudson's Bay Company) who Accompanied Him.* (Ottawa: J. Davie & Son, 1872), pp. 17–18.

103. Burley, et al, *Prophecy*, pp. 128–130.

104. HBCA, B.119/b/1, f. 64.

105. Ibid., f. 100.

106. HBCA, B.119/a/3. f. 60.

107. HBCA, B.119/b/1, f. 36.

108. Ibid., f. 37.

109. HBCA, B.5/a/1; "That Old Rogue, the Iroquois Tête Jaune" by Yvonne Meares Klan, *BCHN* Vol. 34, No. 1, p. 19.

110. HBCA, B.119/a/1, f. 48

111. HBCA, B.188/a/2, letter 22.

112. HBCA, E.24/1, f. 71.

113. Ibid., f. 73.

114. HBCA, B.188/a/2, f. 53.

115. Burley, et al., *Prophecy,* pp. 180–181; HBCA, B.119/a/3, f. 99.

116. *Prophecy,* p. 136.

117. Frederick Merk, ed. *Fur Trade and Empire: George Simpson's Journal, 1824–25* (Cambridge: Harvard University Press, 1968), p. 209.

118. HBCA, B.188/a/2, f. 113.

119. HBCA, B.188/a/2, f. 114–115.

120. HBCA, B.188/a/2, f. 117.

121. HBCA, D.5/1, f. 146.

122. HBRS III, p. 107.

123. HBCA, B.119/e/1, f. 457.

124. HBCA, E.36, Diary of Alexander Grant Dallas, p. 20.

125. Margaret Arnett Macleod, ed., *The Letters of Letitia Hargrave*, Champlain Society Publication XXVIII (Toronto: The Champlain Society, 1947), pp. 20–21, 30.

Chapter Seven: William Connolly

126. Merk, *Fur Trade and Empire*, p. 47. John S. Galbraith, "Sir George Simpson," DCB, VIII.

127. Ibid., pp. 122–123.

128. HBCA, B.188/a/3, f. 1.

129. HBCA, D.5/1, f. 137.

130. Merk, *Fur Trade and Empire*, p. 152, fn. 200.

131. HBCA, B.11/b/1, f. 13–14, Fort Kilmaurs Journal, letter No. 12, Connolly to Brown, May 11, 1825.

132. HBCA D.4/90, as noted in Lorne Foster Hammond, University of Victoria Masters Thesis 1985, "Any Ordinary Degree of System"; the Columbia Department of the Hudson's Bay Company and the Harvesting of Wildlife, 1825–1849," p. 71.

133. "Any Ordinary Degree of System," Lorne F. Hammond, MA Thesis, 1985, University of Victoria, p. 92, 94.

134. Merk, *Fur Trade and Empire*, pp. 36–37.

135. Fanny died December 28, 1843, and at a large funeral ceremony she was buried in the family vault at Pinchi. HBCA B.188/a/20, f. 99, 101.

136. HBCA, D.5/1, f. 165.

137. Ibid.

138. HBCA, D.5/3, f. 313.

139. HBCA, D.5/3, f. 315.

140. Morton, *History of the Canadian West*, p. 719.

141. HBCR X, pp. 17–18.

142. The following year McGillivray and family temporarily replaced John Tod at McLeod Lake. Mrs. McGillivray, her infant son, an Indian child and John Tod's daughter Machoodzay were involved in a canoe accident. Only Tod's daughter survived, because she could swim. William and *engagé* Pierre Eraire drowned while crossing on the Fraser River ice, January 31, 1832. HBCA. B.188/a/15, f. 39; HBCA.B.188/a/17, f. 38; HBCR X, p. 260.

143. Malcolm McLeod, ed. *Peace River, a Canoe Voyage from Hudson's Bay to Pacific by the Late Sir George Simpson*. (Ottawa: J. Durie & Son, 1872), p. 17.

144. W.S. Wallace, ed. *John McLean's Notes of a Twenty-Five Year's Service in the Hudson's Bay Territory*. (Toronto: The Champlain Society, 1932), p. 164; Hall, *The Carrier*, p. 65.

145. HBRS X, p. 48, fn.1.

146. HBCA B.188/a/12, f. 82–83.

147. HBCA B.188/a/12, f. 94–95.

148. Jean Murray Cole, *This Blessed Wilderness: Archibald McDonald's Letters from the Columbia, 1822–44* (Vancouver: UBC Press, 2001), p. 49.

149. HBRS XXX, p. 182.

150. HBRS X, pp.17–25.

151. Ibid., pp. 28–29.

152. Ibid., p. 39.

153. Ibid., p. 40, fn. 2.

154. Ibid., p. 44.

155. Nicky Brink and Stephen R. Bown, *Forgotten Highways* (Calgary: Brindle & Glass Publishing, 2007), pp. 67–87.

156. Silvia Van Kirk, *Many Tender Ties,* (Winnipeg: Watson & Dwyer Publishing Ltd, 1980), p. 187.

157. HBRS X, pp. 237–238; HBCA, D.4/122, fos. 27–30d.

158. HBRS X, 240, 243; B.188/d/2.

159. HBCA B.188/d/14.

160. HBRS IV, pp. 32–33.

161. Add. MSS 2718, Letter 218, George McDougall to John McLeod, March 8, 1828, BCA.

162. J.G. MacGregor, *John Rowand, Czar of the Prairies* (Saskatoon: Western Producer Prairie Books, 1978) p. 83, 88–89; Barker, Burt Brown, *Letters of Dr. John McLoughlin*, p. 87; Cole, *This Blessed Wilderness*, p. 76. Margaret Harriott married John Rowand, Jr., January 1848, and her widowed father married Nancy Rowand, Margaret's sister-in-law. See Van Kirk, *Many Tender Ties*, cover illustration of Margaret, and p. 1(a), 98, 158.

163. HBRS III, p. 288.

164. Wallace, *Documents*, p. 167; Cole, *This Blessed Wilderness*, p. 256; HBCA, D.4/44.

165. Van Kirk, *Many Tender Ties*, pp. 188–89.

166. Ibid., pp. 240–41.

Chapter Eight: Peter Warren Dease and Peter Skene Ogden

167. William R. Sampson, *"Peter Warren Dease,"* DCB. IX.

168. HBRS IV, p. 230; James R. Gibson, *The Lifeline of Oregon Country* (Vancouver: UBC Press, 1997), pp. 66–67, 169.

169. Merk, *Fur Trade and Empire*, p. 331.

170. HBRS IV, 111.

171. M.L. Tyrwhitt-Drake, "David Douglas," DCB VI.

172. A.G. Harvey, "David Douglas in British Columbia," *British Columbia Historical Quarterly*, IV, No. 4, p. 229.

173. Ibid., p. 231.

174. Ibid., p. 253.

175. Ibid., p. 239. Douglas set out from Fort Vancouver in October 1833 to return to England via the Sandwich Islands. While hiking across the mountains in Hawaii he fell into a wild cattle pit and was found dead.

176. HBCA B.188/a/18, f. 9.

177. McLean, *Notes*, p. 147.

178. Edward Ermatinger Correspondence, Add MSS 2716, letter 83, BCA.

179. William R. Sampson, "Peter Warren Dease," DCB IX

180. Van Kirk, *Many Tender Ties*, p. 140.

181. T.C. Elliott, *Peter Skene Ogden: Fur Trader* (Portland: The Ivy Press, 1910), p. 17.

182. D.A. McGregor, "Old Whitehead—Peter Skene Ogden," Vol. XVII. *BC Historical Quarterly*, p. 195.

183. Ogden, Peter Skene. *Ogden's Snake Country 1824–26*, ed. E.E. Rich (London: Hudson's Bay Record Society, 1950) Vol. XIII; *Ogden's Snake Country Journals 1826–27*, ed. Frederick Merk. (London: Hudson's Bay Record Society, 1961) Vol. XXIII; *Ogden's Snake Country Journals 1827–28 and 1828–29*, ed. Glyndwr Williams. (London: Hudson's Bay Record Society, 1971) Vol. XXVIII.

184. HBRS XXX, p. 193.

185. Cline, *Ogden*, p. 127.

186. HBRS XXX, p. 216.

187. W.S. Wallace, ed., *John McLean's Notes of a Twenty-Five Year's Service in the Hudson's Bay Territory* (Toronto: The Champlain Society, 1932), pp. 167–68.

188. HBCA, D.5/7, fos. 4a–6a.

189. Judith Hudson Beattie and Helen M. Buss, *Undelivered Letters to Hudson's Bay Company Men on the Northwest Coast of America, 1830–57* (Vancouver: UBC Press, 2003, pp. 315–319.

190. HBCA, D.5/5, f. 49; D.5/4, f. 322.

191. Walter N. Sage, "Peter Skene Ogden's Notes on Western Caledonia," BCHQ 1 (January 1917), pp. 47–48.

192. HBCA, D.5/6, f. 27; B.188/a/19, f. 5,18.

193. Ibid., f. 4, 5, 41.

194. HBCA, D.5/6, f. 43.

195. HBRS XXIX, p. xi; HBCA, D.5/5, f. 118.

196. HBRS XVIII, pp. xcii-xciii.

197. Sage, *"Ogden's Notes."* p. 55.

198. HBCA, D.5/6, f. 28.

199. HBCA, D.5/6, f. 295.

200. HBCRS XXIX, p. 30, 54.

201. Ibid., p. 90.

202. BCA A/B/20/K1Za.

203. HBCA D.5/6, f. 27; HBRS IV, pp. 214–215.

204. W. Kaye Lamb, "Alexander Caulfield Anderson," DCB XI; HBCA B.188/a/19, f. 103.

205. Sage, "Ogden's Notes," pp. 45–56.

206. Ibid., p. 49.

207. Ibid., p. 53.

208. Ibid., p. 50.

209. Cline, *Ogden*, pp. 143–149, 156.

210. Ibid., pp. 186–196.

211. Molly Forbes. *Lac La Hache, Historical Notes on the Early Settlers.* (Quesnel: Big Country Printers Limited), n.p.

Chapter Nine: Donald Manson

212. HBRS XVIII, p. 227–228, 229, 231; *WHQ*, XVII, p. 271.

213. HBCA, D.4/35, f. 81.

214. Ibid.

215. HBCA, D.4/35, f. 32, f. 110.

216. Nobili correspondence, Mo. Sax. Vol. 1. VI, 4 (a), ARSI; Marie Elliott, "Mission to New Caledonia," unpublished manuscript, pp. 2–92; HBCA, D.5/16, f. 467.

217. HBRS IV, p. 173. McLoughlin was reluctant to give land to HBC men at first.

218. Nobili correspondence, Mo. Sax. Vol. 1, 4 (a), ARSI.

219. Ibid.

220. Ibid.

221. Ibid.

222. Ibid.

223. Ibid., Elliott, "Mission to New Caledonia," pp. 92–162.

224. Ibid.

225. Ibid., pp. 190–203.

226. Ibid.

227. HBCA, D.5/27, f. 358.

228. HBCA, D.5/21, f. 201.

229. Ibid, f. 202.

230. Ibid.

231. HBC XIX, p. 2, fn. 1.

232. Ibid., p. 2, and HBCA B.188/a/20, f. 48.

233. HBCA, D.4/39, f. 192.

234. HBCA, D.5/6, f. 45.

235. HBCA, D.5/24, f. 275.

236. R.C. Harris and H.R. Hatfield. *Old Pack Trails in the Proposed Cascade Wilderness*. Okanagan Similkameen Parks Society, n.d.

237. HBCA, D.4/39, f. 121.

238. HBCA, D.5/24, f. 365.

239. Lorne Foster Hammond, *"Any Ordinary Degree of System,"* pp. 64–66, 97.

240. HBRS XIX, pp. 4–5.

241. Ibid., p. 2, 215.

242. Ibid., p. 215, 234.

243. HBRS XXIX, p. 111.

244. HBCA, D4/45, f. 2.

245. HBCA, D.4/43, f. 225.

246. Ibid., p. 194; D.4/40, f. 188.

247. HBCA, D.5/36, f. 323.

248. Ibid., f. 324.

249. Ibid., f. 323.

250. HBCA, B.188/c/1, f. 2.

251. HBCA, D.5/36, f. 320.

252. HBCA, D.5/41, 108.

253. HBCA, D.5/37, f. 328.

254. BCA, Add MSS 182, Yale Family Papers 1820–1928.

255. HBRS XXXII, p.195n.

256. HBCA, B.223/b/42, f. 168.

257. H.S. Lyman, "Reminiscences: Mrs. Anna Tremewan," *Oregon Historical Quarterly,* IV, p. 264; HBRS XVIII, pp. 238–39.

258. H.S. Lyman, "Reminiscences," *OHQ,* IV, pp. 261–4.

259. *Champoeg Times,* Vol. 6, 3, pp. 2–3; "Reminiscences," *OHQ,* IV, p. 264.

Chapter Ten: The Gold Rush Years

260. Margaret A. Ormsby, *British Columbia: a History* (Vancouver: The Macmillans in Canada, 1958) p. 150.

261. Ibid., p. 150; Hamar Foster, *Times-Colonist,* February 6, 2008, p. A11.

262. Ormsby, *British Columbia,* pp. 150–151.

263. *The British Colonist,* December 23, 1862, p. 3.

264. BCA Colonial Correspondence, F1421/8.

265. HBCA, B.188/c/1, f. 1.

266. HBCA, B.5/d/c, f. 83.

267. HBCA, B.226/c/2, f. 357.

268. HBCA, A/E/OR3/B77.21; Edward Sleigh Hewlett, "The Chilcotin Uprising of 1864," *BC Studies* 19, pp. 70–71.

269. BCA, Colonial Correspondence, F390; GR 218, Vol. 188; HBCA B.171/c/1, f. 256; Irene Stangoe, *Cariboo-Chilcotin; Pioneer Places and People* (Surrey: Heritage House Publishing Company Ltd., 1994) pp. 55–56.

270. HBCA, B.5/c/6, f. 61; B.5/d/2. f. 83.

271. Rosemary Neering, *Continental Dash* (Ganges: Horsdal & Schubart Publishers Ltd., 1989) pp. 53–57.

272. HBCA, B.226/c/2, f. 361–378.

273. Neering, *Continental Dash,* pp. 126–131, 196–197.

274. HBCA AM, Biographical Records; *Colonist,* November 28, 1877, p. 3; British Columbia Sessional Papers, 1880, Lillooet District Voters List, p. 129.

275. British Columbia *Sessional Papers,* 1885. Daughter Maggie married James Todd of Kamloops in 1896 and daughter Elisabeth married John Rae Hamilton of Lac La Hache in 1887. BCA, Vital Statistics.

276. HBCA, B.171/c/1, f. 242.

277. HBCA, AM B.171/c/1, f. 242.

278. Ibid., f. 36. 118.

279. HBCA B.226/c/2, f. 406.

280. HBCA B.171/c.l/f. 49. Trounce had leased Fort Alexandria from 1867 to 1868. HBCA, B.171/c.1/f. 396; B.226/c/2, f. 407.

281. Richard Mackie, "James Allan Grahame," DCB XIII.

282. HBCA, B.171/c/1, f.104; B.226/c/2, f. 410.

283. HBCA, B.171/c/1, f. 104.

284. HBCA, B.171/c/1, f. 118.

285. HBCA, B.226/c/2, f. 458.

286. HBCA, B.171/c/2, f. 23; Mackie, "James Allan Grahame," DCB XIII.

Chapter Eleven: The Company in Slow Decline

287. BCA, GR1304, Box 77, Probate Papers for Peter and Peter Skene Ogden; Cline, *Peter Skene Ogden*, pp. 216–217.

288. Cline, *Ogden*, p. 217.

289. HBCA, B.188/c/1, f. 6; B.171/c/2, f. 109, 116.

290. HBCA, B.171/c/2, f. 20.

291. HBCA, B.171/c/2, f. 5.

292. Art Downs, *Paddlewheels on the Frontier* (Surrey: Foremost Publishing Co. Ltd., 1967). pp. 48–49; Elliott, *Barkerville*, pp. 126–127, 128; Audrey Smedley-L'Heureaux, *From Trail to Rail* (Vanderhoof: Northern BC Book Publishing, 1990), pp. 40–41.

293. HBCA, B.171/c/2, f. 25; L'Heureaux, *From Trail to Rail*, p. 48.

294. Charles George Horetzky, *Some startling facts relating to the Canadian Pacific Railway and the north-west lands* (Ottawa, 1880), pp. 22, 25, 48, 80–94; W.A. Walker Charles George Horetzky, DCB.

295. William Francis Butler, *The Wild North Land* (New York: Allerton Book Co., 1922), pp. 270, 334–335.

296. George M. Dawson, *The Journals of George M. Dawson: British Columbia, 1875–1878*, Vol. 1, eds. Douglas Cole and Bradley Lockner (Vancouver, UBC Press, 1989) pp. 99–101.

297. Ibid., pp. 272–276.

298. Ibid., p. 253, 276.

299. Forbes, *Lac La Hache*, pp. 7–9. Some of Peter Ogden's children were: Peter Skene, Margaret, Isaac, Mary, Christine, Charlie, Henry, Sarah and Rachel Sarah. Phristine died in 1899 at age 72. BCA, Vital Statistics.

300. British Columbia, *Sessional Papers,* Department of Mines Report, p. 244.

301. David Mulhall, *Will to Power: the Missionary Career of Father Morice* (Vancouver: UBC Press, 1986), p. 16, 35.

302. HBCA, B.188/e/6, f. 2.

303. HBCA Bibliography; R. Geddes Large, *The Skeena, River of Destiny* (Vancouver: Mitchell Press Limited, 1958), p.117; BCA Vital Statistics files.

304. BCA, Vital Statistics Marriage Registration. Fort Grahame was likely first established and operated briefly during J.A. Grahame's term of office at Quesnel, 1868–69. Bear Lake Outpost, built by A.C. Murray, had reverted to the name Fort Grahame by 1913 when Frank Swannell photographed it while surveying the Finlay River. Jay Sherwood, *Surveying Northern British Columbia* (Prince George: Caitlin Press Inc., 2004), pp. 116–117. HBC post records under Bear Lake show that Fort Grahame was closed on May 31, 1949, and Fort Ware

on May 31, 1953 (as noted in HBRS VIII, p. xxvii, f2). It may have been operated sporadically.

305. HBCA, B.188/e/6, f. 1.

306. National Archives of Canada, R7344-O-X-E; Biography/Administrative History for MacFarlane posted on NAC website 2007; Letter from Roderick MacFarlane to David Laird, December 24, 1880, posted on NAC website, Ref. No. MG29, A11, vol.1, pp. 808–809.

307. HBCA, B.226/a/3.

308. HBCA, B.280/e/1.

309. HBCA, B.226/e/6.

310. Ibid.

311. Lynne Stonier-Newman, *Policing a Pioneer Province* (Madeira Park: Harbour Publishing, 1991), pp. 62–63; Ronald Greene, "'C' Battery and the Skeena Incident," *British Columbia History*, Vol. 40, 1, pp. 2–6.

312. HBC, B.226/e/6.

Chapter Twelve: The Depression Years of the 1890s

313. K. Douglas Munro, *Fur Trade Letters of Willie Traill, 1864–1894* (Edmonton: University of Alberta Press, 2006), p. 251.

314. Mulhall, *Will to Power*, pp. 80–81, 133.

315. BCA, A/D20/S2k.

316. Munro, *Fur Trade Letters*, pp. 291–292.

317. Marie Elliott, "Robert Borland," DCB 1920–1929.

318. Munro, *Fur Trade Letters*, pp. 300–301.

319. Downs, *Paddlewheels on the Frontier*, p. 50.

320. HBCA, B.171/b/4, f. 485; B.181/b/6, f. 256.

321. BCA, A/D20, Vi3.

322. BCA, A/D20, Vi3.

323. BCA, A/D20, F86.

324. *The Autumn and Winter Catalogue, 1910–1911, of the Hudson's Bay Company* (Winnipeg: Saults & Pollard Limited, 1977).

325. BCA, A/D40AC3.

326. HBCA Post Mark: C.7; HBCA Biography for William Ware.

327. HBCA, B.119/a/10, f. 15.

328. HBCA, Ibid.

329. HBCA, B.249/a/2, f. 12.

330. BCA, A/D20/B38.

331. HBCA, B.226/b/533/S, File 1, 237; Patterson, *Finlay's River*, pp. 88–92.

332. HBCA, B.226/b/533/T, 7475.

333. *Finlay's River*, pp. 93–95.

334. BCA, GR55, Box 8.

335. Ibid.

336. Ibid.

337. Ibid.

338. Marie Elliott, *Gold and Grand Dreams* (Victoria: Horsdal & Schubart, 2000), p. 144.

339. HBCA, B.280/e/1.

340. HBCA, B.171/b/4, f. 472.

341. Ibid., f. 666, 674.

342. Ibid., f. 847; B.226/b/53.2.

343. HBCA, B.188/a/22–23.

344. BCA, AD20/Vi3, Hall to Murray, December, 1894.

345. HBCA, B.188/e/6–11, p. 396.

346. HBCA, B.226/b/53.2/f. 232.

347. "William Sinclair," Dictionary of Canadian Biography, Volume IX; *British Colonist*, November 26, 1899, p. 5, and December 3, 1899, p. 5.

348. HBCA, B.226/b/53.3/a, f. 161.

349. Ibid., f. 1458.

350. HBCA, B.226/b/53.3/S 2971.

351. Ibid.

352. HBCA. B. 226/b/53.3/5, File 1, 2755.

353. HBCA, B.188c/11.

354. HBCA, B.188.c.

Chapter Thirteen: The New Century

355. BCA GR 429, Box 9, File 3, 3180.

356. "Old Days at Fort George," John B. Daniell, *The Beaver*; BCA GR429, 775/02, 833/02; 1047/02.

357. BCA GR429, 1940/03.

358. "Plea for the Beaver," *Colonist*, February 5, 1904, p. 4.

359. Douglas Harris, *Fish, Law and Colonialism* (Toronto: University of Toronto Press, 2001), p. 74.

360. "Relief Measure for the Indians," *Colonist*, November 2, 1905, p. 7; PAC, RG 10, Volume 6735, File 420–3; *British Columbia Gazette*, February 2, 1905, and January 11, 1906.

361. HBCA, B.226b, 53.2c/f, file 1.

362. HBCA, B.226b, 53.2/a, file 2.

363. Ibid.

364. Ibid., file 3.

365. Frank Leonard, "Grand Trunk Pacific and the Establishment of the City of Prince George, 1911–1915" *BC Studies* LXIII, p. 32; Russell W. Walker, *Bacon, Beans 'N Brave Hearts* (Lillooet: Lillooet Publishers Ltd., 1972), p. 14; John B. Daniell, "Old Days at Fort George," *The Beaver*, Autumn 1957, p. 41.

366. *Prince George Free Press*, "Paddlewheel Playgrounds," September 23, 2001, p. B3.

367. Walker, *Bacon*, p. 110; Leonard, "Grand Trunk Pacific," pp. 33–37.

368. HBCA, B.226/b/533.3/S, File 2, 207, 233.

369. HBCA Biography for E.S. Peters.

370. HBCA, B.226/b/53.2/f. 232.

371. Martin Robin, *The Rush for Spoils* (Toronto: McClelland and Stewart Limited, 1972), p. 99.

372. HBCA, B.226./b/53.3/W, 9064, 13717.

373. Mike Nash, *Exploring Prince George* (Surrey: Rocky Mountain Books, 2004), p. 201.

374. HBCA, B.226/b/53.3/W, 11708.

375. *BC Sessional Papers 1905*, p. J105; B.226/b/53.3/G, 8477; B.226/b/53.3/U, 12651, 12663, 12669, 12779, 16033.

376. Jay Sherwood, *Surveying Northern British Columbia* (Prince George, Caitlin Press Inc.), pp. 18–19, 26–27; HBCA, B.226/b/53.2/S 10469.

377. HBCA, B.226/b/53.3/G, 12411.

378. Art Downs, *Paddlewheels on the Frontier*, pp. 49–5, 13368.; HBCA, B.226/53.3/b/T, 1347, 13368.

379. HBCA, B.226/b/53.3/f. 73.

380. *BC Sessional Papers 1903/04*, Fisheries Commissioner Report, F11.

381. HBCA, B.11/a/7.

382. HBCA, B.188/b/10, f. 352; B.226/b/53.3/T, 4933, 20; *A Tribute to the Past* (Quesnel: Spartan Printing and Advertising, 1985), pp. 99–101; *Paddlewheels*, p. 50, 55.

383. HBC, B226/b/53.3/a/201.

384. HBCA, B.226/b/53.3/U, 998, 8413.

385. Ibid.

386. HBCA, B.226/b/53.3/U, 12793.

387. HBCA, B.226/b/53.3/U.

388. PAC, RG 10, Volume 6735, file 420–3.

389. F.S. Swannell, "Ninety Years Later," *The Beaver*, Spring 1956, p. 33.

390. Patterson, *Finlay's River*, p. 124.

391. HBCA, B.188/b/11.

392. HBCA, B.226/b/53.3/U, 3196, 4818.

393. HBCA, B.226/b/53.3/U, 4895.

394. HBCA, B.226/b/53.3/U, 1487, 708, 4444, 4512.

395. Ibid.

396. HBCA, B.226/b/53.3/U, 4894.

397. HBCA, B.226/b/53.3/U, 5119, 7478.

398. Ibid., 6952, 6958.

399. HBCA, B.226/b/53.3/U,6019, 6410; Sessional Papers, 1907.

400. BCA, Add MSS 491, E.O. Scholefield Papers.

401. *BC Sessional Papers 1912*, Provincial Game Warden's Report, p. J9.

402. Baity, *I Remember Chilako*, p. 168.

403. W.T. Munro and Murray Fyfe, *Preliminary Beaver Management Plan for British Columbia* (Victoria: Ministry of Environment, 1979), p. 12.

404. Lukin Johnston, *Beyond the Rockies* (Toronto: J.M. Dent & Sons Limited), pp. 117–119.

405. Frieda Klippenstein, "Constructing Reality: An Example from the Fur Trade at Fort St. James, 1929," paper presented at the Fifth Biennial Rupert's Land Colloquium, Winnipeg, February 1992.

406. Parks Canada, *Fort St James Management Plan* (Ottawa: Parks Canada, 2002).

Appendix I: The New Caledonia Forts

407. F.W. Laing, "Hudson's Bay Lands on the Mainland," *BCHQ* Vol. 3, pp. 96–97; HBCA, McLeod Lake File; Map of McLeod Lake, CM A1260, BCA.

408. Laing, "Hudson's Bay Lands," *BCHQ*, Vol. 3, pp. 96–97; Donald A. Harris, *Manuscript Report Number 228: The Archaeological Excavations at the Site of Fort St. James, British Columbia, 1972* (Ottawa: Parks Canada, 1974), pp. 45, 120–121; Canada, *Fort St. James National Historic Site of Canada Management Plan* (Ottawa: Parks Canada, 2002), p. 2.

409. Laing, "Hudson's Bay Lands," *BCHQ*, Vol. 3, 1939, p. 36.

410. Jean Murray Cole, ed., *This Blessed Wilderness* (Vancouver: UBC Press, 2001), p. 31.

411. Mary Balf, *Kamloops, A History of the District up to 1914* (Kamloops: Kamloops Museum, 1969), pp. 7–17.

412. G.P. De T. Glazebrook ed., *The Hargrave Correspondence, 1821–1843* (Toronto: Champlain Society, XXIV 1938), p. 276.

413. Laing, "Hudson's Bay Lands," *BCHQ*, Vol. 3, 1939, pp. 96–97.

414. L.R. McGill, "Fort St. James Once Hudson's Bay Centre," *Province*, June 12, 1927; Laing, "Hudson's Bay Lands," *BCHQ*, Vol. 3, 1939, p. 96.

INDEX